The English at Play
In the Middle Ages

Teresa McLean

British Library Cataloguing in Publication Data
McLean, Teresa
    The English at play: in the Middle Ages.
    1.Sports—England—History. 2.Games—
    England—History
    I.Title
    796'.0942   GV605

    ISBN 0–946041–06–7

Published by The Kensal Press,
Shooter's Lodge, Windsor Forest, Berks.
Printed in Great Britain by The Hollen St. Press, Slough

Contents

List of Illustrations

39. Butterfly-chasing in the margins of a falconry scene. July depicted in a sixteenth-century calendar. *The British Library* Add. MS. 24098, fol. 24b.

40. Boys chasing butterflies. *Bodleian Library, Oxford* MS. Douce. 276, fol. 61v.

41. Girls catching butterflies in their hoods. From the Alexander Romance. *Bodleian Library, Oxford.* MS. Bodl. 264.

42. A reading party in a flower-garden. From the Alexander Romance. *Bodleian Library, Oxford* MS. Bodl. 264. Holkham 324, fol. 159.

43. A formal garden in the making. Note the marginal game of rattles. March depicted in a sixteenth-century calendar. *The British Library* Add. MS. 24098, fol. 20b.

44. April lovers in a garden. Note the bat and ball game played in the margin. From the sixteenth-century calendar. *The British Library* Add. MS. 24098, fol. 21b.

45. Playing chess in a little pleasure garden. From an English MS. of Marco Polo's *Travels*, *c.* 1400. *Bodleian Library, Oxford* MS. Bodl. 264, fol. 258.

46. Outdoor merels on a faintly marked board. From the Alexander Romance. *Bodleian Library, Oxford* MS. Bodl. 264, fol. 76v.

47. The Gospel game showing a central block of hunted pieces, and surrounding hunters, in a stylised lay-out. *Bodleian Library, Oxford* MS. CCC. D. 122, fol. 5v.

48. Game of chess. From the Alexander Romance. *Bodleian Library, Oxford* MS. Bodl. 264, fol. 112.

49. A fourteenth-century chess game, showing a small board and crude pieces. Add. 12228, fol. 236.

50. Board games, one of which may be draughts, with a form of merels on the right. From the Alexander Romance. *Bodleian Library, Oxford* MS. Bodl. 264, fol. 60.

51. A late medieval game of cards. *The British Library* Add. 12228, fol. 313v.

52. A tonsured clerk hymns the greatest Lord with the aid of hired minstrels. Initial of Psalm 80 Exultate Deo in the Bromholm Priory Psalter, *c.* 1325. *Bodleian Library, Oxford* MS. Ashmole. 1523, fol. 99.

53. Musicians. Initial of Psalm 80 in the psalter of Robert of Ormesby, monk of Norwich Cathedral Priory, *c.* 1325. *Bodleian Library, Oxford* MS. Douce. 366. fol. 109.

54. Musicians. Left to right: bagpipe, hurdy-gurdy, cornet or recorder, portative organ, kettle drums, From the Alexander Romance. *Bodleian Library, Oxford* MS. Bodl. 264, fol. 180v.

55. A costumed jester before his employer. *Bodleian Library, Oxford* MS. Douce. 18, fol. 113v.

56. The Court of Mirth from the *Roman de la Rose*. By Robinet Testard for Charles d'Orleans and Louise de Savoie. *c.* 1490. *Bodleian Library, Oxford* MS. Douce. 195, fol. 7.

57. Contortionist performing. *Bodleian Library, Oxford* MS. Douce. 5, fol. 18.

58. Disreputable japes. From the Alexander Romance. *Bodleian Library, Oxford* MS. Bodl. 264, fol. 74.

59. Gladiatores performing a stylised Sword Dance. *The British Library* Royal 4 E III fol. 89.

60. A king entertaining his guests with music and a story during a meal. *The British Museum* Royal 14 E III fol. 89.

61. Mumming in long-tailed hoods. *Bodleian Library, Oxford* MS. Bodl. 264, fol. 129.

62. Mummers with beast's heads. *Bodleian Library, Oxford* MS. Bodl. 264, fol. 181v.

63. A pole-wife looking for custom. From Marco Polo's *Travels.* *Bodleian Library, Oxford* MS. Bodl. 264, fol. 245v.

64. Boys riding hobby-horses. *Bodleian Library, Oxford* MS. Douce. 276, fol. 124v.

65. A prostitute inviting a client into her hut. From the Alexander Romance. *Bodleian Library, Oxford* MS. Bodl. 264, fol. 83, fol. 204.

66. A couple Maying, he is carrying a blossomy bough, she has hers carried by a servant. *The British Museum* 2467 Add. Ms. fol. 46.

Weights

One ounce (1 oz.)	thirty grams (30 gms.)
three ounces (3 oz.)	one hundred grams (100 gms.)
one pound (1lb) = sixteen ounces (16oz.)	four hundred and fifty three and a half grams (453.5gms.)
two pounds two ounces (2lb. 2oz.)	one kilogram
two pounds (2lbs.)	one kilogram sixty grams (1k. 60gms.)
one quarter (1 qtr.) = eight bushels = twenty-eight pounds = one quarter of a hundred-weight (½ cut.)	fourteen kilograms eight hundred grams (14.8 kilos)
a grain measurement, also convertible into liquid measure	
one quarter = sixty four gallons (64 galls.)	eight centilitres ninety six litres (8.96 cltrs.)
one gallon (1 gall. = eight pints (8 pts.)	four litres four decilitres eighty millilitres (4.48 litres)
one and three quarter pints (1¾ pts.)	one litre (1 litre)
one pint (1 pt.) = twenty fluid ounces (20 fl. oz.)	five decilitres sixty millilitres (5.6 decils.)

Miscellaneous

a loaf of bread weighed about 2¾ lbs.	one kilo four hundred and fifteen grams (1 kilo 415 gms.)

These are all approximated because they don't work out evenly.

Medieval	Modern
one half penny (½d) three farthings (¾d.)	Too small to have an equivalent modern coin
one penny (1d.)	one half penny (½p.)
two pence (2d.)	one penny (1p.) [just over]
six pence (6d.)	two and a half pence (2½p.)
eight pence (8d.)	three and a half pence (3½p.)
nine pence (9d.)	four pence (4p.)
one shilling (1/-) = twelve pence	five pence (5p.)
two shillings (2/-)	ten pence (10p)
florin = two shillings	ten pence (10p)
five shillings (5/-)	twenty five pence (25p.)
half a crown = two shillings and six pence (2/6)	twelve and a half pence (12½p)
one crown (5/-)	twenty five pence (25p.)
one mark = six shillings and eight pence (6/8)	thirty-three pence (33p)
two marks = thirteen shillings	sixty-six pence (66p)
one pound = twenty shillins (£1/-)	one pound = one hundred pence (100p)
one ducat = nine shillings (9/-)	forty-five pence (45p)
three ducats = one pound seven shillings (£1.7.0)	one pound thirty-five pence (£1.35)
one noble = six shillings and five pence halfpenny (6/5½)	thirty two and a half pence (32½p)
eight nobles = two pounds thirteen shillings and four pence (£2.13.4)	two pounds sixty six pence (£2.66)
one hundred shillings (100/-) = five pounds (£5)	five pounds (£5)

Length

one foot = twelve inches	thirty centimetres (30 cms)
one inch (1″]	two and a half centimetres (2.47 cms)
one yard = three feet (3′)	90 centimetres (90 cms)
one yard four inches (3′ 4″)	one metre (1m.)
one mile = one thousand seven hundred and sixty yards	one kilometre three hundred and seventy five metres (1.375 kms)
⅝ mile	one kilometre (1 km.)
one league = three miles (3m)	four kilometres 800 metres (4.8 km)

CHAPTER ONE

Out of Doors

Nobody bothered to distinguish games from sports in the Middle Ages. Both were played primarily for amusement, as diversions from the endless struggle to survive. And amusement, like survival, was a whole-hearted business. Medieval sports and games were played with an abandon, almost an urgency, which they have lost today because their players today do not struggle at first hand with famine, flood and harvest catastrophe in their work as medieval players did. We no longer need such tumultuous diversions.

The old English word 'game' meant a gathering or participation for fun, and the Medievals were passionately addicted to fun. They played games with passionate delight. Game, sport, mirth, passion and fun were inseparable associates. It was not until the sixteenth century that the word 'sport' acquired the specialist meaning it has today of an outdoor physical game. Using the word in that sense helps to pick out sports, as they are now understood, from the multitude of medieval sports and games.

Medieval sports, then, had three distinguishing characteristics: they were essentially physical, they were played outdoors out of necessity, not choice, and they were usually played by large teams, often consisting of whole villages and parishes. Most medieval sports were a recreational form of gang warfare, fierce with ancient rivalries. The word sport comes from the latin *desporto*, meaning to carry away, and much of the fun lay in carrying victory away from the neighbouring community. Some landowners played sports privately, on their own property, but they and their sports were a small minority. Wide open spaces and wild tribal contests were the stuff of medieval sports, and they frequently involved their players in injury, even murder, and their supporters in drunkenness and vengeance.

No spaces were wider, and no contests wilder, than those of medieval ball games, which have been the basic sports in most ages, the Middle Ages included. The most basic of these was camp-ball. Originally, in Anglo-Saxon times a camp was a contest or fight, and camp-ball a kind of warfaring rugger, resembling the Ancient Greek game *harpastum*. It survived in Norfolk, Suffolk and Essex until the late eighteenth century. The competing villages lined their players up opposite each other, and a ball about the size of a cricket ball, made of thong and leather, was thrown up between them. Whoever caught it rushed for the opposing goals, and the camp was on.

There were two goals on each side, anything up to 200 yards apart, marked by village landmarks like the church and the market cross, and if the competing villages were miles apart, so were the goals, and the players might number hundreds. Points were awarded for scoring goals and trapping opponents in possession of the ball. This was where the fun became lethal, and the game had to be first modified, then eventually extinguished. In its medieval prime, its spectators were as dangerous as its scrums, and camping grounds were appropriated to try and contain it within watchable limits.

In 1472, for instance, the rector of Swaffham, Norfolk, bequeathed the field adjoining his churchyard to the village, as a 'camping-close'. But camping always defied enclosure. It was as naturally expansive as it was unruly. The fifteenth-century monk poet, John Lydgate, described what it felt like to be pitched out into nothingness as being 'boulstered out of length and bread [breadth] like a large camping ball'. Large balls, made of pigs' bladders, had become popular by this time because they were easier to handle than small balls. Filled with dried peas, and sometimes covered with cloth, they could be kicked as well as thrown over the huge stretches of camping ground.

And so football evolved. Until 1486, when the term 'football' was first used in England, it was known as kicking camp, which makes it impossible to tell when kicking as distinct from kicking and throwing, or pure throwing camp began to be played. All three were savage. In his eighth-century *Life of St Cuthbert*, Bede says that Cuthbert used to play keenly at ball with his companions until one day he was warned, in the middle of a game, to abandon 'vain play'. There is a twelfth-century illustration of this scene which shows a game that looks like a mixture of both kinds of camp, hurling and all-in wrestling. [Illustration 1]

Many medieval ball games must have been just this sort of amalgam, only gradually refined into separate sports: hockey, rounders and so on. They were traditionally played on Shrove Tuesday, a great medieval drinking, eating and debauching session before Lent. 'The London youths annually upon Shrove Tuesday go into the fields [Smithfields] immediately after dinner (nine to ten o'clock) and play at the celebrated game of ball' [Fitzstephen, twelfth-century chronicler]. Bands played and spectators sang and danced as they went.

Camping was such a fierce game that in 1321 two brothers called Oldyngton, from Darnhill, Cheshire, played it with the head of one John of Boddeworth, a servant of Vale Royal Abbey nearby, whom they had murdered. It was more usual for death to occur during play. The Medievals were heavy, some of them fatal, tacklers. While the Oldyngton brothers were kicking their victim's head about in Cheshire, a canon of the Gilbertine monastery of Shouldham in Norfolk, one William of Spalding, was 'run against' by another William during a game of kicking camp. Canon William's dagger wounded the other William so badly that six days later he died, and Canon William was punished with suspension from his clerical duties. On appeal to the pope, however, he got his suspension lifted and was declared blameless. Officially the Church was disapproving of clerical sports, but most of its clergy played sports, most sportsmen enjoyed risking their lives at play, and few Church officials had the heart to censure them.

The government legislated against camping, especially kicking camp, because it was so dangerous, sapped the fighting energy of the nation, and distracted men from useful sports like archery. But play defied laws. Churchmen played seculars; landlords played labourers, and already by the thirteenth century, perhaps earlier, the passion for football consumed every class of society. St Hugh of Lincoln was a thirteenth-century aristocrat and bishop who became a popular hero, and people sang pop songs about him playing football:

kicked the bà [ball] with his right foot,
and catched it with his knee,
and through-and-through the Jew's window
he gard [watched] the bonny ball flee.

[*Ballad of St Hugh*]

As early as the thirteenth century, English football was predominantly urban. Sprawling and violent though it was, it preferred the streets to the fields. Many of the most full-blooded medieval football matches were played by gangs of apprentices and mobs of students, in the streets. Football released the tensions of urban life, so effectively that the hooliganism it engendered was one of the reasons the authorities gave for condemning it. In 1303 an Oxford student called Adam of Salisbury was killed by a team, or gang, of Irish students 'while playing ball in the High Street towards Eastgate'.

On Sundays, feast-days and holidays, which were holy days when no one worked, the whole sporting population of towns, guilds, parishes or whatever the local playing area was, played football, and by the fifteenth century both Church and lay authorities had more or less given up trying to forbid it, and restricted themselves to forbidding people to bet on it on holidays.

Churches were the social centre of every medieval parish, and churchyards were the most popular parish sports grounds. Many a congregation spilled out of church straight into a football match, using stretches of the churchyard walls as goals. In 1403 at Salmerston, and in 1404 at Chidham, both in Sussex, players broke legs playing football after baptisms.

Rectors of big churches came the nearest one can find to referee status in the Middle Ages, when they ordered players in churchyards to refrain from breaking gargoyles, windows, and even indoor statues, from playing during services and from playing in the nave of the church itself. Law and order was never a medieval strongpoint, and where sport was concerned, it never had a chance; where camping in any of its forms was concerned, realistic authorities aimed at containing what they could not prevent.

Indeed one man of authority, the Prior of the Augustinian

monastery at Bicester, near Oxford, appears to have been the first recorded manager of a professional football team. On St Catherine's Day, November 25th, 1425, and on other saints' days in subsequent years, he paid 4d. to a team of footballers. By this time, highly organised urban institutions such as gilds had teams with definite numbers of players and with training and playing programmes. The fraternity of the football players of the London Brewers' Company hired a hall in 1418 and again in 1419, at a cost of 20d. a time, probably for a team supper or party. Teams like the Brewers were the precursors of club football, and may well have arranged their matches with rival clubs in league divisions and championships.

Scottish, like English, football teams were based in centres of population; Scone was one of the main ones. Every medieval Scotsman from the King down played football. Gavin Douglas's late fifteenth-century poem, *King Hart*, features the King of Scotland suffering from a bruised arm and a broken shin, as a result of playing 'fute-ball'. Despite being busy with border raids in 1497, the King gave one James Dog the handsome sum of two shillings to buy him a football (good ones were made of leather) while he was staying at Stirling. It took more than war to stop the Medievals playing at camp, with hands or feet.

By this date, in fact by a century earlier, a number of different sports had developed from camping, each characterised by the use of a different piece of equipment. As time passed, these derivatives became more specialised and sophisticated, and among their modern descendants are golf, hockey, handball and all kinds of racket and bowling games. All these existed in some form in the Middle Ages, but only the most robust and gregarious of them count as sports.

The most sporting of them were stoolball and handball. Stoolball was played between young men and women, for prizes of kisses and tansy cakes, the women sitting on milking stools to defend themselves from the men's bowling. It is still played in some areas with a lively folk memory. Handball was played by both sexes, singly and in gangs, against church walls and in the open. Children play a simple form of it today; it is too basic a game to disappear.

The use of courts and rackets soon turned handball into the more aristocratic game of tennis, leaving simple handball a popular game with all classes. Most basic sports underwent this process of refinement, by means of enclosure as well as equipment, into specialised derivatives, and since it was only the privileged minority who could afford these means of refinement, sports tended to split into two categories: those which remained primitive and popular, and those which were well equipped, and quickly developed sophisticated rules. Early medieval sports were primitive and popular, and the first piece of equipment added to them was a bat, to go with the ball most of them used. A bat was really just a curved stick. One of the St Cuthbert's companions in illustration no. 1 is wielding a curved stick, which was known as a bandy. Bandy-ball was basic bat and ball, played with a wooden bat, a small wooden ball and far distant goals. It was pretty well the county sport of medieval Devonshire and, like most medieval bat and ball games, had elements of hockey, cricket and golf, and was played with bloodthirsty contempt for definition and restraint.

In 1450 there was a papal enquiry into the miracles said to have taken place at the tomb of Bishop Osmund of Salisbury, and some of the evidence submitted concerned bandy-ball and its dangers. A man called John Combe of Quidhampton told the enquiry how he and his neighbours had been playing ball some ten years earlier with big sticks or clubs, in Bemerton village. A quarrel had broken out, he had intervened to stop it coming to blows, and one of them hit him so hard over the head with his club that he was paralysed for three months. Only his friends' prayers and offerings at Bishop Osmund's tomb effected his recovery. John Combe's story was corroborated by twenty-eight witnesses, which suggests a sport rather than a game, or at any rate a game watched by a lot of people. If there were wickets or goals, neither were mentioned in the story. It was a sort of street bandy-ball such as contemporary illustrations show.

A straight stick like the one used to hit John Combe, was called a crick in Anglo-Saxon times, and that is the origin of the word cricket. When the game originated is impossible to say for certain as there are no mentions of it by name in medieval records, but plenty of mentions of sports that sound like cricket.

In the royal wardrobe accounts for 1288–89 Master John de Leek, chaplain to King Edward I's young son, was paid one hundred shillings expenses for organising the 'prince's playing at creag [crick] and other sports at Westminster on March 10th'. Later in the month he was paid £1 more for similar expenses at Newenton, a village on the edge of the Weald. Some kind of cold weather and barebones combination of stoolball and club-ball, which may or may not have been an early form of cricket, was being played before 1300 in cricket's traditional Wealden heartland.

Medieval beginnings can more confidently be claimed for another bat and ball sport: golf. A sport called bittle-battle appears in the Domesday Book, and a bittle stick with a head, also called a camboc or cambuc. By the mid fourteenth century camboc was on the list of forbidden sports and was as popular as all the other forbidden sports. The use of clubs with more delicate heads, and playing courses, refined it into golf, pronounced 'goff', but it was played by most people in its simple form. The first reference to golf does not come until 1457, when it was decried by the Scottish authorities for interfering with archery practice, along with football.

Like football, it was royally played in Scotland. In 1503 King James IV spent one shilling on a club and eight shillings on two dozen balls, made of leather stuffed with feathers, for a game of golf with the Earl of Bothwell.

Illustrations only show camboc and golf being played by men and boys, whereas most bat and ball games are shown being played by both sexes: men and women; boys and girls; monks and nuns. Maybe camboc was too rough, and covered distances too long, for women, who do not seem to have played much bandy-ball either. [Illustration 2]

A sport had to be very rough indeed before it was too rough for medieval women, who played and disported, as they hunted and worked, alongside the men. Most sports were played by all ages (John Combe was forty when he suffered his injury), all kinds and classes of people, and both sexes. The omnivorous desire to stop work and 'make you and me a right good sport' [Cely Papers 1481] was strong enough to overcome all but the most impassable social barriers.

Climatic ones too. Freezing winters brought the sporting Medievals out of their homes on to the frozen waterways to play curling, ice camping, ice bandy-ball, sports of all sorts. The fens were the best ice sports grounds, especially the great 'fin' at Finsbury, north of London, which was frozen for fourteen weeks in 1410.

'Great companies of men go to sport upon the ice,' wrote Fitstephen, 'and bind to their shoes bones.' Skates were made of horse and cattle bones, sharpened on the bottom and flattened on top so they could be stood upon. Some were strapped on, but most not; there was no need for straps because the feet were not lifted off the ice. 'They hold stakes in their hands, which sometimes they stick against the ice.' In this way skaters pushed themselves across the ice. Great numbers of medieval skates have been found in archaeological sites, dating from the eighth century right through to the fifteenth, belonging to men, women and children. The excavations at College Street, Ipswich, in 1899 unearthed the sad little find of a woman skater's skeleton, complete with skates, in the mud of the former river course.

Women who did not play sport watched sport, and medieval spectatorship was so keen that it constituted secondary participation. Crowd hooliganism was endemic, and bloodthirsty interruptions to alter the course of play or change the results were common. It is often impossible to tell whether those involved in sporting riots and injuries were players or spectators, and with sports like camp-ball it is misguided to try. In such sports, teams consisted of whole communities, not fixed numbers, and whole gangs of spectators might suddenly join in, in the partisan heat of the moment.

Medieval artists always show sports being played in front of, or in the midst of, spectators, and the larger-scale and the more primitive the sport, the harder it is to tell player from spectator. Sportsmen seldom wore uniforms because it was unnecessary to distinguish friend from foe in community sports. As time passed and sports refined themselves into sophistication and a smaller scale, some were played on clearly marked grounds, which might be the usual fields, churchyards or streets, but were increasingly often enclosed sections of field, or purpose built courts and yards. In the later Middle Ages spectators were walled off from players, the better established of whom began to play in distinctive team formations and uniforms.

The more aristocratic a sport, the more organised and spectacular it was likely to be. The later the date, the more dramatic these tendencies.

Brilliantly dressed ladies of high society in the late Middle Ages inspired the sportsmen they watched from pavilions and balconies ablaze with coloured flags. Humbler spectators at this date often watched their sports from decorated enclosures. Every medieval sports crowd liked to indulge in display, re-enacting, gambling, hero-worshipping, abusing and avenging, blaspheming and singing and dancing.

All these could be indulged at wrestling, a sport which made up for its small numbers of contestants, usually one or two pairs at a time, by the intensely physical nature of its contest. The Medievals flocked to see men wrestle for prize rams, or occasionally cocks, which symbolised the virility of the victor. Wrestling was compulsively crude, which is why reformers preached against it so loudly and so uselessly; it was 'a foul and unthrifty occupation' [Bromyard, the fourteenth-century Dominican preacher]. [Illustration 3]

Unthrifty it certainly was, for gambling on wrestling was as heavy as attendance. Few could resist the chance to back their local champion against their neighbours' champion, and summer was a feast of wrestling matches, played in natural arenas like town squares and churchyards. The London wrestlers gave a public display each year outside the city walls, on St James's Day, July 15th, for the prize of a ram. One of them was killed in a fifteenth-century bout, wrestling for the London Grocers' Company, and he was one of a good number of medieval fatalities in this most brutal of sports.

The chronicler Matthew Paris gives a vivid description of the same London wrestling contest three centuries earlier, in 1222, and that too ended in deaths. When the Londoners won the day, riots broke out between their supporters and those of their Westminster opponents. The struggle had been hard, with innumerable 'castings', but the riots that followed it were harder, and only suppressed by the Chief Justice and a force of armed men hanging the main ringleaders and cutting off the hands and feet of most of the others. Such was local competitive pride.

Different regions prided themselves on their different local styles. The most famous was the Cornish and Devonian, where the opponent had to be thrown so that he hit the ground with three 'points', a style which gave menace to the old Cornish threat 'to give a Cornish hug'. Next most famous was the 'tight-holding' style of Cumberland and Westmorland, then the fast-moving, catch-if-you-can Lancastrian style. But the one most often illustrated is the 'loose' style of Norfolk and Bedfordshire, where the open hand grasped the body, tunic or scarf of the opponent, and attempted to pull him down. This was pretty well the standard medieval wrestling style, and countless variations of clothing and technique were developed from it. In 1423 the city of Norwich sent seven wrestlers to appear before the King, equipped with new hoods which were, apparently, indispensable to their performance.

Except for accessories like these, and loin-cloths, wrestlers fought naked, with oil on their bodies so they were hard to get hold of. Illustrations show 'loose-style' wrestlers grasping loin-cloths, cloths round the neck and in the hand, and even clubs in the hand. For less serious occasions there was shoulderback or chairtop wrestling. [Illustrations 4, 5]

Essential strength lay in the hand, especially with 'loose-style' wrestling. The one stylistic comment Matthew Paris made about the London-Westminster match was that it was fought 'with a strong hand'. Dextrous, masculine and aggressive, medieval wrestling was the favourite small-scale sport of villages and towns: men, women and children alike.

The sports derived from it were never as popular. 'Tugging' was presumably an extension of the cloth pulling of 'loose-style' wrestling, played over all sorts of obstacles and developing into tugs-of-war, on land and ice. Cudgel play was later known as quarter staffs; 'hippas' was a children's version of shoulderback wrestling. All classes of children played wrestling games, but the adult wrestlers described in the records are all franklins and labourers. Middle- and upper-class interest in wrestling was probably non-combative.

In wrestling's most dangerously armed derivative, sword and buckler play, it was indignant. A gentleman's sword was the instrument of his honour, and its use in sport made light of his honour. English kings and their councillors condemned it, from the chivalrous thirteenth century onwards, as 'a trade of subtlety derogating from true and natural valour'. Sword and buckler play was an adolescent's sport, a street game that degenerated, rather than developed, into a sport by virtue of being played in gangs. Sword and buckler play sometimes wore the costumes and posed in the postures of chivalry, but it was basically boyish, best played with wooden swords and shields. [Illustration 6]

It was gangs of boys 'walking by night and assaulting those they met' [1281 writ from Edward I to the Lord Mayor of London], rather than any offence against the sensibilities of the knightly class, that caused the sport to be condemned. City sheriffs made nocturnal 'sweeps', arresting all sword and buckler players, but many eluded them. Fencing masters held schools in taverns, boarding and private houses which were closed down, only to reopen a few years later.

In 1310 Roger le Skirmisour was charged with keeping a school of arms in London and 'enticing thither the sons of respectable persons'. It transpired that a number of his pupils had been involved over the years in serious breaches of the peace, including killings and knifings. Roger was a typical medieval fencing-master. He was imprisoned, but released after a short while. He was, as his name suggests, a skirmisher, not by medieval standards a public danger, and was accordingly lightly punished. As one fencer, John Felered, servant of one Oliver Howe, put it in 1442, 'the game vulgarly called sword and buckler or piked staff . . . comes from merriment of heart.'

So, in English folklore, did the most romantic of medieval English sports, one which was played with real, deadly weapons, but enforced by the same kind of statutes that forbade sword and buckler play. Archery was the official national sport.

Merry it was in green forest,
Among the leaves green,
Where that men walk east and west,
With bows and arrows keen.

This is the opening of the ballad of *Adam Bell* [the northern Robin Hood], *Clym of the Clough and William Cloudesley*, which may date back from as early as 1220, and which gave the English imagination its first yeoman-archer heroes. The most popular of them, Robin Hood, is still a folk hero today.

Archery is inextricably associated in the English imagination with life under the greenwood tree, the yeoman, his longbow and his quiver of arrows. There is no medieval reason to change that picture, except by adding to it. Medieval archery was a military as well as a sporting exercise; it was played, in varying degrees, by both sexes and by all classes, in churchyards as well as woods and towns as well as villages. Some of the best archers were Welsh.

The story of English archery begins back in the Anglo-Saxon period, when bows were used for hunting and, possibly, for sport in their own right. As the centuries passed, archery began to be used for national defence as well. Saxon bows were short and stout, easy to use on horse-back, and this style of bow was used right through the Middle Ages, though superseded in popularity by the longbow. Some bows were made of one wood, and known as self-bows; most were made of two woods.

When the chronicler Gerald of Wales visited his homeland in 1188, he reported that the Welsh bows were made of wild elm and were 'unpolished, rude and uncouth, but stout.' Nearly a century later Edward I was so impressed by what he saw of the shooting power of these bows in his Welsh invasion of 1277 that he made them the standard infantry weapon in his army. The traditional English longbow may have developed from the Welsh bow, the Saxon bow or the Norman bow; there is no way of telling; most likely it developed from all three. But whatever its origins, it had begun its life in English romantic history by the reign of Edward I, and kept its place there thanks to royal patronage all through the medieval period, helped by its military importance. It became a symbol of English prestige.

From the reign of Henry I onwards, any archer who killed someone passing between him and his practice targets was declared free of the charge of murder. Anyone with forty shillings' worth of property had to keep a sword, a bow and arrows and a knife in his house 'for to keep the peace', and royal statutes subsidised the sale and manufacture of archery equipment to encourage bowmen.

Crossbows were much slower and more complicated to fire, were never a major English weapon, in war or in sport, and were never subsidised like longbows. They were popular on a small scale, with women and boys who went fowling. They were also popular with boys in big towns, who used them to pick off pigeons, gargoyles and shop signs, because they were easy to carry and run away with. Country clergy used crossbows for leisurely shooting expeditions; in 1299, Archbishop Winchelsey issued injunctions to the prior and canons of Leeds, including one which stated that none of them was to go into the garden after compline with crossbows and stonebows.

The longbow was an altogether different proposition; a serious marksman's weapon, respected and highly valued. Its stave was about six feet high and about one-and-a-half inches wide at the centre, tapering at the ends, where it was cut with nocks to hold the string. It was a bow to shoot with on display. It might be made of ash, wych-elm or hazel, but was best made of the slow-growing mountain yew, grown in England in the early Middle Ages then, as demand outgrew supplies, imported from Spain, Portugal, Italy and Prussia. The light-coloured sapwood just under the bark was used for the back, or convex, side of the bow, and the heartwood for the belly. The sapwood resisted stretch, the heartwood resisted compression, and the two combined to give a balance and tension that could draw 100 lb. weight and shoot an arrow over 225 yards.

The strings were made of hemp or flax impregnated with beeswax and whipped with fine thread at the end, to prevent fraying and repel rain and dew. For maximum power the bow was drawn back to the ear, not to the breast as was the custom of the Ancients, and this permitted the release of an arrow from twenty-seven inches to thirty-nine inches long. Arrows were made of birch, aspen and oak, but were best made of ash, which gave a swift, heavy flight. Bow staves were often knobbly, but arrows were always smoothly rounded. The heads of sporting arrows were pointed with iron, and sharpened by a file kept down the boot.

The brown, wing feathers of the peacock, not the colourful eye feathers, were the best for fletching arrows. Some archers preferred the rare feathers of the grey goose's wing; those of the swan, crane and (later) the turkey were less popular. Feathers were cut straight and angular, and three of them six inches to eight inches long, were bound or glued to either side of the arrow. Two dozen made a sheaf, but most archers carried smaller bundles in quivers or tucked under their belts.

The fully equipped longbowman was the pride of medieval England. But he was expensive to maintain, and preferred to play football or some less demanding sport. Statute after statute ordered him to practise his sport. Town and village authorities set up practice grounds, and their officials tried to supervise practice on them once a week. The standard practice grounds were butts, which were wedge-shaped mounds made of fibrous earth, such as peat, taken from the common, which held arrows well. Many English place names include the word butts in them, testimony of their medieval archery use, and late medieval churchwardens' accounts are full of entries like 'beer and bread for those who make the butts'. Butts were usually set up in churchyards, and practice took place against the church walls, which were also used for sharpening arrowheads. Archery was one of the Sunday sports played in village churchyards all through the Middle Ages, in all seasons, amidst all sorts of other sports, games and festivities.

But official practice was never enjoyed as much as the more informal sort played on village greens and in back alleys, using rose garlands, artificial parrots, dead or wooden cocks and circles of coloured cloth as targets. More popular still was shooting at a prick, which was a wooden peg, usually made of hazel, either stuck upright in the ground or fixed in the centre of a white, straw-stuffed, canvas disc about eighteen inches in diameter. The archer improved his shooting 'to a length' by trying to cleave the pin, in the manner of Robin Hood. The length concerned might be anything up to 200 yards.

But most popular of all was practising by roving, which meant shooting at random targets over any distances. It was really a kind of rambling play with the bow. Gangs of people went roving on holiday afternoons. In 1480 the prior of a monastery near Coventry complained that his corn and grass had been damaged by citizens on roving expeditions, to which the Mayor replied that many towns permitted their citizens to practise by roving. Coventry, however, was not one of them, as the prior pointed out, and butts had been set up there fourteen years before in accordance with royal command.

Commands were increasingly necessary in the later Middle Ages, as archery lost the popularity it had enjoyed so resplendently during the Hundred Years' War, when English longbows put the old-fashioned, crossbowed French to shame. In the reign of Edward III archery legends and romances proliferated, and by the time the poet Langland wrote, in 1377, Robin Hood was his favourite hero. The yeoman archer had his golden age. As time passed, landowners and aristocrats took to archery as a sport in its own right, apart from hunting, and disported themselves in the style of Robin Hood, while yeomen and smallholders let the sport languish.

The household accounts of John Howard Duke of Norfolk for the years 1462–1469 give some details of one such late medieval aristocratic archer and his style. On his rides round his estates, Sir John liked watching the village bowmen competing, and often took a hand himself. He bought huge quantities of shafts, for arrows, as well as bowstrings, feathers and arrowheads. He paid bowyers, stringers, fletchers and handymen to make and mend his equipment. His style was lavish, his equipment flamboyant. On March 27th he paid '2d. to have some shafts feathered, 2d. to the fletcher as a tip, two shillings to a bowyer for mending the bows.' He had his bows painted (the paint preserved as well as decorated the wood), and cut with ivory and horn nocks. For a few real showpieces he may have had silk strings. He also had his arrows painted (this helped to identify them, and was known as cresting) and 'plumed with peacock'. Some of his bowcases and quivers were pelissed with otter fur, and his arm bracers were embossed with leather.

For all his display, the duke enjoyed himself most when playing with his tenants. On a typical day he paid 'to Thomas of York, for losses at the pricks, 8d., losses at the butts 8d., to Richard Crowthe at the butts, 12d., for bread and ale for all, 4d.' He never seems to have won his archery bets, but he never stopped making them. Few Medievals could resist a bet.

As more and more of them resisted the lure of archery, and opted for cheaper and easier sports, the English kings intensified their support and patronage of the sport that had been a royal amusement and pride ever since the days of Henry II who, according to one of his chroniclers, was never idle; his hands 'were always full of bow or book.' The keenest royal archer of all was Henry VIII, the exhibitionist patron of a dying art. He and all his court played bows and arrows with expensive elegance. In 1532 he paid 'to Scawseby, for bows, arrows, shafts, broad heads, bracer and shooting glove for my Lady [Anne Boleyn] 33/4d. . . . to the King's bowyer for four bows for my Lady Anne, at 4/4d. a piece, 17/4d.' Within a year Anne Boleyn was buried, headless, in a box of elmwood made for storing arrows. Within a generation archery was almost a dead sport. It survived in sporting use two centuries after the introduction of the gun, but barely. As the preacher Latimer lamented, in an uncharacteristically nostalgic and worldly sermon preached to the young King Edward in the 1540s, 'Men shall never shoot well, except they be brought up it.' Puritanical as he was, Latimer was overcome by the beauty of good bowmanship. 'It is a gift of God, that he has given us to excel all other nations withall.' [Illustration 7]

It is from this period that the only definitive treatise on archery dates: *Toxophilus*, written by a yeoman's son named Roger Ascham who, like Latimer, had learnt his bowmanship from his father and was loathe to see it die out. His treatise is an epitaph on a sport that was once too well known to need written description, and once so well known that it gave the English language a host of expressions, some of which have lasted until the present day: 'highly strung', 'bracing' oneself for something, 'being a butt' for someone, knowing the 'upshot' of something (in archery, not the final result but the best shot so far).

The last word on archery comes from the old popular song that celebrated it in its golden age. This is the last verse of *Adam Bell, Clym of the Clough and William of Cloudesley*:

Thus endeth the lives of these good yeomen;
God send them eternal bliss.
And all that with a hand-bow shooteth,
That of heaven they never miss. Amen.

1 The boy St Cuthbert, too fond of playing games, is warned in a vision to be more serious. From Bede, *Life of St Cuthbert*, Durham, *c.* 1120–30. *Bodleian Library, Oxford* MS University College, 165, p. 8.

2 A bat and ball game played by both sexes. Marginal illustration from an illuminated MS. of the Romance of Alexander. *c.* 1340. *Bodleian Library, Oxford* MS. Bodl. 264, fol. 22.

3 Wrestling before an audience. *Bodleian Library, Oxford* MS. Douce. 202. fol. 180.

4 "loose" wrestling, with one of two wrestlers wearing a cloak and holding a stone club. *The British Museum* Royal 2 E VII. fol. 168.

5 Wrestling before a big crowd, for the prize of a cock, in the standard "loose" style, which included grabbing the opponent' scarf. *The British Museum* Royal 2 B VIII. fol. 160v.

6 Boys playing at sword and buckler. *Bodleian Library, Oxford* MS. Douce. 6, fol. 4.

7 Boating in May, with marginal archery. From a sixteenth-century calendar. *The British Library, Oxford* MS. Bodl. 264, fol. 50.

CHAPTER TWO

Animal Sports

The Medievals played, as they worked, in harness with animals.
Never a day passed them by without some part of it being spent
with animals. If it was not time spent following the plough, it
was time spent driving carts, herding stock, catching fish, scaring
birds, riding to deliver a message or fight in a battle, pulling a
heavy load, or doing any of the countless other jobs which medieval life demanded. Man and beast functioned together, sometimes in harmony, sometimes in enmity, and it was only natural
that they should play together in the same ambivalent way.

Medieval animal sports were basically of two kinds: ones
where animals partnered men and ones where they competed in
front of men to provide bloodthirsty spectator sport. In the first
kind, men took as active a part as their animals; in the second
kind, they were onlookers and gamblers.

As far as the first kind is concerned, man's closest playing
partner was also his closest working partner: the horse, and the
top sport for this partnership was horse-racing. Hunting was a
distinct sport in its own right.

Horse-racing belonged to all classes. It had the wildness and
at the same time the human attachment of the horse itself. It was
thrilling and gratifying to successful owners, trainers, punters and
riders. Nothing in the sporting world appealed to so many people
as a horse-race. Right from the earliest recorded times the English
have been racing horses, and breeding and training horses to race.

Queen Boadicea's people, the Iceni, were famous as horse
breeders and lived in the traditional horse-breeding country of
Cambridgeshire, Norfolk, Suffolk and Huntingdonshire. If they
raced their horses, it was probably in chariots; the British skill at
chariot racing greatly impressed their Roman conquerors. It is
impossible to tell exactly what breeds of horses there were in
England in this early period, but Iceni coins and horse bones from
Roman camps on the Scottish border are evidence that there were

sturdy forest ponies, slighter Celtic ponies and Libyan-Arab style horses, which could have come to England from Gaul, or been imported by the governor, Septimus Severus. The Romans were addicted to horse-racing and set up altars to equestrian goddesses at Silchester, Caerleon and other settlement centres.

But the first reference to a horse race in England comes from the seventh century, when chariots were a thing of the past, and the bold warriors in *Beowulf* raced 'with their horses in rivalry over the fallow fieldways'. By the eighth-century there is a reference to a jockey falling off: no less a figure than Abbot Herebald of Tynemouth. When he was a young man he could not resist joining in with the rest of Bishop John of Hexham's retinue to 'gallop and make trial of the goodness of their horses . . . I struck in among them, and began to ride at full speed,' recalled the Abbot ecstatically. But in trying to clear a hollow in the plain over which they rode, he fell off and concussed himself on a stone.

'Running horses' such as the Abbot rode 'with saddles and bridles of yellow gold' were sent to King Athelstan in the early tenth century by the French King, Hugh Capet, starting a fashion for horsey presents between kings, but there is no other mention of horse-racing before the Conquest.

After it the mentions are legion. William the Conqueror brought heavy Norman and Spanish warhorses to Britain, and possibly Arab racers too. Henry I bred his stable stock from Arab sires, and in 1110 sent a white one to the King of Scotland. By the mid twelfth-century English racehorses were attracting buyers from all over Europe. Fitzstephen has left us a marvellous description of the famous Smithfield horse fair held every Saturday, of the kinds of horses to be seen there, and most vividly of all, the selling races held to demonstrate the horses' fitness as well as entertain the crowds.

'When a race . . . is about to begin,' he wrote, 'horses of the baser sort are bidden to turn aside. Boys . . . curb the horses' untamed mouths with jagged bits, aiming to stop their chief rival getting the lead. The horses likewise lift up their spirits. Their limbs tremble; impatient of delay, they cannot stand still. When the signal is given, they gallop off. The riders, hoping for renown and victory, lash them with switches and excite them with cries.'

The starts were obviously a case of every man for himself, some of the horses were unbroken, and the riding was hell for leather. There were medieval race officials, but their control was negligible. Richard I used to sponsor and steward meetings. He once put up a purse of £40 'in ready gold' for a three-mile race, run at Whitsun, the height of the medieval racing season. Most of the big meetings seem to have taken place at the Easter and Whitsun festivals, and in the favourite medieval month of May. But racing of some sort doubtless went on all the year round, like most medieval sports. There is no specific mention of racing being divided into seasons, still less jumping and flat seasons, as it is today. In fact racing over jumps is not mentioned at all, and chroniclers like Fitzstephen always reckon the best courses to be the flattest ones. But medieval races were very long, three miles being the shortest in the records, and the longer races over seven or more miles of country must have entailed the jumping of some obstacles, like the hollow which unseated Abbot Herebald. Even so, flat racing alone is on record, because that is what suited the fast, lightly built Arab horses Richard I brought to England in large numbers after the Crusades, when racing became very fashionable and records were kept in earnest.

Richard and his successor, John, filled their stables with 'fast running horses', the best of them known as palfreys, from the Latin *paraveredus*, a fast relay horse. These were priced above all other types of horses. Many were probably bred at least in part from heavy stock, to combine stamina and strength with their speed. The most famous horse of medieval romance, and one of the very few recorded by name, was Arundel, so called because his owner, Sir Bevis of Hampton, came from Arundel.

In the course of many adventures together, Bevis and Arundel found themselves taking part in a Whitsuntide race meeting for mounted knights.

A great course there was do grede [prepared]
For to try there all their steeds,
Which were swift and strong.

[*Romance of Sir Bevis*]

Arundel was generously blessed with both these qualities. The course was seven miles long, and when he reached the start,

> Two knights had the course stole,
> That they were two miles before,
> Ere any man it wist y-bore [realised it].

But he won by 'half or more', though the author does not say whether it was half the course or half a length. Nor does he say what breed of horse Arundel was; only that he was a palfrey.

If his swiftness was Arabian, his strength may have come from the heavy *destriers* imported into England throughout the period. 'Costly destries of graceful form and godly stature, with quivering ears, high necks and plump buttocks' [Fitzstephen] fetched high prices at the Smithfield fairs.

There were royal studs for all sorts of breeds in Oxfordshire, Berkshire, Buckinghamshire and Middlesex. The kings employed bloodstock agents from Normandy, Castile and Aragon, Portugal, Scotland and England to buy and sell for them. The royal accounts are full of equestrian trading, recorded in entries like 'an Arab or bay, which the King had by gift of the Emperor' (1237), 'eight horses bought from Blanche of Castile' (1242), 'broken and unbroken horses and mares from Scotland' (1347).

The royal studs had specialist individual managers, like Garsias de Ispania, keeper of Queen Eleanor of Provence's stud in 1291, and general managers, like William Beauxamys, who was in charge of all the studs in 1313. Horse prices were sky-high, exports had to be licensed, and buyers were protected by elaborate legal provisions, including the right to trial ownership for periods of up to a year.

Most races were probably selling races, where the winner was auctioned, but these could be very valuable and were always hard fought. In 1377, when Richard II was still Prince of Wales, his horse was beaten in a selling race by a horse called Arundel, whose owner, Sir Alured de Vere, had named it after Bevis' legendary champion, and who sold it to Richard in the bidding after the race for a huge sum. When Richard became king, he sent Sir Alured to Tower Hill, as if he still resented the defeat.

out and another pair of cocks fought. The survivors of the two fights then fought each other, and the process continued until there was only one cock left alive. His victory won his owner freedom from flagellation during Lent and the right to free other boys from flagellation whenever he chose during that season. It was life or death to the cocks, power or subservience to their young owners. [Illustration 8]

Some victorious apprentices celebrated by beginning the eating of the dead cocks. The fighting and celebrating took place in school rooms, backyards, streets like 'le cockplace' in fourteenth-century Lincoln, and most commonly in churches, where side-chapels made ideal cock-pits. If the Medievals built cock-pits, they never mentioned them in their records; the word is not recorded until the sixteenth century. Like so many killer entertainments, cock fighting was especially popular in towns, where fighting with nature to survive was less directly ferocious. Cocking became a synonym for any fighting or wrangling, and grew ever more popular.

All cock sports had the same appeal. Cock throwing and beating were the most popular variants, and both belong uncompromisingly to the second category of animal sports, with man the spectator and gambler on animal performances. Cocks were chased and 'thrown', beaten with sticks until disabled by a hit, when they were propped up with sticks or forks and 'thrown' to death. The best sport was in trying for the first hit, while the cock was still able to try and escape, though its chances of doing so were, to say the least, remote. The boys of Wye School in Kent in the fifteenth century bought back from their grammar masters for 'cock shying' the cocks they had given him for fighting. [Illustration 9]

Shying, like fighting, was very rowdy. In 1409 a group of parishioners from St Denis Bakchurch, London, bound themselves, under penalty of a £20 fine, to refrain from 'collecting money for a football, or money called cocksilver, for a cock, hen, pullet, capon or other bird or for any other use, and that they would not thrash any hen or capon or any bird in the streets and lanes of the city.' Cocks were the only savage animals within easy reach of the medieval English, and since fights without savagery were fights without interest, cock sports were a major interest.

Bear-baiting was a lesser but still very popular savage sport, especially in towns. The Domesday book records that in Edward the Confessor's time the city of Norwich gave the King a bear and six dogs to bait it, every year. By that time the native bear was extinct in Britain, and bears were imported, so only wealthy householders, city corporations and 'bear-wards' under the patronage of one of these two could afford to present the sport.

The dogs used were usually greyhounds, in gangs of five or six at a time. These were also beyond most peoples' means, and any fast dogs with sharp teeth could be used in their place. Or smaller numbers of bigger dogs, like mastiffs. 'In winter on almost every feast-day before dinner either foaming boars and hogs, armed with tusks lightening swift . . . fight for their lives, or fat bulls with butting horns, or huge bears, do combat to the death against hounds let loose upon them' [Fitzstephen].

Cold winter days, empty patches of suburban ground, and walled yards in aristocratic households were the stark settings for medieval baitings. There is hardly any mention in the records of the boar baiting described by Fitzstephen, but bulls are often mentioned. By the late Middle Ages, most towns had a 'bull-ring mayor' or 'warden of the shambles' to make sure bulls were baited before they were slaughtered, despite the butchers' objection that the flesh of unbaited bulls was more wholesome. Fifteenth-century Coventry is typical of many late medieval towns in having a bull-ring next to its Great Butchery. The municipal authorities at Norwich provided a rope for the bulls baited there in 1375–1376 and again in 1387–1388, but there is no mention of a bull-ring, and the baiting was probably in the churchyard or the streets.

Town streets, full of pigs, dogs, fowl, rubbish and traders, traffic and travellers, were the setting for bull running, a derivative of bull-baiting that was popular in Lincolnshire and Staffordshire. It is said to have originated in Stamford, Lincolnshire, in the reign of King John, when William, Earl of Warenne, looking down from his castle walls, saw two bulls fighting for a cow in the meadow below him. A town butcher, who owned one of the bulls, set one of his mastiffs, the traditional medieval butchers' dogs, on the bulls to separate them, whereupon his bull broke loose and ran through the town, pursued by all the butchers' dogs, all the town's butchers, and crowds of people who joined the pursuit from the streets. Earl William jumped on his horse and joined it too. He so enjoyed the sport that he gave the meadow where the fighting had started to the butchers of the town as a perpetual common, provided they found a mad bull each year, to continue the sport.

So bull running became an annual event at Stamford, and was organised by the gild of St Martin, on their patronal feast, November 11th, or on the feast of St Brice just after it, November 13th. The meadow survived and was called 'Bull Meadow' until the beginning of this century; it still belongs to the town as a common right. The sport enjoyed some local popularity in the Midlands. John of Gaunt, who was a generous patron of bear baiting, was much taken with it, and developed his own peculiarly insatiable combination of baiting and running. He gave a charter to the king of his minstrels at Tutbury Manor to make a bull mad by sawing off its horns, cropping his ears, smearing his body with soap, and blowing pepper into his nose. He was then to be chased, and if caught, to be baited and killed, and served at a banquet given by the Prior of Tutbury for the Lancaster family, to which all were invited. There was never any suggestion of restraint in medieval sports, least of all in combative ones.

The ideal was exotic savagery, and since that was virtually unattainable in England, most people settled for savagery. Second best was exoticism which, like savagery, most people could only get in a diluted form, with domestic animals added.

A tiny minority of really rich Medievals could either import exotic animals directly or by means of personal and diplomatic contacts abroad. The absolutely basic sport for courtiers with a taste for the exotic was making a menagerie. Henry II seems to have started the fashion for this by filling the royal park at Woodstock with lions, leopards, lynxes, camels, most of them sent by his brother-in-law, Frederick II of Naples, and a porcupine, sent him by William of Montpellier, and the wonder of the chronicler at Malmesbury. Menageries became courtly status symbols, and the more exotic their inmates the more they paid tribute to the social distinction of their owners.

Not surprisingly, royal owners did best. Henry III seems to have done best of all. In 1237 he got a leopard-house built within the grounds of the Tower of London, and assigned 18/7½d. for the expenses of 'two of the King's leopards and two of their keepers, with four horses and three grooms, for ten days.' Where he got the leopards from and how long they lived we do not know. Henry had close political ties with the King of Sicily, who seems the most likely source of supply. At any rate, by 1240 he had turned his attention to lions, assigning 'fourteen shillings to William the lion-keeper, for chains and other things he bought for the use of the lion.' In 1244 he raised William's expense allowance for the lion and lioness from 1½d. to 2d. a day, allowing William himself ½d. a day.

Two years later he developed an interest in bears, and the Tower menagerie was extended to accommodate one sent him by the Mayor of Northampton. Where the mayor got it from we have no way of knowing. The royal records seldom mention the provenance of the royal zoo animals, and it is safest to assume that most of them were presents from other European rulers, or brought back from the Crusader territories.

In September 1252 the King assigned 4d. a day to the upkeep of a white bear and its keeper, both of whom he was sending to London. In October he ordered the steward of the Tower to get a muzzle for the bear, which he said had been sent him from Norway. A muzzle was the bare minimum for safety, since the bear was obviously given the maximum freedom, to help it adjust to its new surroundings. It was to be 'attached to an iron chain when out of the water', and to 'a long and strong cord when fishing in the Thames.' Whether it was the chains, the fish or the Thames that did not agree with the bear, it never appears in the records again.

The case of the King's elephant is an even sadder one because there is documentary evidence of its demise. Like most of the exotic imports, this most ambitious one only lasted a few years. It came to England as a gift from Louis IX of France, probably originally from the Near East or Sicily, in 1254. It was met at

Dover by the King's steward, who had to arrange for its transport to the Tower, preferably by water, if he could find a boat and crew able to take it. Whether he found one or not, he somehow got the elephant to the Tower safely by 1255, and installed it in a building forty feet by twenty feet which had been erected for it. A group of keepers was appointed to look after it. But life was too cramped for the homesick giant, and its last appearance in the royal records, three years later, is a posthumous one.

The King must have liked it a lot because it was given an honourable burial within the Tower bailey, and in 1258 he ordered the Constable of the Tower to dig up its bones and give them to the Sacrist of Westminster Abbey, who got personal instructions from the King as to what he should do with them. It is not known what his instructions were.

Such was the over-ambitious partnership between men and exotic animals. It was a persistently popular one, failures notwithstanding, because it was spectacular. When the Earl of Derby, later King Henry IV, went to Prussia and the Holy Land in 1390–1393, he was given a leopard on his way home by the King of Cyprus, and spared no pains to get it home safely. Uniformed keepers kept and fed it on board ship, where it had a cabin built of 'ropes and tables'. In Italy he bought oil, spices and horse-irons for it, and at Treviso an expensive mat. In Calais he bought candles, wine and milk to support the keepers during their vigils with it, and at other stops sheep for it to eat, and spices for its medicine. New leggings for the scratched keepers were a recurrent expense.

Wherever he went on his journey, the Earl was presented with exotic and expensive animals, including a wild bull, three young bears and an elk, but there is no record of what happened to them when they got back to England. Only bears had once been native to Britain, of the exotics, and they had a special place in English hearts and in English sports.

Quite a few medieval English noblemen had 'bear-wards' who trained bears to dance, walk on two legs and gesticulate like humans, do acrobatics and tricks, alone and with other animals, and fight. Anglo-Saxon entertainers often had animals in their travelling circuses, and often had a bear amongst their animals.

In England it was the only savage animal most Medievals were ever likely to see.

In the first year of his reign Richard III appointed one John Brown to be 'guider and ruler of all our bears and apes', and as a reward for his 'diligent service' in this capacity, granted him the privilege of wandering about the country with his bears and apes, receiving 'the loving benevolence and favours of the people.'

No one could resist either bears or apes. The ape's vocation in medieval life was to be a grotesque parody of man, satirising him by imitation. Medieval art delighted in showing man his absurdity by showing apes doing all the most absurd and base human activities: stealing, pouring urine out of flasks, farting, acting as doctors and dentists, and preaching and listening to sermons. Apes were trained to do human tricks like acrobatics, dancing and performing with animals. Mockery was good sport and good for the soul, and none was better than self-mockery. Kings and noblemen kept apes to perform alongside their jesters; queens and noble ladies kept apes to offset their beauty and carica-ture their lovers; church dignitaries kept apes, as one monastic chronicler put it, 'to dispel their anxieties'. In 1361 the Prior of Durham spent thirty-one shillings on a monkey, which he bought at York, for the amusement of his household. [Illustrations 10, 11]

This was a considerable, but not an exorbitant sum for a man of his eminence to spend on amusement. Apes were mid-way between animals that were rare and exotic and animals that were common and had to be made exotic by training and presentation. The latter were naturally far more numerous, and for every menagerie there were scores of circuses. The margins of medieval manuscripts team with horses and dogs, the most domesticated and easily trained of these animals, doing tricks in company with humans or other animals, or on their own. Animal musicians were the most popular of all, followed by animal dancers, tumblers, stilt-walkers and even animals teaching men to perform. Goats, pigs, rabbits and birds, and the occasional ram and ox, are portrayed as less popular performers than horses and dogs. [Illustration 12]

Animal circuses seem to have been one-man shows, though usually with a boy helper, and often one-horse shows as well, with two or three dogs, and perhaps a monkey or a goat. The horse was the main attraction, and was colourfully saddled and draped to do his dancing and kicking. The dogs wore brightly coloured collars, often with bells attached, to do their dancing, jumping and riding. The most common accessories for animal performers were hats, jerkins, sticks, tambourines and drums; for human performers whips, sticks and drums. When the animals had finished doing their tricks and human imitations, the humans put on animal head-dresses and imitated animals, and danced and cavorted with them. These shows were especially popular around Christmas time, when churchyards, market-places and the halls of great houses competed to accommodate them. The rest of the year they made what living they could on tour, usually as part of a minstrel's show. This was considered the vulgar side of minstrelsy, and got much of its support from villagers and poor townsmen.

By contrast, simple riding was popular with everyone. It combined animal and human partnership with animal and human display, and though it was often just a part of work, it was also a sporting pleasure. Even the most involuntary of journeys became a procession when there were onlookers.

So Chaucer characterised his pilgrims by describing what kind of horses they rode, conjuring up the spectacle horse and rider made together. The nun's priest and the canon made the poorest spectacles, riding respectively a jade and a hackney. 'What though thine horse be foul and lean,' wrote Chaucer of the nun's priest, for a jade was any hack or draught horse ridden when there was no riding horse available. The hackney was hardly more esteemed, being lean like a jade, right for a man who cared little for appearances. It was common and useful, and was sometimes bought by a wealthy buyer looking for a light horse, particularly if he was buying for a woman. In the second half of the fourteenth century, when Chaucer wrote, society women took to riding about in chaises or chariots, luxuriously upholstered and drawn by hackneys. But in general the hackney was not the first choice of those who could afford to choose.

Nor were the mares ridden by Chaucer's cook and ploughman. When a horse was referred to simply as a mare, it meant it was undistinguished, otherwise it would have been further described, as a trotter, or a mare of a specific colour. One of the very few times a mare is distinguished by a name in the records, it is an insulting name. In 1392 Thomas Duke of Gloucester inherited 'a mare called Gillard, worth ten shillings, with a saddle and bridle in poor condition, worth two shillings.' The mare must have been in similar condition, to have fetched so small a price, and to have been given that name, for a Gill was a medieval nickname for a worthless female.

A 'stot', which is what Chaucer's reeve rode, was also used on occasion as a derisory nickname, but a relatively inocuous one, with the same meaning as the type of horse it described: a sort of all purpose old faithful. 'This reeve sat upon a full good stot, that was all pomely [dappled] grey,' wrote Chaucer approvingly, of a horse he thought just right for a reeve.

The shipman had more genteel pretensions, for he rode a rouncy, which was a trotting horse something like a modern cob, ridden by knights and gentlemen. It was almost certainly the rouncy that Fitzstephen described as 'horses that best fit for esquires . . . they raise and set down the opposite feet, fore and hind, first on one side then on the other.' They were primarily riding, not working or racing horses, and though they were used for tourneying and leisurely hunting, they were best suited to riding round estates or on journeys where there was company to impress. They were therefore good sporting horses, though the shipman had trouble disporting himself as he would have liked on his, and had to ride it 'as he couth', i.e. jogging.

More expert riders chose the rouncy to show off their skills, mastering their rhythmic, high-stepping gait. A king would often reward his steward with one and buy a good many for his own stables. By the fifteenth century, a distinct breed of rouncy, known as the trotter, had been established in Norfolk. It had a diagonal trotting gait and became very fashionable. The Earl of Derby bought himself a pair of trotters, in advance of fashion, for his expedition to the Holy Land.

Those who preferred walking to trotting bought amblers. In the *Clerk's Tale*, Lord Mark set his wife upon a 'horse snow white and well ambling.' Chaucer's Wife of Bath, on the other hand, 'upon an ambler easily she sat' to show her contempt for the male sex, a whip in her hand, telling stories of how to deal with five husbands. Some fifteenth-century illustrators emphasise her earthiness by painting her astride her horse, since by that time it was the fashion for women to ride side-saddle. This is said to have been brought to England by Richard II's queen, Anne of Bohemia, in about 1388. Many fashionable late medieval ladies rode side-saddle, including Chaucer's nun and prioress.

The best amblers were showpieces for rider and horse alike, like the 'two beautiful horses which are delicate, supple and good to handle' Henry III bought from his steward in Gascony in 1238. Amblers were the only riding horses Sir Thomas Urstwick kept in his fashionable stables in Essex in the late fifteenth century, and he kitted them out proudly with tack made of Hungarian leather, including 'two pillions for gentlewomen, and a stirrup', which implies that pillion riders rode side-saddle. The word pillion does not appear until the late fifteenth century, and then always with reference to women riding side-saddle. If the early Norman centuries did miss out on pillion riding, they missed out on one of the most romantic medieval pastimes, which later artists depicted in gay colours, rich clothes and summer sunshine, with birds and flowers round about, and often with hawks on wrists. [Illustration 13]

The best saddle horses of any kind were palfreys. They had 'class', which meant speed, beauty and breeding. Rich buyers left standing instructions with their agents to buy all the best palfreys that appreared at big sales like the Smithfield one, where Fitz-stephen saw 'ambling palfreys, their skin full of juice, their coats a-glisten, as they pace softly . . . .'. Chaucer's monk rode a palfrey.

> Full many a dainty horse had he in stable,
> And when he rode men might his bridle hear
> Jingling in a whistling wind all clear.

Here was the medieval sporting rider *par excellence*, the churchman on the rich churchman's traditional mount, riding for pleasure and display. By giving his monk a palfrey, Chaucer put him on a par with the bishops and monastic heads, and all the grand householders who have left household accounts full of the expenses of buying, keeping and riding choice palfreys.

They cost twice as much as most saddle horses, and were carefully put through their paces before purchase. In 1308 Bishop Swinfield's favourite palfrey was injured, and he and his friend, the Abbot of Gloucester, tried all the Herefordshire and Gloucestershire horse-owners and dealers in an effort to find a replacement. Sir Gilbert le Sauvage had a bay palfrey the Bishop liked, but he refused to sell it; only after his death did the Bishop manage to get it, together with an unbroken colt which he hired a trainer to break in for him. A really good saddle horse was part of a man's very self. As the most valuable of a gentleman's possessions, palfreys were taken as mortuaries, and bequeathed to heirs and closest friends. In 1314 the Bishop of Norwich sold one for £26.13.4d. – an enormous but by no means exceptional sum.

Purchase was only the beginning of the expense. Dignitaries like Swinfield kept permanent servants whose sole job was to look after their palfreys. They were paid money, food, drink and usually a lavish 'livery' or uniform, sometimes two or three a year. Extras included mattresses, so the palfreyers could sleep in with their charges if need be, expensive whips and spurs, to distinguish their uniforms still further from those of the other grooms, and choice foods and medicines for sick palfreys.

No cost was spared when it came to sick treatment. In 1232 Henry III ordered the Bishop of Carlisle to 'find the necessary to cure the royal palfrey dying at Harrow, whatever the expense'. The most common medicines were grease and ointments for sore limbs, often made of suet, butter or bacon fat, and doses of honey and linseed for poor coats; cumin, resin and alum for sore stomachs, and a host of nameless purges and herbal potions.

If the palfrey recovered, he was ridden on parade or to hunt in magnificent costume, with linen covers for saddle and bridle, carved leather girths and stirrup leathers, coloured girthwebs and rump cloths, and countless brasses, plumes and hangings. To match these, riders wore velvet riding jackets and hoods, fustian doublets, brilliantly coloured short gowns and stockings, and leather or skin boots. Both sexes rode in spurs, gold and jewelled ones if display demanded it, and often in dress gloves, with optional dress collars, purses and caps. These last became all the rage for society ladies when Anne of Bohemia was queen. Both sexes rode to hunt and take the air in narrow velvet caps with turned-up borders festooned with bright feathers.

But it was the horse whose colour mattered most. The few medieval horses recorded as having had names were named according to their colour, which was the attribute the Medievals valued most in horses. The monk's palfrey was 'as brown as is a berry', that is to say bay, a very popular horse colour, advertised in names like the Bishop of Norwich's 'Palfrid Bai' and King Edward III's 'Bayard Stakes'. Sorrels and duns were also popular, but not chestnuts or black horses, which appear much less frequently in names, pictures and stories. Horses of more than one colour, and with markings like stars or white feet, are also rare in illustrations, but get affectionate mention in written records. Henry III was especially fond of 'bald' (piebald) palfreys.

But everyone liked greys best. The Medievals distinguished at least five shades of horse grey. White was as precious as it was rare, and few owners outside romance were lucky enough to own a white horse. Grissel, or pale grey, was next best, and Edward III paid a princely sum of £24 for a horse called 'Grissel de Borton', named after its colour and previous owner, in 1340. He paid 20 marks (£13.6.8d.) for a grey called 'Lyard de Burgh', which he bought from Raymond de Burgh. Liards were horses spotted with grey and, like grissels, were much sought after, and snapped up as soon as they came on the market. Dappled greys were popular, as is evidenced by the number of synonyms for their colouring, such as spotted and pomelled. Ferrant, or iron grey, was either an unusual shade or one which few bothered to distinguish from liard, since it only appears occasionally in the records.

A single adjective, if not of colour then of speed, is all the description the Medievals ever give of their horses. They knew them too well to need written descriptions. 'Knights knoweth the goodness of horses,' wrote one fifteenth-century chronicler succinctly. The medieval reticence on horse riding is testimony of its familiarity. Phrases like 'he rode a great wallop' [Malory's *King Arthur*] were enough to invoke a complete picture of horsemanship.

One of these incidental little phrases about horse riding is
enough to sum up the understood indissolubility of the sporting
partnership between medieval man and his horses. The phrase
comes from Malory again: 'It is Sir Lancelot, I know it by his
riding.'

8 Cock-fighting. Marginal illustration from the the Alexander Romance. *Bodleian Library, Oxford* MS.
Bodl. 264, fol. 50.

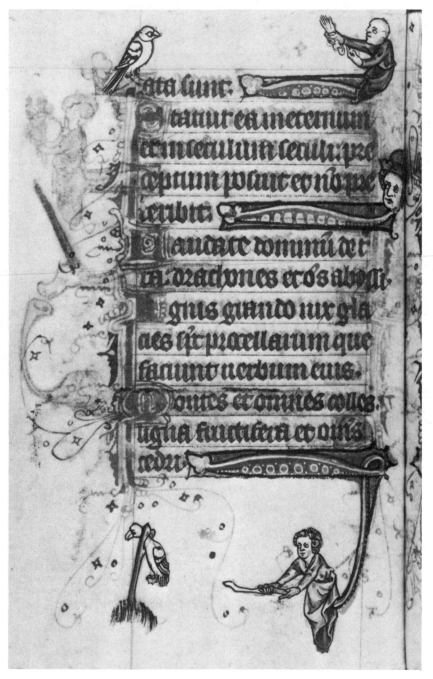

9 Cock-throwing with a stick. *Bodleian Library, Oxford* MS. Douce. 6, fol. 156.

10 An ape in mock combat with a man in grotesque ape costume. By the Master of Mary of Burgundy in the Book of Hours of Englebert of Nassau. *Bodleian Library, Oxford* MS. Douce. 218, fol. 132v.

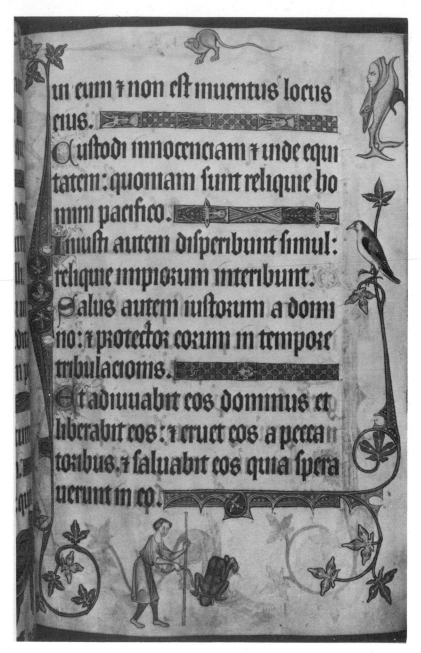

in eum ⁊ non est inuentus locus
eius.

Custodi innocenciam ⁊ uide equi
tatem: quoniam sunt relique ho
mini pacifico.

Iniusti autem disperibunt simul:
relique impiorum interibunt.

Salus autem iustorum a domi
no: ⁊ protector eorum in tempore
tribulacionis.

Et adiuuabit eos dominus et
liberabit eos: ⁊ eruet eos a pecca
toribus. ⁊ saluabit eos quia spera
uerunt in eo.

11 A travelling player with his performing ape. *The British Library* Add 42130. fol. 73.

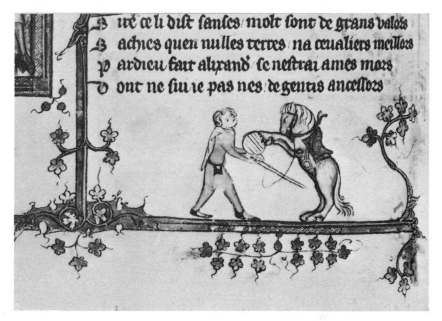

B ue ce li dist sances molt sont de grans valors
B achies quen nulles terres na cevaliers meillors
P ardieu fait alixand ce nestrai ames mors
O ont ne suie pas nes de gentis ancestors

12 Performing horse. From the Alexander Romance. *Bodleian Library, Oxford* MS. Bodl. 264, fol. 96v.

13 Pillion riding in the summer, the women riding side-saddle. *The British Library* Add 38126, fol. 5v.

CHAPTER THREE

Hunting, Hawking and Fishing

'By God's body, I had rather that my son should hang than study latin! For it becomes the sons of gentlemen to blow the hunting-horn well, to hunt skilfully, and elegantly to carry and train the hawk' [a fifteenth-century nobleman]. The medieval aristocracy never changed its hunting cry. From first to last it gloried in hunting as the most noble, manly and sporting of all occupations. Hunting was the heart of a nobleman's education and delight; it won the heart of his lady; it was far and away his favourite sport. He ate, drank, slept, loved, prayed, and hunted with hawk and hound. Already, before Britain was conquered by the Romans, its noble heroes had famous hunting dogs, which they gave personal names and to which they were strongly attached. British, especially Irish, hounds were exported all over the continent in the first century B.C., and were much esteemed; when the Anglo-Saxons took over most of Britain, they took over its ancient sport of hunting with horses, hawks and hounds. It is clear from Anglo-Saxon records that this was a nobleman's sport, requiring a nobleman's resources of time, land and animals. Kings Ethelred and Canute forbade hunting on Sundays, and Edgar's canons forbade any priest to 'hunt, hawk or dice . . . rather he should study his books . . .' But landowners and clerics hunted irrepressibly throughout the period.

King Alfred's friend and biographer, Asser, related proudly how well Alfred hunted wild boar before he was twelve years old, and now he had a fine slogan for the chase: 'If thou hast a sorrow, tell it to thy saddle-bow and rise thee, singing, forth.' Asser was a monk from Wales, where the British hunting tradition was proudly upheld. There were game laws protecting and evaluating the famous British hounds, of which the Welsh King Howel the Good distinguished four kinds in the early tenth century. Athelstan demanded some of these 'sharp-scented dogs' and some hawks, as part of his tribute from the Welsh King after the battle of Brunanburh in 937.

The chief huntsman was one of fourteen people at the Welsh court who sat in armchairs in the palace. His dogs were worth the same as the King's, and his allowance included regular hornfuls of liquor and meat meals; in winter he was supplied with oxskin, to make leashes, and in summer with cowskin, to make boots. The needle he used to 'sew up torn dogs' was one of three 'legal needles' in the land, the other two being the Queen's sewing needle and the palace doctor's needle, each of them valued at 4d.

Hunting in dense forests was on foot, using stone slings, spears, short bows and crossbows, hunting swords and knives, and three-pronged forks. In thinner forests and in open country, hunting was on horseback, using all these weapons and also long-bows and javelins. Hunting was the one secular amusement of the austere Edward the Confessor. It was the national passion, dominated by King, court and country. The first concern of the Norman kings, as it had been of the Anglo-Saxon kings before them, was to restrict hunting as far as possible to themselves and their noble entourages.

They therefore distinguished three main types of hunting and restricted the right to each of them. The most important type was forest hunting, and it was declared a royal monopoly. This meant that the four forest beasts: red deer, fallow deer, roe deer and wild boars, and in some areas hares too, were royal monopolies. Foresters, woodwards and verderers were appointed to plant and maintain the forests and their animals, often walling them in to make parks, for the royal enjoyment. Forest justices were appointed to deal with those who broke the forest laws, most commonly by poaching and trespass. Pretty well all dogs except sheepdogs were banned from royal forests unless they had one foot mutilated, so they could not chase game. King John not only greatly extended the already vast acreage of Britain under forest – about two-thirds of the country – but also ordered that all the dogs in every forest of the kingdom be slaughtered. Edward I eventually relaxed these laws to remove only those dogs that were too big to pass through a dog-gauge about seven-and-a-quarter inches by five inches. But human hunting trespass remained absolute anathema, and penalties for it varied from substantial fines to execution.

The second type of hunting was that of the chase, which was a piece of forest, often in the form of an enclosed park, granted away to an individual, who could hunt it, and allow others to hunt it, as he liked. He usually kept the right to hunt the forest beasts, but might grant away the right to hunt the others, which were bucks, roebucks, martens, badgers and wildcats.

The third type of hunting was that of warren, which was quite distinct from those of forest and chase, for it was hunting in the open countryside, and in theory everyone had a right to it. In fact, the right to warren on big estates was often granted away privately, but on unclaimed land it and its small animals were open to all.

There was a fourth type of hunting, but it was never defined and regulated like the other three because it was not considered a sport. This was the hunting of vermin, and people were not only allowed, but encouraged, even compelled, to undertake it, since vermin destroyed game, and so spoilt good hunting. The hunting of vermin was the only brief by which most people were allowed to enter the royal forests.

But the royal forest monopoly could not last. The English nobility just would not submit to exclusion from hunting the best game, and broke into it by winning and buying numerous grants from the Crown. Every nobleman wanted his right to 'vert' (greenwood) and venison.

> For in his hunting hath he such delight,
> That it is all his joy and appetite
> To be himself the great hart's bane
>
> [*The Knight's Tale*]

In the thirteenth century the barons not only forced King John to sign Magna Carta but also forced Henry III to sign a follow-up to it known as the Forest Charter, in 1217. This ended the royal monopoly and reduced the amount of royal forest. Henry III then relieved his cash problems by relaxing the forest laws still further, in favour of clergymen worth £10 a year, and burgesses. The golden age of the hunting parson had dawned.

What chance had the reformers' strictures against the seductive pleasures of the chase? How could they hope to quench the enthusiasm of men like Reginald Brian, a fourteenth-century Bishop of Worcester, who wrote to the Bishop of St David's about some hounds the latter had promised to send him, 'Let them come, oh reverend father, without delay! let my woods re-echo with the music of their cry and the cheerful notes of the horn, and let the walls of my palace be decorated with the trophies of the chase!'

If prayer was the first duty of the cleric, hunting was his first sport, and doubtless a fair share of his prayers were addressed to St Hubert, the patron saint of hunting. As a nobleman and a cleric, Hubert was the ideal saint for the job. He was born in Aquitaine in about 656, and was a passionate hunter. So much so that he went hunting on Good Friday in 683. Just as he was blowing his horn at the death of a fine stag, he had a vision of a stag with a luminous crucifix between its antlers, reproaching him for hunting on so solemn a holy day. He returned home, entered the Church, and later became Bishop of Liège. Nothing in his story says that he gave up hunting, and medieval portrayals of it take great relish in its hunting details; his patronage was obviously considered sympathetic rather than curative.

He had plenty of clients in England. Church prelates had to accommodate the royal hounds whenever the royal hunt was passing in their direction. When they died, their hounds went to the King as a mortuary. Church and lay magnates were equally keen on hunting and equally manificently equipped for it, with animals, weapons and clothes.

The most important of these were animals, and the most important animals were hounds. There were three basic hunting methods in the Middle Ages, and hounds were vital to all three of them, whereas horses could be dispensed with in two of them, and even in the third, most popular method when the game hunted was small.

The least popular method was hunting from artificial hedges, or hays, with nets and snares concealed in them, on the edges of the chase. The game was driven towards the hays, and caught, or shot with bows, by the waiting hunters. It was too static and unsporting to offer much enjoyment, and was only practised a little, towards the end of the period, as a change from the chase. But its increasingly elaborate hays, sometimes shaped like horses and mounted on wheels, were no substitute for the chase. More popular, but still too static to offer real sport, was the similar method of hunting from stands, known as stables, armed only with bows, and without the help of snares. But the real sportsman hunted by chasing, usually on horseback but sometimes on foot, until he had exhausted or trapped his quarry and managed to kill it. This was the only method that gave genuine sport, with all its thrills and strains, as described by Edward Duke of York, known as the Master of Game, after the treatise of that name which he wrote between 1406 and 1414.

Like all the English hunting writers, he put the hare top of his list of game, but the English were alone in Europe in preferring this 'good little beast' to the stag, the king of the forest. They preferred him because he was hunted all year round, across all types of countryside, and if he was to be caught, subtle skill was required. Hunting the 'cunning, devious little hare' was the best possible training for hounds. One thirteenth-century poem listed all the names by which the English knew the hare, and they give an idea of English respect for it. The list reads like a hunting litany. 'The hare . . . the way-beater . . . the go-by-ditch . . . the steal away . . . the grass biter . . . the late-at-home . . . the woodcat . . . the wind-swift . . . the sitter . . . the grass-hopper . . .' The hounds who had to cover 'four swift miles' to catch it were greyhounds and running hounds, the same ones that were used to chase stags.

All the hunting writers devoted long, loving chapters to hounds, and their favourites were always greyhounds and running hounds. An early Welsh proverb declared that a gentleman might be known by 'his hawk, his horse and his greyhound.' Only a gentleman would be able to accommodate and care for greyhounds in the manner recommended by the Master of Game and Twicci, Edward II's huntsman. There had to be two-storey kennels, fitted with 'straw coloured stones to piss against, and gutters', enclosed in sunny grass yards, looked after by kennel men familiar with herbal medicine. [Illustration 14] Greyhounds living in such luxury had to be

headed like a snake,
and neckled (necked) like a drake,
footed like a cat,
tailed like a rat.

[Dame Juliana Berners, c. 1496]

Medieval illustrations show beautifully kept greyhounds of all sizes, though medium sized was best liked, and a variety of colours, white being the rarest and most valuable. When Froissart, the French chronicler, went home from Scotland in the late fourteenth-century, he took with him 'un blanc levrier' (a white greyhound), one of four he had named in the heroic tradition: Tristam, Hector, Brun and Roland. Next most highly prized were black and tan greyhounds, then plain sorrels and greys. The name greyhound does not refer to their colour, but to their 'grae' or 'high grade' (Celtic and Old English respectively). From early Celtic to Tudor times, they were the aristocrats of English hunting. [Illustration 15]

They always worked in pairs, their couplings attached to ornate collars. In 1400 the wardrobe accounts mention 'two collars for greyhounds, le tissue white and green with letters and silver turrets'. The hounds were 'slipped', or let loose, from their collars to course hares.

They were also used to turn back bigger game from passes to the main chase, and to take over the chase relay in open country from a pack of 'running hounds', towards the end of a hunt, in order to pull down the wounded game. They were speed relays, hunting by sight.

Running hounds hunted by scent, in packs of large and small dogs, the small ones known as kennets, raches or harriers, because they harried small game such as hares. Medieval illustrations show a variety of breeds of harriers. White or pale biscuit was the most common colour, often with black or mottled markings.

The native long-eared was the progenitor of the beagle, and

there were what Edward II called 'our bow-legged hare hounds of Wales which can well discover a hare', and a variety of Danish, Saxon and Norman imports. Though chiefly used on small game, English harriers had an international reputation and were just as well treated and carefully trained as stag hounds. Chaucer's prioress fed her small hounds with 'roasted flesh or milk, and wastel [best wheat] bread', a diet recommended by hunting writers and used by some hound masters. Bread was the hounds' staple food, and it was either made of wheat flour, bran flour or oats, which made hard bread, like dog biscuits.

The finest running hounds were trained to hunt bigger game than hares, in particular the hart, the royal red deer of five years old or more, with antlers of ten points, the 'fairest hunting that any man may hunt after' [*Master of Game*]. Mounted parties of both sexes went out to hunt harts during the hart hunting season, officially from Midsummer's Day, June 24th, to Holyrood Day, September 14th, but actually extended to begin in May. The season was known as the 'time of grace' and was the huntsman's heaven. The wood and huge woodland parks that had been stocked with deer ever since the close of the last season were his to disport to his heart's content.

Bishop Swinfield took his packs of hounds and his thirty or forty horses on summer hunting tours. When he reached a place where he did not have kennels, he paid the villagers to accommodate his hounds and dry the oats for their food. He bought huge consignments of beer for his 'men out hunting in the July sun', and was careful to compensate the locals on the rare occasions when his highly disciplined hounds killed one of their domestic animals. When he died, his hounds had to go to the King as a mortuary, but while he lived, he hunted.

The hart hunts he went on would have been big, elaborate, colourful pageants. They began at dawn, when the hunt officials met to get their instructions from the Master of Game. Kennel and huntsmen assembled before the Master with straining leashes of hounds, to be despatched to their stations. The grooms of the hunt and local foresters were sent off to watch the deer in their feeding places, and estimate the size and whereabouts of their coverts. The central officer in this, and in all the preparatory stages of the hunt, was the lymerer, so called because he held the hounds tightly bound in a 'liam', or leash, until he found the hart's lair, or 'ligging'. His hounds were called lymers, and their job was to scent the quarry, then later to frighten it into breaking cover by barking. Lymers were not a breed. They were a type, often including mongrel greyhounds. But the best of them, with the best noses and black and tan colouring, were descended from St Huberts or Talbots, from St Hubert's monastery in the Ardennes, the foundation stock of medieval Southern Hounds and modern bloodhounds, pointers and setters.

The Master of Game explained in detail how the lymerer used these hounds to 'know a great hart by the fumes [excrements] . . . by the place where he hath frayed his head . . . by his traces [footprints] . . . and by his bellow.' He then explained how the lymerer was to discover the whereabouts of the hart's covert, and whether the hart was still in it or not, leaving a complicated system of signs made of broken twigs and branches to convey this information to the huntsman and his hounds when they came by later.

The huntsman presided over his grooms, palfryers, kennel men and berners (houndsmen), across the dinner table, in the middle of what the Master of Game said should be a 'fair green mead with trees all about'.

The hunters made elaborate personal preparations for the chase, and ate elaborate picnics, while the presiding lord and the Master of Game received the reports of the lymerers and foresters about the whereabouts of a good hart. Examining the fumes they brought back, the lord and Master of Game decided which hart would make the best hunting, in which direction they should hunt him; and where to station the berners with their relays of hounds.

If the hunt was by stands and stables, these were positioned, and the hunters with their bows went off to occupy them. If the hunt was 'by strength' (chase) alone, it was still customary to carry a short- or crossbow, easily slung across the shoulder. A hunting knife was absolutely basic, and the foot berners often carried spears, swords and other weapons for the kill.

Huntsman and berner alike rode horses that were the pride of their stables. Under Norman rule, heavy hunting horses became fashionable in England, many of them 'coursers swift as any thought' [Chaucer's *Legend of Good Women*], originally bred for charging and war. What was required of a good horse, wrote Dame Juliana, was a mixture of the three qualities of men and the three qualities of women – the men's to be bold, proud and hearty; the women's to be fair-breasted, fair-haired, and easy to leap upon. English coursers seem to have been well qualified. Illustrations show them with small heads, strong, low quarters and long tails. Those with the highest-ranking riders had their manes neatly plaited. Once leapt upon, they were ridden without spurs, with a curb-chain, frontlet, and occasionally a throat-latch, for extra control and turning power at speed. The saddles had raised backs, or cantles, for extra support, and were hung with gorgeous trappings, often including the family arms.

Most hunting women wore simple clothes, long and loose dresses and short over-jackets, slit up to the hip, allowing them to ride at speed and astride without any trouble. The men wore much the same, but those of lower class wore shorter, knee-length tunics like the ones worn by the berners and assistants on foot. Gloves were the other hallmark of nobility. Colours might be brilliant, the servants wearing the rich velvet liveries of their masters, but were more often predominantly green, for camouflage.

It was therefore essential that the huntsmen, lymerers and berners had horns with which to blow their whereabouts, and that of the hart, during the hunt. All the hunting writers give detailed descriptions of the different types of horn, which were favourite status symbols. Medieval wills and inventories are full of items like 'a horn covered with silver and gilt' [William Carent, Somerset, 1406] and 'a horn with a "bugil" harnessed with silver' [Thomas Halle, Somerset, 1457]. A 'bugil' horn was the simplest kind, just a polished cattle horn. Other sorts included ruets, from the French rouette, a small wheel, horns so curved that they were almost circular, and some with stoppers attached so they could be used to carry fumes or, more refreshingly, drink.

One after another, in descending order, the officials of the hunt sounded their horns, and the lymerer and his hounds advanced on the hart until he broke cover. Finders helped to find and separate the chosen hart from the others near him. The first relay of hounds was then released and the chase began. It was supreme sport, its language compulsively lively. Educated noblemen knew more hunting cries than they did horn blasts, and certainly more than they did Latin verbs. During a chase the forest rang with a unique combination of bloodthirsty English, Norman French and hunting Latin: 'Cy va, cy va [There he goes] . . . So howe, so howe illeoque [Back there] . . . Ha cy douce [Softly does it]'. Sending the hounds off his true line of running was the stag's only good chance of escape, and the Medievals esteemed him as they did because he had so many ways of doing this. He could double (double back on his tracks), beat (swim) up rivers, foil down (go downstream), go to soil (stand in water), and change places with another hart, a manoeuvre known as rusing. If all these failed, and his leaping and running could not save him, the hart turned his head and stood at bay.

This was the great moment. If any one creature can be said to have borne aloft the pride of the Middle Ages, it was the stag at bay. Winning a victory over it was the huntsman's highest ambition. All the huntsmen gathered around the bay, holloaing and blowing their horns, to 'break the bay' and kill the hart. This was done either by stabbing him from the shoulder to the heart, with a sword, or more commonly, because it was safer, shooting him with a bow and arrow. If the hounds caught him before he could turn at bay, he was killed quickly in one of these ways. As soon as he was dead, the lord or Master of Game 'blew the death', and his head was cut off and held by these two dignitaries. They held its antlers, the nostrils trailing the earth, and the body was cut up according to a set scheme, the various parts of it being given to various of the huntsmens' officials, and to the hounds, who had been coupled up by the berners before the kill.

This ritual flaying and carving up was one of the skills of a good woodsman, but in the words of the *Master of Game*, 'It is well suiting to a hunter to be able to do it.' It marked out his triumph, and in the fourteenth-century *Romance of Ipomydon*, it was the sight of the hero performing this ritual that finally won him the love of the lady he sought.

The lady looked out of her pavilion,
And saw him dight [cut up] the venison;
There she had great deynte [delight, dainty satisfaction]
. . . . . .
And thought in her heart then
That he was come of gentle man.

The hart's head was carried back in triumph to the lord's hall, where the final call, known as the menée, was blown, and all the huntsmen, wrote the Master of Game with tired simplicity, were to have good suppers. They were to have wine, not ale, and if earlier hunting had been successful, venison to eat. It was good to eat both fresh and salted, but it was not the chief reason for hart hunting. The chief reason was noble and sporting.

It had long been the custom for packs of royal hunting hounds and teams of royal hunting horses to move round the country to wherever the King wished to hunt, but Edward III was the first to establish separate packs of hart and buck hounds (bucks were young male deer) in permanent kennels at Windsor. His Master of the Buckhounds and of the Horse was Sir Bernard Brocas, a highly paid officer and a personal friend of the King. He was in overall charge of buying, selling and breeding the royal hunting animals, and maintaining supplies of game.

Deer hunting precedence was itemised by Henry IV in his household accounts: 12d. for the Master of Hart Hounds each day; 12d. for the Master of Buckhounds; 12d. for the Master of Harriers; from 4d. to 9½d. a day for huntsmen, depending on the exact nature of their job; 4d. a day for horse yeomen; 1½d. or 2d. a day for foot berners; 1½d. or 2d. a day for fewterers (greyhound attendants); 2d. a day for bercelettars (hunting dog attendants), and 1d. to 3d. a day for chace-chiens (dog boys), grooms, pages, foresters and parkers.

The hart was the only deer that was chased; bucks and does were hunted. There were seasons for every kind of hunting, and naturally they operated on all kinds of different scales. Most of the hunting in medieval England was probably done by little hunting parties of two or three, holding their own hounds, and often hunting on foot. Costs for big hunters were so great that there were few of them. [Illustrations 16, 17, 18]

In the early fourteenth century, hounds cost ½d., ¾d. or 1d. a day to keep, plus the cost of their keepers, and medical and transport expenses. Royal huntsmen hired horse-litters to transport hounds, and in 1277 the King paid John the Berner 3/6d. 'for his expenses going to Dover to bathe six sick braches by the King's order and for staying there twenty-one days.'

The number of deer taken by big hunts was enormous. In nine days of 1252 Duke Richard of Cornwall took thirty-two bucks in Rockingham Forest, an average score for one of his rank and resources. Not surprisingly, deer as well as the horses and hounds to hunt them were moved from park to park and wood to wood.

If the supply ran low, the season closed, or over-indulgence inspired a desire for change, there was always the wild boar, which was hunted in the wild winter months and was the only beast that ranked alongside the hart as a chaseable forest beast. Boar were hunted in England in Charles II's reign, but they were already less common at the time the Master of Game wrote than they had been when Fitzstephen wrote, and wild boar roamed the woods near London. In the later Middle Ages the appeal of boar-hunting was mainly that of the rare and the exotic, though all through the period it also had the appeal of the gory and the masculine.

The thrill of boar-hunting lay more in the kill than the chase. Henry VIII had a collection of boar spears, about three hundred of them 'dress' spears, covered in velvet and fringed with silk, and three hundred 'knotted and leathered' for real hunting use. Boar spears were broad headed, with cross-bars just below the heads to stop them entering the flesh too deeply and impaling the hunter on the boar's tusks. The more cautious used nets to hold the boar for the kill.

Sir Bevis of Hampton hunted boars as well as riding race-horses, and his story gives an unforgettable taste of what it must have been like to be faced with a creature:

at his mouth five tusks stood out,
each was five inches about,
his sides were hard and strong,
his bristles were great and long.

All round his den were the bones of men he had slain in the wood:

eaten their flesh and drank their blood . . .

Bevis went for the kill by driving his spear against the boar's shoulder. It broke in four pieces without even piercing the hide, and Bevis was forced to fight 'against the boar so grim' all day until evensong, but which time the boar's mouth was pouring foam and 'God's grace and his virtue' came to Bevis's aid. He dented two tusks and cut off a slice of snout.

So the boar so loud cried,
out of the forest wide and side . . .
his sword Bevis hastily
in at the mouth then pressed so
and carved his heart even unto.

It was all over bar the beheading, which Bevis did at once, putting the head on the handle of his spear as a trophy. He had proved his strength and bravery. All boar-hunters sought to do likewise; they were a dedicated minority, and were always paragons of manhood.

They needed exceptionally tough hounds, and the best for the job were alaunts, or alans, and veutrers. According to the Master of Game, alans were like greyhounds except that their heads were bigger and shorter, with small eyes and sharp, upright ears. They had the speed of greyhounds, three times the biting power, but had to be taught to keep hold of their prey, in the case of boars most understandably. They were very strong, ferocious and warlike.

They probably got their name from a Caucasian tribe called the Alani, who invaded Gaul in the fourth century, thence Spain, where the best medieval alans were found. They came in many colours, but white was the best, with black spots about the face. Almost certainly these were the original English mastiffs, but they were known to huntsmen as alans and to most people as butchers' dogs or bandogs, who brought cattle in from the countryside to the butcheries, and recaptured them if they escaped. They fed on discarded butchers' offal, and if starved of this for a few days, made champion bull and bear baiters, and boar-hunters.

There was a similar type of dog called a veutrer, or velterer, also used for guarding butcheries, baiting and boar-hunting. The Master of Game warned rather alarmingly that they were inclined to run at everything and everyone, including men and hounds, but it could be said in their favour that they were so heavy and ugly that it did not matter if they were slain by a boar.

With that, he passed on from boar to wolf-hunting, which apparently needed as many as four relays of hounds for the chase, and mastiffs for the kill. The wolf was the most common and dangerous form of vermin, especially in the early Middle Ages, when the Anglo-Saxons called January wolf-month because they lost so many cattle to wolves during the frozen weather. Anyone could hunt the wolf, though chances of success were remote, for it was inexhaustibly fast and cunning. Forest and chase owners hired wolf-hunters to rid their game reserves of wolves, by putting down pitch to trap them and their whelps.

The Master of Game put foxes after wolves in his book, classing them as a similar type of vermin, particularly dangerous to domestic fowls, that could be killed by a similar array of unsporting methods, including traps, snares, poison, nets and suffocation. William of Blatherwyk, known as William de Foxhunte, was Edward I's 'fox-dog keeper' and had a kennel of twelve hounds, to which he added another twelve at the height of the September to April season, and a load of fox-nets and a horse to carry them to the foxes' covert in Clarendon Park. Nets were seldom used in any sort of hunting because deer might trip over them and injure themselves, but William used them to surround the foxes' part of the woods, so that the foxes could run into them when flushed out of cover by the hounds.

Edward I also had an otter-hunter called John, whose job, like William's, was a cross between hunting and pest extermination. Just as foxes preyed on poultry, so otters preyed on fish, and so, in the Master of Game's words, 'men take them in rivers with small cords as they do the fox with nets and other gins.' There were royal otter-hunters from the reign of King John onwards, right through the Middle Ages, as well as countless unofficial and unrecorded otter-hunters.

Licences to hunt vermin in royal forests were plentiful; everywhere else, such hunting was unrestricted. For the purists, it had official seasons, but it was in fact permissible all year round. It covered badgers, wildcats and rabbits too. Fox- and wolf-skins had to be strongly tawed before they could be used to make collars and cuffs because they smelt so strong; the community at Whitby Abbey in 1396 had fourteen wolf skins dressed for them, at a cost of 10/9d., but they were unusual in bothering. Wildcat fur was easier to use, and hunters used it to trim their winter clothes. Rabbit- or cony-skins were occasionally used to make warm linings, great numbers of them stitched together, but the Master of Game could not bring himself to give rabbits even a dismissive chapter in his book, 'for no man hunteth them unless it be bish [fur] hunters, and they hunt them with ferrets and with long small hayes [wire tunnel traps disguised as hedges].'

In fact ferreting was not just a bish hunter's ploy; it was a popular small sport, like fowling, the catching of birds in snares and traps. Like all hunting that used these methods, it was basically unsporting, but it became a sport in its own right with noble women and children, who made their own traps and found sport in trying to make them work. It was the miscellaneous end of hunting. [Illustration 17]

Dame Juliana Berners, a late fifteenth-century sporting writer who was probably the abbess of a convent, and enjoyed the traditional monastic sport of hunting, gave a hunting vocabulary at the end of her treatise which captures delightfully the character of all these different kinds of hunting. According to Juliana, foxes congregate in skulks, like thieves and friars; moles congregate in labours; ladies and roes in bevies; women and geese in gaggles and nuns in superfluities.

Juliana was particularly fond of the small, feminine end of hunting, and devoted a section to hawking, which was the sport of both sexes but was a feminine speciality because it used small, graceful animals and because female falcons were better chase-birds than male falcons. Falconry and hawking were interchangeable terms. They were almost the same sport, except that hawks were slightly shorter, with more rounded wings and tails. Both falcons and hawks were very expensive to buy, keep and train, and hunting with them was an aristocratic sport.

The hawk had been a noble, indeed a sacred bird, since the time of the Ancient Egyptians, if not before, and was the noblest of noble possessions throughout the Middle Ages. Nowhere was this more so than in Wales, where peregrine falcons were famous, and where the falconer who trained them was one of the aristocrats of the court. He was only allowed three draughts of ale from his honorary horn in any one day in case he got too drunk to do his duty. Falconry was the exercise of excellence.

Like hunting, it was the passion of the Anglo-Saxon and Celtic nobility, and the scourge of the reformers. The first trained hawk is said to have been sent to England by Boniface when he was Bishop of Mons in the eighth century, as a present for King Ethelbert of Kent. Hawking immediately became a royal sport. William the Conqueror and his court displaced a hunting nobility, bringing with them famous Flemish falconers with new breeds of bird on their gloved fists. Norman hawking was more international, luxurious and formal than Anglo-Saxon hawking, but even after the Conquest British peregrines continued to be especially highly prized at home and abroad. They were exported and exchanged all over Europe. Henry II's favourite hunting birds were Welsh peregrine eyasses.

It was an élite trade, king to king, court to court, passing between the East coast ports and Flanders, Scandinavia and Normandy. In 1232 Henry III instructed the bailiffs of Yarmouth to keep all birds coming into the country from 'Norway or other lands', so that William of Hauvill, the royal falconer, could take them for the King if he liked the look of them. That year he had a choice of lannerets (Mediterranean falcons), sparrowhawks (small hawks that prey on small birds such as sparrows), gyrfalcons (large, white falcons which fly at prey such as herons and are northern visitors to Britain), goshawks (large, short-winged hawks) and falcons gentle (female and young of the goshawk). Local hawk dealers quickly made big enough fortunes to start collecting hawks themselves. In one typical case in twelfth-century Lincoln, it was decided that Outi the chaplain (his name suggests he was a Scandinavian) would have to pay one hawk for the right to recover four hawks and four falcons from Godwin the Rich and William, son of Englebert. But Outi could not pay the hawk he owed because he was away in Norway at the time, hawk-trading.

Hawks were very expensive. In 1361 Edward III drew up a list of prices for his new buyer in East Anglia, and he put falcons gentle at the top, at twenty shillings each, and lanners bottom, at half a mark each (3/4d.). But it was nothing to pay £5 for a good bird, plus the expense of having it escorted to its new home by its keeper. Owners liked to keep their birds in expert hands, and paid to have them bought, transported, trained and kept by experts.

There was a special satisfaction in hawking with a bird that came from one's own estates and had been caught young and trained by one's own falconer. Bishop Swinfield had a bird-keeper called Harpin, the only man in his ample staff who had what sounds like a nickname, *harpin* being the French for a boat-hook. He was the Bishop's favourite, and was given a house of his own on the edge of the Bishop's estates at Ross-on-Wye. Part of his job was to catch young falcons as they left their nests, and he went on long falcon-catching expeditions, taking nets and an assistant with him.

Even those who went in for grandiose falconry, like Edward I with his eleven falconers with two horses each, and six falconers with one horse each, liked to buy untrained birds and have them trained by their own men. This was a painstaking process, and Juliana left detailed instructions about it, including one that hounds should be kept away the first time a hawk is taken out to fly at prey, because many hawks dislike hounds. Most owners preferred to accustom their birds to hounds from an early age, and hawks and hounds kept close company in the halls, and in the hunting, of medieval sportsmen.

Training could be long and expensive. Henry III once paid eleven marks (£3/13/4d.) for two gyrfalcons, and ten marks (£3) to have them trained, and provided cranes for them to practise on. Poorer owners provided woodcocks. Besides teaching the bird to stand on its perch, fly off to attack, and return, the trainer had to teach it to work at speed, from horseback, and in close human company. Taking a hawk to church on one's wrist was a favourite way of accustoming it to human company; reforming clerics objected strongly, but most clerics were unreformed.

A hawk on the wrist was part of an owner's nobility; taking it into church was a parade of rank. Juliana had a table of rank for hawks and their owners, starting with a merlin hawk as a bird fit for an emperor, then a gyrfalcon or tercel (male) gyrfalcon for a king, down through a long list to a sparrowhawk for a priest, and a kestrel, the humblest of all, for a knave or servant.

Most of the noblest hawks she categorised as 'hawks of the tower, to be called and reclaimed from a perch', and most of the humblest ones as 'flying from the hand over fields of stubble'. In fact hawking from perches and from the hand was done both on horseback and on foot, by riverside and across the fields. Riverside hawking was the most popular sort, and was an English speciality. Chaucer's Sir Thopas could hunt deer 'and ride on hawking by the river, with grey goshawk in hand.' [Illustration 24]

Having a hawk on the wrist was having it 'on the creep', and slaying thus was slaying 'on the creep'. Alternatively, the hawk could be left on a nearby hillside while the hunter crept across to a river full of birds and called the hawk across, scaring the prey into the air by banging a tabor (a small drum) and calling out. The tabor was the favourite instrument for scaring prey, and was used in all sorts of hawking. [Illustration 19]

The bigger the prey, the nobler. And crane, heron and partridge were ranked the noblest. Hawks could be trained to catch prey on land, especially hares and vermin, but this was less sporting and less popular than catching in the air. Every hawk had its own style of flight, attack, killing and training, all of them detailed by Juliana, together with a list of specialist nouns describing the feathers, flights and physical features of hawks.

A hawk might hunt a sage of herons or bitterns, a nye of pheasants, or a dropping of sheldrakes. It 'dantylleth' (stretches its wings along its leg), 'joukyth' (sleeps), and 'rouseth' (shakes its feathers and body). Its tail feathers were called a beam, the small white feathers under its tail 'brallys', the wing feathers next to its body 'flags'.

The equipment for hawking was minimal but extravagant. It consisted basically of a swivelling perch, attached by rings called 'terrets' to leather or silk strings called 'jesses', which the hawk wore round its legs when not in flight. Some people preferred to hunt without perches, and wore the terrets round their little fingers. Either way, hawkers always wore big, handsome, leather gloves. While a hawk was being trained to fly at prey, a long lead called a 'creance' was attached to it, so it could be reclaimed easily, and sometimes attached to its prey, to make capture easier.

It had been the custom of falconers in the East to hood their birds while they were not in use, to keep them relaxed and fresh for flight. After the Crusades this custom spread to Western Europe, and hawks were hoodwinked with little silk hoods, sometimes exquisitely embroidered or feathered, in the colours of their masters' livery. The more fashionable of them wore little bells on their legs, which rang and sparkled as they flew. Some owners put bells on their jesses too. Everything about hawking was flamboyant and dramatic.

It was also very personal, more so than any other form of hunting. Owners took their hawks into their chambers and dining-halls, along with the rest of their noble companions. Society ladies displayed their hawks on perches in their rooms. Phillipa of Hainault, who came to England from a country famous for its falconry, to be Edward III's queen in 1328, had a magnificent collection of birds, and was personally responsible for their management. Other women of her class did likewise. Hawks were a mark of noble femininity and a coin of noble currency. They were commonly used in the payment of noble rents. Henry

IV granted the Isle of Man to Sir John Stanley in lieu of the 'cast [couple] of hawks' he usually paid him.

Noble hawks were highly strung, and needed doting care. Hawks were always protected birds. Penalties for stealing or damaging hawks' eggs or eyries were harsh, and Edward III raised the penalty for killing a hawk to death.

'Hawks are tender and must have rest,' wrote Juliana, 'so it is a good thing to bring them in from their eyrie to a clean, warm place.' It was important to do this before they began to mew (moult), and the places they were brought into, known as mews, were built facing south for sunlight. They were always spotlessly maintained, and were often luxurious. Henry III's hawks at Nottingham had a mew hollowed out of the rock below the castle for them in 1236, but it was at Charing Cross that the royal mews reached the last word in comfort and ostentation.

Edward I liked falconry better than any other field sport, and between 1274 and 1277 he had two chambers built at Charing Cross, one for falconers and one for chaplains, backing on to an enclosed, turfed garden with a lead bath for the birds, with a metal image of a falcon in the middle. Water was conveyed to the mews in an aqueduct, and poured into the bath through four brass spouts shaped like leopards' heads. The falcons were kept in little cages or cabins, fed on doves from dovecots in the mews gardens, and kept in training with a supply of cranes to fly at. From time to time the clerk of the works at Westminster bought blocks for the falcons to stand on, and renewed the curtains that kept their cages shady. There was also accommodation for hounds, and, later in the century, horses. These mews were a mixture of retreat, holiday home and health farm.

While there, hawks were fed on pieces of chicken, kid or eel, tied to pieces of string and pushed into their cages. While a hawk was mewing no one but its keeper was allowed near it. If it was sickly or convalescent it was fed on pork and pigs' liver, and purged with a favourite medieval laxative: butter and herbs.

The fastidious care lavished on sick hawks was described by Chaucer in his *Squire's Tale*. A young princess, Canacee, finds an injured hawk and takes it home:

And softly in plasters gan her wrap . . .
. . . herbs precious, and fine of hue,
To heal with this hawk . . .
And by her bed's head she made a mew,
And covered it with velvets blue . . . . . .
And all without the mew is painted green.

Royal falconers watched round the clock with sick hawks, kept them warm and made offerings at shrines for their recovery. Edward I paid Simon Corbet of Shropshire, one of a great sporting family, 16d. for '1 qtr. [512 lb.] of coal, to burn a light for four days for one of the King's sick gyrfalcons', and 18d. for 'wax to make an image of a gyrfalcon to offer at the shrine of St Thomas of Cantilupe in Hereford Cathedral.' He paid a further 6d. for 'gifts made at the shrine of St Thomas of Hereford and the one of St Thomas of Canterbury, for the said sick falcon, at the King's command.' He sent Thomelin Corbet down to Hereford from court for eight days, to take the falcon to the shrine there.

Sick and healthy hawks alike bathed every three days in hot weather, once a week in winter. They were fed on the best meat, and rewarded with portions of the neck and brain of the prey they had caught. Gentle training started with flying at game flushed out of cover by small dogs such as spaniels.

Spaniels became popular in England in the sixteenth century. Before that there were relatively few of them, and most belonged to noble ladies. 'Small hounds' included spaniels, but more often meant other small breeds. They were beloved of nuns because they hawked well and were affectionate, faithful companions; Dame Juliana went hawking with small hounds, and she was probably the Prioress of Sopwell Nunnery in Hertfordshire. In 1387 William of Wykeham made a complaint of the sort echoed by countless visitors to medieval nunneries, that the nuns of Romsey 'bring with them to church birds, rabbits, small hounds and such like frivolous things, whereunto they give more need than to the offices of the church.'

The Master of Game reckoned small hounds were inclined to bark too much, and could not keep a straight line while running, which they could only do after partridges and quails. But within these rather effeminate limits they could be taught to be good couchers (from the French coucher, to lie down), to swim and dive well in rivers, and to be expert covert dogs.

They preferred hawking on foot to hawking on horseback. On foot it was more subtle, on horseback more exhilarating. Hawking horses had to be steady, strong and fast, able to cover long distances at speed. In 1240 Henry III ordered the Sheriff of Essex to repair any bridges along the length of the River Lea that were not in perfect condition, so that he could hawk its length 'expedite', at speed. Horse and rider needed steady nerves. In 1243 Henry's falconer, Gilbert de Hauvill, was paid 5 marks (£3/ 13/4d.) for training one of his chief gyrfalcons, and money to replace 'the two horses he lost therein.'

Juliana's real love was a gentler sport than either mounted hawking, hawking on foot or hawking 'on the creep'. She gave all forms of hawking and hunting the respect and interest they deserved, but not her heart. This belonged in more tranquil disport. 'Hunting as to my intent is too laborious, for the hunter must always run . . . He bloweth till his lipblister, and when he weneth [thinks] it be a hare, full oft it is a hedgehog.' As for the fowler, 'in the hardest and coldest weather . . . he is wet shod unto his tail.' The falconer had the neurotic nobility of his birds to contend with. 'When he would have her to fly, then will she to bathe.' So anyone wanting 'good disports and honest games' should take up 'fishing, called angling, with a rod and a line and a hook.'

Angling was nothing like as popular as hunting or hawking, and for all her enthusiasm, Juliana made her section on it an appendix to her sections on the other two. Because most people fished to help them survive, few did it for sport. Like hawking, angling was aristocratic and clerical, but unlike hawking, it was also unfashionable, inexpensive and undramatic, or as Juliana would have it, unpretentious. 'The angler . . . hath his wholesome walk and merry at his ease . . . He heareth the melodious harmony of fowls. He seeth the young swans, herons, ducks, coots and many other fowls with their broods.'

Angling was the only sort of fishing Juliana counted as a

sport, the others being too much like hard work. On the rare occasions when medieval man fished for sport, it was usually with a rod and line. Fishing with nets could also be sporting, as contemporary illustrations show, but usually it was subsistence work. What made angling a sport, in Juliana's opinion, was that it was peaceful and meditative, more concerned with the catching than the catch. 'In quietness you may serve God devoutly in saying affectuously your customary prayer.'

Monks and nuns enjoyed angling in the stews that were also fished seriously to provide their communities with food. Gentlemen and women angled in their estate stews. Most estates had at least one stew to provide them with carp, bream, perch and other fleshy fish during Lent and on meatless days, and sometimes these stews were landscaped into watery pleasure gardens, where one might sit, and perhaps angle.

But anglers like Juliana thought little of angling in ponds, even if they were natural ones, and positively despised it in man-made stews. It was bad sport. 'A pond is but a prison for fish and they live there for the most part in hunger like prisoners, and therefore it is the less mastery to take them.' But angling in rivers and streams, especially 'stiff' streams, near weirs and waterfalls, and in the quiet, bankside water of streams, was sport indeed. It was health-giving, since anglers rose early, and it was invigorating and relaxing at the same time. It was richly varied but simply equipped.

Rods were usually home-made, though towards the end of the period manufactured ones began to appear on the market. Better ones were made of wands cut from hazel, willow or aspen trees, sharpened at one end and hollowed at the other, so that they fitted into each other and made a three-tier line with some give in it. The simplest ones were made of twisted horsetail hairs, dyed brown, ranging in thickness from one-ply for minnows to two-ply for gudgeon to twelve-ply for large trout and fifteen-ply for salmon fishing. It took several lengths of hair knotted together with a knot that tightened when pulled and wetted, a water-knot, to make a line.

Hooks ranged from tiny pieces of bent wire for light lines to bent shoemakers' and saddlers' needles for the strongest lines.

Juliana liked to see them bound to the lines with fine red silk, but hers were counsels of idealism. Most medieval illustrations show lines with cork floats attached; only ground lines, for trout and low-swimming fish, were weighted down, with leadweights, and some had neither float nor weight.

Salmon and trout gave the best sport and the best-tasting reward if the sport was successful. They were big, agile, handsome and delicious. Caterpillars, worms and minnows were the commonest bait for catching them. Grayling were the next best thing to trout, and were an important item on medieval menus. Of the remaining freshwater fish, eels were consumed in vast numbers, but were caught almost exclusively for that purpose, not for sport. Chub, bream, perch and roach, and in particular the strong-toothed pike, were good sport as well as good fleshy eating.

Those who took time over their angling made artificial flies, as well as collecting bait. Most flies were made of dyed wool, with insect wings or tiny feathers attached. Flounders, dace and other flat fish splashed about a good deal but did not 'labour' long and hard enough to give really good sport. Small fish like ruff and gudgeon were children's sport. Angling seems to have been more popular with children than with adults, and to have been a childhood household hobby as much as a sport.

It was too cool, calm and colourless to be a popular bloodsport, and too much a part of working life to be a popular sport with labourers, though more people may have angled than medieval literary records suggest; there is no way of knowing. As Chaucer said in his *Complaint of Mars*:

And like a fisher, as men all day may see,
Baiteth his hook with some pleasance
Till many a fish is wooed, till that he be
Seized therewith; and then at erst [last] hath he
All his desire . . .

14 A hunting kennel. *Bodleian Library, Oxford* MS. Douce. 335, fol. 46r.

15 Medieval hunting greyhounds, wearing ornamental hunting collars. *The British Library* 27699, fol. 34.

16 Searching out a stag. *Bodleian Library, Oxford* MS. Douce. 335, fol. 57.

17 Hunting hares on foot. *The British Library* Royal 2 B VII. fol. 155v. Ladies ferreting *The British Library* Royal 2 B VII, fol. 156.

18 A small ladies' hunting party, on foot. *The British Library* Royal 10 E IV. fol. 41.

19 Using a tabor to scare duck into the air for hunting. *The British Library* Royal 10 E IV. fol. 77v.

CHAPTER FOUR

Tournaments, Jousts and Tilts

William Marshall was a knight errant. For fifteen years he earned a princely living, fighting tournaments all over Europe. Henry II appointed him the chivalric companion of his son, the young prince Henry, whom he took on a jousting tour of the Continent. When he retired from active service he had five hundred tournament victories to his credit, and those in the fierce, dangerous tournaments of the twelfth century. Medieval knights in armour really did exist, and really did joust to the death, in tournaments and jousts.

The word 'tournament', usually abbreviated to tourn or tourney in the Middle Ages, comes from the Old French *tournay*, to turn or wheel about, and was the name for 'a military exercise, wherein lies no hatred, done for military practice and to display personal prowess' [The chronicler Roger of Hoveden, late thirteenth century]. This description fits jousting as well as tourneying, and the only difference between the two is that a tourn involved lots of knights, a joust only two. The names were often used interchangeably and the events staged together. William Marshal was a champion at both. But in his time tournaments were more popular, and jousts tended to replace them as time passed.

These games trained and glorified knights and would-be knights, and from the mid-thirteenth-century onwards were run according to an increasingly elaborate code of chivalrous conduct, in increasingly spectacular armour, costumes and settings, with sumptuous celebrations. Of the reasons Roger of Hoveden gave for tourneying, the second one, that of personal display, predominated in the later part of the period.

But earlier it had been very much the reverse. 'A youth must have seen his blood flow and felt his teeth crack under the blow of his adversary and have been thrown to the ground twenty times . . . thus will he be able to face real war with the hope of victory' [Roger of Hoveden]. Such were the brutal beginnings of chivalry and its tournaments.

They probably came to England with the Normans; The early Anglo-Norman chroniclers called them *batailles françaises*. They were officially forbidden by the Crown because they were politically dangerous. Post-conquest England was ruled by a handful of powerful barons, each with rival ambitions in Normandy and England. In such a situation, armed noble assemblies were the last thing the king wanted, and young knights wanting to tourney had to go abroad, especially to France, where tournaments were welcomed as showpieces of chivalrous high society.

But they gradually won a little more royal support in England, despite their dangerous political potential. Henry I began the fashion for heraldry in 1126, when he knighted his son-in-law, Geoffrey of Anjou, and hung round his neck a shield of gold lions. Thereafter most knights adopted shields of arms and distinctive trappings for their horses and weapons. Young nobles were tutored by men like William Marshal until they were ready to be knighted and given their own emblems, usually at the age of twenty-one, but younger if they were very distinguished socially. William's princely pupil was knighted when he was nine.

The first description of an English tournament dates from Henry III's reign, when Fitzstephen described the Sunday games 'representing battles and going through a variety of warlike exercises' played by London boys with padded shields and headless lances. 'At the same time many young nobles who have not yet received the honour of knighthood came from the king's court and from the houses of the great barons, to make trial of their skill in arms, the hope of victory animating their minds.' By the late twelfth century, knights were a vital force in the defence of England, and Richard I, alarmed at their military inferiority to French knights, and perhaps inspired by his crusading exploits, allowed knights and young men aspiring to knighthood to tourney.

But only at five fixed sites, on payment of fines, and without any foreigners participating. Tournaments were still politically dangerous, and (martially) they were absolutely lethal. Melées of fully armed knights mounted on war horses aimed to kill or incapacitate their opponents. They fought in enclosures known as lists, but more often in the open, and there were few rules. William Marshal and Prince Henry used to pretend they were taking no part, then charge when everyone was occupied. 'A sport which they call a tourn, but the better name would be a torment,' wrote one chronicler, and the Church condemned it unreservedly.

But also ineffectively. The thirteenth century was the great age of English tournaments. After Magna Carta in 1215 the Crown had to give them its reluctant blessing, and they developed into artistic performances as well as chivalrous games and political meetings. Different kinds of tournament were distinguished, and rules and conventions drawn up for them.

Still, crude tournaments were little more than scrimmages. In 1215 there was a grand tournament at Rochester for French and English knights, at which the English set upon the French with staves, beat them and chased them through the town, to avenge similar rough treatment they had received at a similar event in France.

Nevertheless, tournaments aimed more and more at knightly excellence. Wooden lists about 60 paces long and 40 paces wide, at least seven feet high, so they could not be jumped by horses, were set up on hard, level ground near castles and towns. They faced east-west, so the sun would not get in the combatants' eyes, and spectators watched from outside the barriers, the most important of them from a stand halfway along the south side. Heralds from the sponsors' household proclaimed the tournament all through the neighbourhood with the help of trumpets, minstrels and horses clothed, like themselves, in the household livery. Some tournaments were open to all comers; some were only for invited individuals, who might come from abroad. Participants presented themselves before the presiding king and queen, or lord and lady, and entered the lists in opposing groups numbering anything from twelve to twenty, when the opening fanfare was sounded.

They waited at opposite ends of the lists while attendants checked their armour, weapons and horses. If the contest was *à outrance* (to the death), they were encased in plate armour from top to toe. Most important of all was the helmet, or helm, either worn over a sort of chain mail wimple or padded and worn next to the skin. The face was always the main target, and well armed knights like Guy of Warwick, in the thirteenth-century romance of that name, had helms 'on every side stiff and stark.' [Illustration 20]

They also had chain mail or leather hauberks all over their bodies, and front and back plates over the top of those. Their legs were protected by plate chausses, riveted to bend at the knees, and their feet by plate shoes. They seldom wore spurs, in case they injured themselves or their horses, which they stirred into action with the touch of an armoured heel. In the second half of the thirteenth century there was a fashion for ailettes, which were little upright wings on top of the shoulders, attached by cords. But these were more common in tournaments *à plaisir* (of courtesy, with harmless weapons) than tournaments *à outrance*.

The accounts of one such tournament *à plaisir*, held in Windsor Park in 1278, survive to give some details of their sporting armour. The tournament was fought between thirtyeight 'cavaliers', many of whom had fought with Edward I in the Holy Land, and some of whom were from France and the Low Countries. Their outfits cost from seven to twenty-five shillings each and included leather hauberks, breast and back plates made of buckram, leather ailettes costing 8d. a pair, and gilded or silvered leather helms costing two shillings each. Big strong leather gauntlets were an essential part of every suit of armour.

By about 1300 it had become standard practice to have three courses with lances, three with swords and three with axes, and these remained the basic tourney weapons all through the Middle Ages. At first lances were just poles made of soft wood so they would splinter easily on impact, but by 1300 they were usually embellished with vamplates, which were wooden cuffs to protect the hands. In tournaments *à plaisir* these were tipped with coronals, or flat wooden crowns, and in tournaments *à outrance* with sharp metal points.

If the lance courses were not decisive, or if one of them unhorsed the opposition, the contest was continued with swords. In the Windsor tournament *à plaisir*, these were made of whalebone and parchment with silvered blades and gilded hilts, but it was more usual for them to be made of steel for this kind of tournament, with blunted ends. For bloody combat they were sharp enough, according to romance writers, to send sparks into the air when struck against armour, and strong enough to pierce right through saddle and horse and then the ground to a depth of a foot or more. That is why a knight needed

> a right noble targe [shield],
> it was great, strong and large,
> like Guy of Warwick's.

By the thirteenth century English shields had already developed their distinctive tapered triangle shape, which made them so easy to manoeuvre, but also made it more than ever essential that they be so manoeuvred. In 1390 the Earl of Pembroke was too slow using his during a jousting practice, and was struck in the groin and died.

Shields were painted with their owners' coats of arms, sometimes on a leather covering. The shields for the Windsor Park tournament were made of wood and cost 5d. each, plus the cost of emblazoning them.

Axes were long handled and topped with roundel, point, spike and *bec-de-faucon*. They were used in the last of the tourney courses, when the combatants were too tired to do much more than haul them up into the air and hope they would crash down on to a dent or fault in their opponent's armour. Some preferred to replace them with knives; some used neither. There were no absolutely fixed rules of play until the fifteenth century, and even then they were taken more as guides than controls. Tourneying did not easily admit of controls.

Mounted tournaments were fewer in the thirteenth century than ever before. 'Strenuous', or active, knights never numbered more than about 2,000, and as knighthood became more decorative it became more expensive. A knight's charger, known as a courser, had to carry heavier armour, more elaborate trappings and more complicated weapons, and heavy coursers were specially bred, at great expense. Mounted tournaments became fewer, slower, less dangerous and more spectacular.

The Windsor Park cavaliers adorned their coursers with coloured bridles crested with plumes, and necklets of little silver bells. Saddles were large and padded, and often emblazoned or hung with heraldic cloths. Courser and rider alike were liveried in a surcoat of coloured cloth which was extended in the four-teenth and fifteenth-centuries to cover the courser's legs and head, but in earlier centuries had left them uncovered for freer move-ment. Courser and rider cut colourful figures as they waited in the lists for tourneying to begin, surrounded by liveried heralds, men-at-arms, minstrels and attendants. By the thirteenth-century most knights wore coats of arms, which had originally been coats covering their armour, as their name suggests, then developed into heraldic devices for coats, shields, saddles and crests.

Guy of Warwick had a helmet 'with a crest of gold well dight' (dressed), and it seems to have been a point of honour with him to cut the crest off his opponent's helmet. Crests were originally simple cameos or plumes fixed on top of the helmet or bridle, then they followed the rest of knightly trappings into a golden age of display.

This age was trumpeted in by heralds, who first appear in English records in Edward I's reign, but were probably taking part in tournaments much earlier, and were referred to in the records simply as minstrels. Heralds and minstrels did the same jobs: announcing tournaments, playing music and dancing to celebrate their masters' victories, cheering the combatants on, attending on the lady spectators and answering their questions about the knights, getting the knights up to go to mass on the morning of the contest, and writing songs to commemorate it afterwards.

Immediately after a contest there were banquets with much music and dancing, at which the lady or ladies in whose honour the tournament had been held presented prizes to the victorious knights. At the Whitsun tournament in Guy of Warwick,

Many a maid there chose her love anon
Of knights that thither were come.

The prizes were all a romantic knight could wish for: 'great worship, . . . a girfauk (gyrfalcon) all swan white . . . and a horse of great bounty . . . and two greyhounds that good be.' Knights who had proved their worth in the tournament might be knighted by the King on the field of combat or afterwards, during the celebrations. The knighting ceremony involved an elaborate ordination ritual, an all-night vigil before the altar and an initiation mass as well as a ceremonial girding on of a sword, a ceremonial kiss, a public proclamation and a feast.

For knighthood was more than a social status by the thirteenth and fourteenth centuries, just as tourneying was more than a battle. Knighthood was the profession of chivalry, and tourneying was its display. Chivalrous romances were written to influence as much as commemorate tournaments, and by the fourteenth century tournaments had become almost entirely romantic dramas; sumptuous, idealised representations of the battles they had once been. Already in the reign of Edward I, English tourneying had reached heights of glamour. Edward saw himself as the father of English chivalry, and made the most chivalrous of all forms of tourneying, the Round Table, the favourite sport at court.

The chronicler Matthew Paris described a Round Table as 'a chivalrous game, not the game vulgarly called a tournament.' It was tourneying à plaisir as described in Arthurian romance, which was the favourite reading of all the aristocracies of thirteenth-century Europe, and soon became their favourite source of sporting inspiration. In 1240 an Austrian knight called Ulrich von Leichenstein went to tour round Austria and Styria, under the name King Arthur, jousting with all comers, many of whom had names like Ivain, Lancelot and Tristan. By the mid thirteenth century Arthurian enthusiasm had reached England.

In 1252 there was a Round Table at Wallenden Abbey, a venue which bears witness to the Church's blessing on this form of tourneying, the perfection of Christian knighthood. Everyone was outraged when Roger de Lemburn was found to have killed his opponent, Arnold de Montigny, with a sharp lance. He had abused knightly ideals by using a real weapon, and even when he vowed on the spot to become a pilgrim and make amends by penitence, people still suspected he was a false and murderous knight, especially when it was recalled that Arnauld had broken Roger's leg in a previous tournament. Victory was glorious, but vendetta anathema.

No one understood this better than King Edward. His promotion of Round Tables was a subtle blend of romance and pragmatic politics. A romantic cult of kingship could only work in his favour, and he made a cult of himself as the heir to King Arthur. In 1278 he and Queen Eleanor went to Glastonbury and had the tomb of Arthur and Guenevere opened, the remains removed for popular devotion, and the tomb closed again for veneration by the High Altar. His publicists pressed the idea of Arthur as king of all Britain, and Edward as a second Arthur. He celebrated all major military victories, like the one over the Welsh in 1284, by establishing Round Tables. They gathered his knights in tribute around him, and placed him among the romantic élite of Christendom's princes.

Round Table celebrations were impressive events, with lavish music, singing, processing and dancing. At the Nefyn Round Table of 1284, celebrating Edward's victory over the rebellious Llewellyn, the last native Prince of Wales, there was so much dancing that the floor fell through. There would also have been story telling, minstrelsy and disguising, and exotic masques performed in front of the tapestried hangings on the walls.

By the late thirteenth century, knights costumed themselves as exotically as the ladies they fought for, and there were allegorical jousts featuring knights with Arthurian names bearing Arthurian devices. New romantic heroes competed with the Arthurian ones, and in 1309 there was a tournament in Stepney between one Giles Argentine, appearing as the King of the Greenwood, and all who would come against him. Prizes became more exotic too. Bears were popular prizes, symbolic of knightly strength. Crests and devices became more involved, and canting or punning devices were especially favoured, like the Oldcastles' castle device, and the Brayboeufs' oxen device.

Tourneying was entering its late medieval phase. In the fourteenth and fifteenth centuries it was part of the festive court life of Christendom. Jousting was far the most popular form of tourneying, and in England the reigns of Edward III and Richard II saw romantic chivalry come to its full, luxuriant flowering.

Court tailoring developed into an ostentatious art. Cloaks replaced long sleeved gowns. The fourteenth century saw a craze for skin-tight hose and long, pointed shoes. Shoulders were padded, waists pinched, and collars set high, with jewels stitched into them and all along the sleeves and gloves. There was little to separate fashion, tournament-fashions and disguises. Courtiers and jousters wore badges. In the late fourteenth century Simon of Burley wore a white leather coat embroidered with the Burley badge of stakes, with fiftyfour buttons, when he was at court. He also had a couple of tabards to wear in the lists, one made of cloth-of-gold embroidered with roses, the other made of scarlet embroidered with the sun and gold lettering. Heralds wore tabards in their masters' colours, and in the fifteenth century most knights wore tabards over their armour.

Colours were brilliant and designs fabulously extravagant. In 1342 Edward III wore a 'velvet tunic of arms, powdered with small Saracens of gold and silver, each having a jewel with the king's motto, and embroidered with trees and birds, and with effigies of two Saracens, holding shields of the king's arms.'

There were politics in the king's panache. Like his grand-father, Edward III emphasised royal splendour when the Crown was at its weakest. Under financial and military pressure during the French and Scottish wars, he held the most magnificent of all Round Tables at Windsor in 1344. Shortly afterwards he instituted the knightly Order of the Garter, enrolling his most powerful nobles as its members.

Heralds proclaimed the Round Table in Scotland, France, Burgundy, the Low Countries and Germany, on trumpets hung with mantles quartered into gold waves. Knights from all these countries, except the old rival, France, attended, as did ladies who watched them from gorgeously decorated pavilions. The jousting and feasting lasted a fortnight, and after it the king built 'a house in Windsor Castle which should be called the Round Table, of a circular form, 200' in diameter' [Walsingham chronicler]. Some time before 1356 he had a round table made for it, out of fiftytwo oak trees for which he paid the Prior of Merton £26/13/4d. King

Philip of France at once had a similar table made, to keep up with his rival.

Edward gave his most powerful nobles permission to practise arms, and pre-empted knightly opposition to the Crown by turning it into an armed society of exclusive chivalry, complete with its own herald, the Windsor herald, who proclaimed its activities throughout Europe. Membership of the Order of the Garter was coveted as the highest distinction of courtly Europe, and Edward praised as the champion of Christendom. There is a tradition that the name for the Order suggested itself to him during a ball held at Calais to celebrate the capture of that town by the English. The king's mistress, the Countess of Salisbury, lost her garter while dancing and Edward at once added it to his own costume, with the words 'Honi soit qui mal y pense.' This became the motto of the Order, and blue garters embroidered with it are mentioned in the royal accounts for the Windsor Round Table, along with silk-covered harnesses, green, blue and white tents, green robes embroidered with pheasants' wings, and other adornments.

Women participated more and more in jousts. Their basic role was still to inspire, and the Countess of Salisbury inspired, if not the Garter, at least one 'feast of jousts which the King of England held for love' [Jean de Wavrin's *Anciennes chroniques d'angleterre*]. This was a grand occasion; the merrymaking lasting fifteen days, but it was also an occasion for mourning, when one of the young aspirants to knighthood was killed in the jousts. For all their artistry, jousts could still be deadly affairs. The ladies applauded and encouraged their champions and favourites, mourned the dead, tended the wounded, and dressed in a style befitting their championship by the knights. [Illustration 21]

Noble spectators were on public display, and by the four-teenth century ladies were expected to judge and present the prizes and also take a leading part in the processions beforehand and the dancing afterwards. Processing reached a glorious peak in the reign of Richard II, and London was the backcloth to numerous masques, mimes, *tableaux vivants* and processions marking all sorts of state occasions.

In 1389 there was a tournament at Smithfield, just after

Michaelmas, in imitation of the one held in Paris to celebrate the entry of the French queen into the capital. Heralds had proclaimed it round Europe, and it was a European pageant, with knights from all countries jousting *à plaisir*. Squires were invited to joust on one of the days; they were just beginning to break in on the knightly monopoly of jousting, and they joined in some of the banqueting, dancing, fêtes and minstrelsy that went on each night until daybreak. Jousting and celebrating together lasted a week, and on the opening day the ladies awarded prizes to the most successful challengers: a gold crown to the best lancer, the Duke of St Pol; a jewelled girdle with a golden clasp to the best all-round jouster, the Earl of Huntingdon. All the foreign competitors were sent home laden with presents, including horses and falcons.

The tournament opened with sixty richly dressed ladies on palfreys setting out from the Tower leading sixty fully armoured, mounted knights attended by sixty mounted squires, on silver chains. 'Those of the king's side were all of one suit: their coats, armour, shields, horses and trappings, all were white harts.' Accompanied by minstrels and trumpeters, they made their way down Cheapside to Smithfield, where the ladies entered their pavilions and the knights set up their tents in preparation for the contest.

They were elaborately armoured, in plumes, buckles, ridges, lacings and huge, brilliantly coloured crests on printed helmets. The wealthier made their armour of laton, a mixture of gold and brass. They also carried elaborate weapons; bows and arrows, knives and maces as well as the basic swords and lances which were worked in intricate designs.

The noise at tournaments was deafening. 'Delightful din upon day, dancing at night'. [*Gawain* poet] In 1305 the chancellor of Oxford University refused permission for a Michaelmas tournament to be held there simply because it would disturb the scholars' quiet. Besides the minstrels and musicians, there were heralds riding up and down calling out messages, attendants buckling on armour and sharpening weapons, and hoofs thundering, blows ringing and spectators yelling themselves hoarse from sunrise to sunset.

In the fifteenth century they got noisier than ever as

commoners began to stage their own jousts, and tourneying became a popular sport. At court, tourneying was between country gentlemen and new as well as old nobility, while away from court all sorts of variations were introduced by humble jousters. In response, courtly tourneying became more and more formal as it lost its social exclusivity. The contest between Lord Scales and the Count de la Roche, known as the Bastard of Burgundy, serves as a model of this formality, being the foremost tournament of the fifteenth century, and the last word in courtly contrivance.

'In the worshipful reverence and help of our Blessed Saviour Jesus Christ, of the glorious Virgin His Mother, and St George, very tutor and patron and cry of Englishmen; in augmentation of knighthood and recommendation of noblesse . . .' That was just the beginning of Lord Scales' introduction to his challenge, which took two years to deliver in full at the Burgundian court. It began one Sunday morning in 1465 when Scales was leaving mass and some noble ladies presented him with 'a gold flower of souvenance', thus requesting him to do some great feat of chivalry. He had no choice but to obey, and no choice of opponent but the foremost knight of Burgundy, since the Burgundian court was the centre of tournament pageantry and drama in Europe, and in close contact with the English court.

The Chester herald was appointed official organiser of the proceedings, and spent the next two years conveying challenges, invitations and instructions to the Bastard and his Burgundian attendants. About four hundred of them finally accompanied him when he landed at Gravesend in May 1467, and their mountain of equipment and clothing was taken by barge to Billingsgate, while the King met them and escorted them in musical procession to St Paul's. There they offered tokens of tournament, in particular shields, on the High Altar, as was the fashion in the fifteenth century.

Lists had been set up at Smithfield 90 yards long and 80 yards wide, surrounded by barriers seven-and-a-half feet high, and in the warm sunshine of June 11th, 'with nine flowers richly tapped', Scales rode into the lists to report his purpose to the King in the royal pavilion. His horse was covered in white cloth-of-gold, with a crimson cross of St George, bordered with a gold fringe. He had a pavilion of blue satin, richly embroidered with his letters and his motto, and hung with banners.

At the upper end the Bastard rode into the lists with seven attendants, on a horse covered in crimson cloth edged with silver and gilt bells. The King gave him licence to set up his pavilion, inspected his weapons, and had the contest proclaimed at the four corners of the field.

It was a fiasco. Both men failed to make contact in the first course, threw away their spears and armguards and took to smiting each other with their swords. The Bastard's horse had armour plating round the nose and cheeks. It ran into Scales' horse and fell down dead, on top of the Bastard, who was pulled out by his valets. Scales rode over to the King, holding his sword on high; the King offered the Bastard a fresh mount, but he declined it and the first day's jousting was at an end.

The next day Scales entered the lists with numerous attendants in gold livery, and set up a blue and tawny gold velvet pavilion with a crimson fringe and a banner on top flying out from the mouth of a gold griffin. His opponent entered and set up a purple and white damask pavilion with a green banner bearing his motto: 'Null ne cy frete' (None so strong).

They fought on foot, with axes, Scales wearing an open visor, which the chronicler considered 'very jeopardous', and the Bastard wearing a closed one; Scales using the head of his axe and the Bastard the small end of his. Eventually Scales smashed in the side of the Bastard's visor, and the King put an end to the contest by throwing down his staff and shouting 'Whoo!' Scales and the Bastard shook hands and left the field. Such was the greatest tournament of the fifteenth century.

At the very least, it confirms that tournaments at this date were feebly fought and highly formalised, a fact which is borne out by Henry IV's royal statute of arms. This limited the number of attendants allowed to each jouster, and the number of liveries allowed to each attendant. It limited weapons to a broadsword, and armour to a muffler, thigh and shoulder plates and a helmet. It hinted at the very active nature of medieval spectatorship when it forbade crowds to come to jousts armed with swords, daggers, staves, maces or stones. The same prohibition applied to minstrels, footmen and arms carriers. Only those squires who usually ate with their lord were to eat with him after the contest.

The statutes were trying to keep tournaments free of excessive embellishment and revelry, and to keep their jousting simple and skilful. Penalties for infringement were severe, ranging from the loss of one's horse to seven years in prison. They were impossible to enforce, and the tendency towards over-elaboration, which they tried to check, was characterised by elaborate regulations such as these as well as by elaborate personal followings and extravagance. Jousting had become less and less military as castles were replaced by palaces and knights were replaced by gentlemen.

Tilts were introduced to stop chargers colliding with each other as they had done in the Scales-Bastard tournament. At first they were ropes or cloths (toiles, whence the word tilts), then wooden walls. They divided the lists in half lengthwise, and the jousters charged at each other down opposite sides of them. This prevented jockeying and tripping as well as colliding. [Illustration 22]

It also meant that only lance courses were possible, the jousters being too far apart for effective swordplay. Only the left side, which was near the tilt, was liable to be struck, and in Edward IV's reign extra bits of armour to protect the left side first appeared in England. The most fashionable of them were made in Milan, which was the armoury of fifteenth-century Europe. Other bits of armour, like the lower leg-guards, were discarded from the left side, in favour of big protective saddle steels.

Tilting lances often had spiked heads and handle ends, these last pressed into a wooden block in the lance rest, so that the shock of striking a blow was absorbed all over the body, not just the wrist, of the jouster. Vamplates were enlarged to protect the lance-arm further, and a metal pad known as a polder miton (from the French *épaule de mouton*, a shoulder of mutton, for that was its shape) was worn over the forearm and the bend of the arm. Tilting was one-armed, one-sided jousting, where victory was in the striking of the blow, and cushions were sometimes strapped round the horses' breasts to protect them if blows went astray.

If was easier to judge than any other form of jousting because it had a more specific object, and was easier to watch accurately. By the mid-fifteenth century it was the main tournament sport, and was played according to a standard set of rules drawn up by John Tiptoft, Earl of Worcester. Tilting often took place in crude enclosures such as fields, or, more often, town squares, with people watching from the windows of surrounding houses. If the tiltyard floor was hard, it was strewn with sand or tanyard refuse, to break the falls. More distinguished tiltyards were graced with all the traditional trappings of gracious jousting.

A couple of the heralds usually acted as the official scorers, one for the challenger and one for the responder. They had score-sheets marked with a diagram of the tiltyard on which they marked each blow struck and received. The best way to win the prize was to unhorse an opponent, the second best to hit the cornal of his lance twice, the third best way to hit him three times in the visor. Otherwise, contests could be won on points, which were awarded for disarming the opponent or breaking his spear with a hit. Points were deducted for hitting the tilt, hitting the opponent below the waist or hitting his saddle. Certain manoeuvres, like hitting an unarmed opponent or one with his back turned, meant disqualification. Tilting was touch play; meticulous, popular and regulated.

Some jousters still fought on horseback with swords, but mainly in the interludes between tilts, and as side-plays and warming-up sessions. The popular follow-up to tilting was jousting on foot, and maces and axes replaced swords as the favourite weapons. Axes got longer and heavier, more like the spears used in tilting. The style too of foot jousting grew more like that of tilting.

'Thrusting is better than smiting, especially at the heart,' wrote the author of *Knighthood and Bataille* in 1458, a treatise in praise of knighthood and its contemporary exercise, tilting. He revealed the extent to which tilting had lost its original knightly qualities when he recommended young knights to learn their sport by tilting at poles stuck in the ground. Gone were the days of learning by knocking out an opponent's teeth at full charge, or, to use a medieval expression, at full tilt.

Tilting at poles was called tilting at the quintain, and had existed in England as early as the thirteenth century, as a gentle kind of practice for boys, and by the fourteenth century it was played as a boys' sport in its own right. Before long, quintains shaped and dressed like Saracens were used, for livelier play, and 'tilting at the Turk' became very popular, sometimes played as a tournament event. The quintain was given a moving pivot, with a figure suspended from one side of it and a wooden shield or lance from the other, so that if the tilter struck his target anywhere but in the face, it swung round and struck him back. Points were awarded according to where on the face the tilter had hit the target. There were also ring quintains, where the tilter had to pass his lance through a ring hanging from the pivot and carry it off with him, and there were all sorts of other variations. [Illustration 23]

Tilting was halfway between a tournament and an outdoor game, and tilting at human quintains was a favourite medieval game. The target had to avoid being knocked off a stool and it all appealed enormously to the Medievals' raucous sense of humour. The players liked dressing up in chivalrous disguise. The fourteenth-century burlesque, *The Tournament of Tottenham*, described with typically medieval irreverence and relish a labourers' slapstick tilting tournament held in the countryside one holiday:

> There hopped Dawkin,
> There danced Dawkin,
> There trumped Timkin,
> And were true drinkers.

They wore armour made of mats, helmets made of bowls and breastplates made of baskets. Their weapons were flails, staves, harnesses and spades, their shields dough troughs. 'He that had no good horse borrowed him a mare.' They fought to win the hand of a farmer's daughter, his brood hen and his dun cow, watched by their women, who sat on grassy banks.

> All the wives of Tottenham came to see that fight,
> To fetch home their husbands, that were troth plight.

By the time darkness fell, everyone was so weary that they could hardly drag themselves to the feast where, in the best sporting spirit, 'Mickle (much) mirth was them among.' And in the best medieval spirit,

> In every corner of the house
> Was melody delicious.

20 Jousting in spectacular helmets. From the Alexander Romance. *Bodleian Library, Oxford* MS. Bodl. 264.

21 King Edward III holds a tournament in honour of the Countess of Salisbury. From Jean de Wavrin's *Anciennes chroniques d'Angleterre. Bodleian Library, Oxford* MS. Laud Misc. 653, fol. 5.

22 June tournament from a sixteenth-century calendar. *The British Library* Add. MS. 24098, fol. 23b.

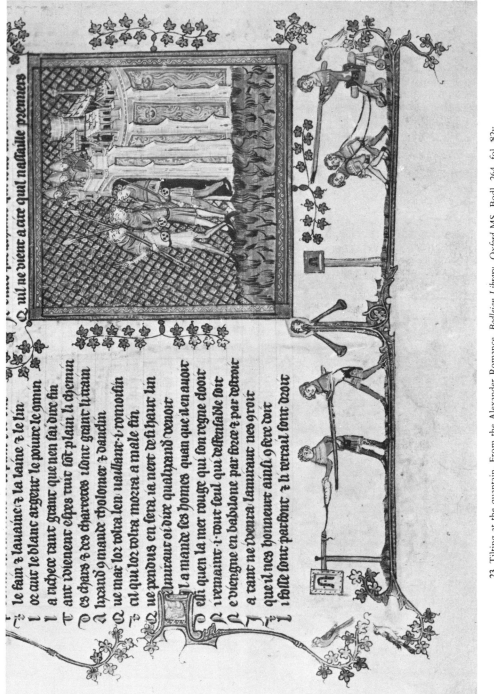

23 Tilting at the quantain. From the Alexander Romance. *Bodleian Library, Oxford* MS. Bodl. 264, fol. 82v.

CHAPTER FIVE

Outdoor and House and Garden Games

Most medieval life was lived out of doors. It took darkness or bad weather to drive people into their squalid huts, and only the few who had better homes went into them willingly. The most popular games were outdoor ones, and all games were played outdoors whenever possible. Those who were tough enough to survive the first few months of existence were tough enough to play games all year round, in all weathers.

But at the same time, the Medievals were out of doors so much that they were far more sensitive to the seasons than people today, and took a special delight in games that could only be played for a month or two each year, the favourite playing month being May.

The well-to-do delighted in alternating between outdoor and indoor games, as weather permitted. But most Medievals played games that were really small-scale sports whenever the weather eased up enough to let them out of doors, summer or winter, rain or sun. The bigger and cruder the game, the more popular it was. Common land was plentiful, and made the ideal community playground. Land enclosed by private householders, requiring maintenance and often equipment to make it playing ground, was scarce, especially in the early part of the period, and so were the games played on it.

Everyone threw stones for sport on village and town fields; it was a typical crude outdoor game. Fitzstephen described the summer games of London boys as throwing the stone, archery, leaping, wrestling, throwing the thronged javelin beyond a mark, and fighting with sword and buckler. Anyone with a bit of time to spare could play these games.

'Throwing the stone' could mean throwing for distance, putting the shot for weight, or a combination of both. Medieval illustrations show stone and bar throwing, and games of catch, which were played with stones if nothing else was available. They also show putting the stone shot.

> The put of the stone thou mayest not reach,
> Too little might is in thy sleeve,

wrote the author of a fourteenth-century hymn to the Virgin, full of pity for her weakness. Throwing tested strength in the same simple way that racing tested speed.

Most throwers, indeed most athletes, came from the labouring majority, not the minority who could afford to prefer more sophisticated sports and games. Stone throwing with a sling was an ancient British skill, but its only sporting use was fowling, for which countrymen, women and boys used slings and stone-bows throughout the Middle Ages.

But the real throwing game for labourers was quoits. It was a kind of discus-throwing to a target, usually an iron pin or a stake in the ground, known as the hob. The quoits were anything from horse-shoes to flat, rounded stones. They were sometimes thrown towards a single hob, sometimes from one hob to another, sometimes even to no target save distance. Played in medieval style, it could be a dangerous game. It was forbidden by royal decree, along with stone- and bar-throwing, not only because it took people from archery practice but also because it took them from their work, and was excessively rowdy. In 1518 Coventry city council forbade its poor craftsmen to play quoits or bowls, though bowling at St Anne's by the Charterhouse was allowed to 'honest persons that will make little noise.'

Richard Wodewell, who was a carpenter in Salisbury in 1409, made worse trouble than noise. On St Mark's day, April 25th, he and some companions were throwing quoits made of 'stone and lumps of iron' in the nearby village of Lavestock. One of their quoits hit a girl called Christina who was standing twelve feet behind the hob. Made of iron and weighing one pound, it struck her lifeless, her brains exposed. Prayers were offered, first to God, then to the Virgin, then to Bishop Osmund, whereupon

Christina instantly recovered, and expressed her gratitude by making an offering of Richard's quoit at the Bishop's tomb.

Bowls was safer, more containable, more aristocratic. It was played in its simplest form, with stone bowls on a stretch of flat land, by all sorts of people all through the period. By the thirteenth century it was being played with little conical jacks to aim at, and by the fourteenth century with jack-balls. In this period at least, each player had just one bowl, usually made of stone. Bowling was a simple game. But that meant it was simple to refine, and as early as the thirteenth century bowls were being made of bone, metal and wood, and played in churchyards and on village greens, later on in specially constructed playing grounds, or alleys between trees or houses. [Illustration 24]

Tradition has it that the oldest bowling green in England is the one in Southampton known as Old Green, which was a recreation close, and possibly a bowling green, in 1299. The first official bowling alley was opened in London in 1455, but bowls were being played in gardens and garden alleys, most notably those belonging to monasteries, long before then. Bowling was the perfect monastic game. It could be easy-paced, contemplative or competitive, according to how it was played, and monastic courtyards and gardens made ideal bowling grounds. The fifteenth-century cloister court and infirmary garden at Westminster were used as grounds for a sort of mini-bowls, played with small balls rolled into small holes in the turf, like outdoor billiards. More typical was the Durham 'gardening and bowling alley belonging to the Common House on the back side of the said house, towards the water, for the novices sometime to recreate themselves.' Bowling spread quickly to the secular world, and became a fashionable garden game for the late medieval aristocracy and fashion-conscious new rich. [Illustration 25]

John of Brabant invited his friends to play bowls with him at home and lost 12d. to them on one game, 6d. on another. He played in summer, and though many people played all year round, the rich played it as a summer game, on new-mown grass or hard earth, with sunshine to warm the bowling fingers.

A lot of medieval ball games were derived from bowls; a few of them, like the 'long bowls' which King James IV of

Scotland used to play at St Andrews, directly, but most of them by way of added equipment. Half-bowl was a late medieval game played with target pins and a sliding wooden hemisphere. Some sort of bowling at pins is probably as old as bowling itself, but it was only recognised as a separate game and given a name of its own in the fifteenth century. In 1477 Edward IV issued an edict against 'various new games called closhes, kayles, half kayles, hand-in and hand-out . . .' Both closh and kayles were forms of pin bowling. Closh was played with a ball and kayles with a stick. Townsmen and country labourers played closh out of doors, sometimes with only one pin, a hoop and a small bat, so that it was more like croquet than bowling. [Illustration 26]

Late medieval ladies played it indoors, with small pins and balls made of expensive materials. This game soon came to be known as skittles, from the Anglo-Saxon scytan, to cast or throw, and in the Middle Ages it was a women's and children's game. In 1472 Queen Elizabeth of Scotland 'and some of her ladies and gentlewomen played in her chamber at the closhes of ivory . . .', according to one chronicler. In courtly circles the game was also known by its French name of *morteaulx*.

Another courtly game with a French name was 'quilles', or pins, also played as a vigorous and popular outdoor game. From six to nine pins were set up in a single row and then thrown down with a stick, which might be a sheep's knuckle bone or a carved piece of wood. Probably because the sticks were often big and heavy, and very vigorously thrown, kayles was consistently forbidden from the fourteenth century onwards, apprentices in particular being warned against it.

Hand-in and hand-out, which was next to kayles on Edward IV's list of forbidden games, was probably a kind of trick catch. It was one of the many medieval ball games widely played and only loosely identifiable.

See what I send to thee, son . . .
A hat and a handball, and a hernepanne [iron pan]

wrote the author of a fifteenth-century romance, and left it at that, with no further details. Popular medieval games belong to the unrecorded hours of childhood, summer evenings and holidays. They are only glimpsed fleetingly, between the lines and in the margins of medieval literature, where more select games are more explicitly represented, and where every passing reference stands for a hundred playing hours.

Tennis is a good example of a sport which has had its history hidden in its records. It has always been thought of as late medieval, aristocratic and not very popular, because these are the characteristics of the records that mention it. But there are just one or two hints in the records that a crude form of it was played much earlier and much more widely. As tennis is basically just one more variation of the basic bat and ball game, we should take the hints for all they are worth.

Primitive tennis was played with the hand, and seems to have been popular in Picardy, and perhaps elsewhere in France, by the twelfth century. It may have been a crusading import; it was played in twelfth-century France under the name *jeu de paume* (palm of hand game), and was a favourite of the upper clergy shortly after the Crusades. The theory that the clergy played tennis in their monastery courtyards, and that these were the ancestors of tennis courts, their walls and cloister-hedges the ancestors of nets, their cloister-roofs and buttresses the ancestors of the sloping roofs, or penthouses, that projected from three of the walls of early indoor courts, cannot be proved from the medieval records, but it does get some support from them.

French tennis was played in courts or courtyards. There was one built at Poitiers in 1230. Played like this, in courts, it was an aristocratic game. But it was also played in yards, alleyways and in the open fields, as a popular variation of handball, known as *longue paume*, the palm game played over long distances, often with up to five players a side.

In 1441 the justices of Pershore, Worcestershire, forbade people to 'frequent the game which is called tennis playing in the King's highway or in any private place.' But the most popular unofficial courts were always churchyards, and the cloister courtyards that may have given birth to the game in the first place. These were pirated from the clergy by anyone wanting to refine their *longue paume* play. In 1447 the Mayor of Exeter received a complaint that the young people of the town played tennis and other unlawful games 'and most at tennis' in the cathedral cloisters during divine service, 'by which the walls of the said cloister have been defouled and the glass windows all to brost [broken]'.

Tennis was played as this kind of bat and ball game, rough and only occasionally contained in courts, for centuries. It was only in the fifteenth century that it established its English identity as the racket and ball game played in courts. In the early years of that century the Crown tried to stop tennis establishing itself because it was a French game, and therefore to be despised. In 1414 the French Dauphin 'in scorn and despite sent to him [Henry V] a tonne [cask] full of tennis balls, because he should have somewhat to play withall' [*Brut Chronicle*]. King Henry considered this a great insult because it implied that he had nothing better to do than play fashionable French games.

By this time tennis was distinct from field tennis. It was played both with and without rackets. Players began to bind their hands with cords in order to strengthen them for hitting the ball, then they inserted strips of wood into the binding, then they 'played racket, to and fro' [Troilus and Criseyde]. In the same way players had started to play shuttlecock with little wooden rackets and corks stuck with feathers. [Illustration 27]

But some preferred to go on using their hands as rackets. As late as 1505 Archduke Philip of Austria, who was being entertained as a royal captive by Henry VII, 'played with the Lord Marquis of Dorset . . . but he played with the racket and gave the Lord Marquis fifteen,' evidently as a handicap to compensate for the Marquis's playing with his hand. The modern scoring system at tennis is medieval, and lends further support to the theory that tennis was originally French, because it is based on the vase of French currency in the early fourteenth-century, when tennis was becoming really popular in France. Bets were laid on it either in small coins called Tours *deniers*, or in bigger ones called *sols*, or *sous*, worth fifteen deniers each. If a player won a point with a *sou* bet on it, he won his backer fifteen *deniers*. Hence the scoring in fifteens. The deuce score comes from the French *à deux*, meaning two points to go in the game. The nil score of love probably comes from the old English saying 'love or money'; if there was no money on the game, it was just played for love.

The derivation of the word tennis from the Old French 'tenys!', meaning hold, or serve, is less clearly suggested in the records, though it is as likely a theory as any other. In the early fifteenth-century ballad of Harfleur, celebrating the English victory over the French there, the battle is described as a tennis game, in which one of the English 'great guns' begins the game by calling 'Tenys . . . hold fellow; we go on to game.'

It is not known who won the game between Archduke Philip and the Marquis of Dorset, but it was watched with keen interest 'from an upper gallery . . . laid with two cushions of cloth-of-gold for the two kings.' It was played in a walled but open court, probably with a net made of rope hung with weights to keep it steady.

The London livery companies, ever anxious to distinguish themselves as leaders of fashionable society, built themselves tennis courts and played each other at tennis, from the mid fifteenth century onwards. In March 1459 the Warden of the Ironmongers Company was paid 59/2d. for tennis balls, which the Ironmongers seem to have sold to the other companies, and which they may have made themselves. They did a thriving trade, selling their tennis balls to buyers all over the city, and in 1463–1464 joined in a petition against the import of 'any woollen bonnets, tennis balls . . . made by artificers and handycrafty men and women.' French tennis balls were hard, made of leather, the best ones stuffed with wool or hair, inferior ones with rags or bran, and they were in demand all over Europe. Despite the English manufacturers' efforts to stop them coming into the country, many English players used them.

By the end of the fifteenth century English and French tennis balls had begun to soften up and be made of tightly bundled rags, a development too late to prevent young John Stanley, the grandson and heir of Sir John Stanley, being killed by a tennis ball which hit him on the head in 1460. Except for grass court-yards and fields, tennis courts were as hard as tennis balls. The best ones were usually paved or, in the case of indoor courts, of which there were a few, planked. Town squares and alleyways remained the most popular courts. By the late fifteenth century, tennis had become the top sporting game in high society, and was played for substantial bets, and with skilled technique. When the London skinner, Richard Skeres, was executed, the chroniclers lamented his death because he had been 'one of the cunningest players at the tennis in England for he was so delver [agile] that he would stand in a tub that should be near breast high and leap out of the same . . . and win of a good player.'

Children played tennis as shuttlecock, just as they played most ball games in a miniature form. Marbles originated as a childish form of bowls, played with nuts and small stones. Penny prick was a children's throwing game which was also played for money by adults. The prick, or target, was a penny hung from a string, at which sticks were thrown. It was one of the games played so dangerously in the cloisters at Exeter, and in 1421 the justices at Maldon, Essex, forbade men to play it because of the danger to their neighbours. Medieval games, whether children's or adults', were never tame.

Top whipping appears in many illustrations as a childrens' game, and in many court rolls as the cause of damage to life and property. [Illustration 28] Apprentices were not allowed to play it because they made it into gang warfare. The author of the fifteenth-century Life of St Christina distinguished a scropelle, or a 'top that children play with', from a street top, which was for bigger and rougher players.

Stilt walking is another children's game that was played by adults. Its appeal was that it could easily be turned into a quarter staffs match, a parade of the grotesque, of which the Medievals were so fond, or a parade of athletic prowess. [Illustration 29]

Games like the ones that fill the margins of fourteenth-century manuscripts gave all ages and both sexes a chance to show off these kinds of prowess trickily and competitively. Men, women and children got a good deal of indecorous fun from acrobatic, balancing and buffoonish games. [Illustrations 30, 31, 32]

For men and boys there were games of strength. Boys played reduced versions of men's games to show how manly they were. Most of these are unidentifiable and best classed simply as boys' games, such as are played in every age. [Illustrations 33, 34]

Swimming was a masculine game. Females took to the water in pools rather than the rivers preferred by men, and they did so to bathe rather than swim. Boys were taught to swim as a preparation for survival, seldom as a game. [Illustrations 35, 36]

Take two strong men and in the Thames cast them,
And both naked as a needle. . . .
Which trowest thou of the two in the Thames is most dread?
[*Piers Plowman*]

Men learnt to swim because they were frightened of drowning, a frequent cause of death in the Middle Ages. And, as Langland says, they did it in the nude. It was therefore a summer game, if leisure permitted. In the hot summer of 1350 Edward III forbade anyone to 'dare to bathe in the fosses of Our Tower of London, or in the fosses near to the Tower, or in the water of the Thames opposite to the same Tower, by day or by night' because bathers were obstructing the royal boats going in and out of the Tower.

Rowing was less popular. Like swimming, it was a strictly masculine sport, and too much of an everyday working exercise to be a popular sporting one. Only a few aristocrats rowed for pleasure. Just about the only medieval reference to rowing as a sport or game is the one in William of Malmesbury's chronicle, repeated in later chronicles and poems, to King Edgar the Peaceable's rowing expedition down the Dee. Rowing was a Scandinavian speciality, and this expedition sounds almost as much like a Viking training-session as a game. Edgar was rowed in state from his palace in West Chester to the church of St John and back again. He got together a flotilla of noble boats to escort him, chose

A good ship and entered into it,
With eight kings, and down they sit.
And each of them an oar took in hand . . .
And he himself at the ship behind
As steersman . . .
[1436 poem]

By the time this poem was written, water pageantry was at its height, and the first pleasure boats were being used to convey noble men up and down the Thames. It quickly became popular with men like John Norman, the Lord Mayor of London, who organised the first water procession to Westminster, in 1453, with himself, like Edgar, seated at the rear, but unlike Edgar, inactive. Rowing had only minor playful importance in water pageantry and sport.

Most boys preferred to hoop, hop or snowball. Hopping in the Middle Ages was a vigorous affair, and often a part of dancing.

More academic boys got together on feastdays 'at the churches whose feast day it is, and the scholars dispute, some in demonstrative rhetoric, others in dialectic' [Fitzstephen]. It was 'nothing but a wrestling bout of wit', and Fitzstephen used sporty language appropriately stuffed with classical allusions, to capture its atmosphere. 'The boys hurtle enthymemes . . . strive against one another in verse . . . hurl abuse and jibes . . . Their hearers, ready to laugh their fill, with wrinkling nose repeat the loud guffaw.' But spectators must have been few, to watch hardworking students debating, when doubtless they too would have preferred to play sportier games.

Most games that did not involve physical strength and danger were played by children of both sexes. Many of them were already old when the Middle Ages began and are still played by children today: skipping, leap-frog; all the medieval versions of hide-and-seek, of which the most common were hunt-the-fox and hunt-the-hare; thread-the-tailor's-needle, where a chain of players run under the arched arms of the leader of the chain, turning him from the leader to the last; five stones (jacks); bob cherry and bob apple, from strings and in tubs of water; cherry stone blowing; blind man's buff, known in the Middle Ages as hoodman blind, and played extremely vigorously; ducks and drakes; swinging; see-saw, known as titter-totter, and a whole host of others. [Illustrations 37, 38]

Some games were distinctively medieval. As well as fowling, snaring and trapping all sorts of game, medieval children spent summer days catching butterflies and sometimes birds and dragonflies, in their hats. [Illustrations 39, 40, 41].

Prisoners' Base, or Bars, was still being played by country children when Shakespeare wrote *Cymbeline*, under the name Country Base. It was mentioned in Edward III's reign as a childish amusement, and as an early game of capture. Two chains of players, usually boys, numbering anything up to twenty or thirty each chain, occupied the spaces between their 'bases'. One of them left his chain and was chased by his opposite number in the other chain. If caught, he was made a prisoner, and the side with the most prisoners at the end of the game won.

Hot cockles was played by children of both sexes and by women, who played it indoors at Christmas time. One player was blindfolded. She laid her hand on another's knees and called out 'Hot cockles, hot!', upturning her hand behind her back. Someone struck it and the seated player asked her 'Who struck?', which was the alternative title for the game. If she guessed rightly, the blindfold was removed and put on someone else; if she guessed wrongly, she had to do a forfeit. One of the reasons for its adult popularity is that the names of lovers were offered in wistful answer to the question 'Who struck?' For women it was flirtatious fun; for children it was rough and tumble.

What strikes a modern observer most about medieval children's games is how energetic and lacking in contrivances they were. They used very few toys, most of them simple ones like tops, clubs or skittles. The best game was making playful use of the animals, fields, trees, water, buildings and streets that adults had to use for work. Toys hardly ever appear in medieval accounts. There is the odd 'whipping top of travelling pedlar', but toys were usually made by the children themselves, even if they could afford to buy them. Medieval play was too fierce for all but the toughest toys. Edward III bought his small son, Henry, 'a small cart for the lord's use as a plaything, 7d.', but it was broken almost at once. Puppets were the most popular toys, and it was only children of Lord Henry's class or thereabouts who bought them. Toys like this belonged to the select life of the indoors, where games were mainly well-to-do, monastic or feminine.

Since women spent more time at home than men, they had more home amusements and fewer sporting ones. Their kingdom was their house and garden. The higher up the social scale, the more time and resources they could spend playing there.

The most obvious place for women to play was the garden, and gardening was the most important feminine amusement of the Middle Ages. Every medieval woman was a garden-wife as well as a housewife and managed, however poor she and her garden were, to plant the garden with a little bit of delight. Cottage gardens were a tangle of herbs and strong tasting vegetables like onions and garlic, to flavour the bread and starchy soup peasants lived off. But they also accommodated some flowery intruders from the wilds, and edible and medicinal flowers, like marigolds, that brightened them in summer. Still, they were basically yards, crowded with chickens, dung heaps and the occasional pig.

Middle-class women could afford to garden more playfully. Herb, fruit, flower and vegetable gardens were often separated from each other by walls, fences and hedges. They were for pleasure as well as practical production, and the most purely pleasant of them was the flower garden, often designed as a 'pleasance' of perfume and beauty.

It would be enclosed within high walls and fences, with entrance doors and gates that led onto sealed paths across the lush, flowery lawns overgrown with daisies, periwinkles, violets and other 'sweet herbs'. There were very few flower beds, and these were raised above the ground and surrounded with palings and fencing. For the most part, show flowers like roses, lilies, irises and wallflowers, grew out of the turf which covered the walls, banks, seats and ground. Occasionally they were planted in pots and stood on the turf along with potted trees and shrubs. Rambling roses and other climbing flowers were trellised over turf seats to make sweet smelling arbours, or 'privy playing places' [William of Palerne, fourteenth century], which were especially suitable for romantic games. The ideal flower garden blended a geometrical lay-out with a perfumed profusion of pretty flowers and trees. [Illustrations 42, 43]

Blossom trees scented and shaded the turfed benches and seats in early summer. One of them often stood next to a central well or fountain, where husbands, lovers, friends sat in the cool.

Flower gardening was a game in itself, and the gardens it made were the playgrounds for some of the favourite medieval games: walking and talking, especially of love; exercising and parading pets; listening to birdsong; playing chess or tables; sitting and lying on the grass. The ultimate medieval garden game was making love, and many a hero and heroine of medieval romance played at it in an enclosed garden. [Illustrations 44, 45]

'After dinner gone they to dance, and sing also.' [*The Franklin's Tale*] Many a summer evening was spent singing and dancing in the garden. Sir John Heveringham was more devotional. He 'said to his wife that he would go to say a little devotion in his garden and then he would dine.' But he was an exception. Most people, however religious, preferred more earthly garden games. When the Bishop of Lincoln visited the Cistercian nunnery of Nuncotton in 1440, he found the nuns there keeping little private gardens; some of them did not come to Compline because they preferred to spend their evenings wandering about their gardens, gathering herbs.

After dinner was another favourite garden time, when people read and told stories, and women gathered flowers to make into garlands for their hair. The best gardens for doing this were flowery meads, or meadows, the simplest kind of pleasance. Flowery meads were enclosed meadows full of flowers, trees and birds. They were favourite playgrounds and favourite settings for enclosed flower gardens. These last were walled in 'strict and close' [*Aucassin and Nicolette*, thirteenth century] under the south wall or the ladies' chambers, so that

Adown the stair anon nigh though she went,
Into the garden.
          [*Troilus and Criseyde*]

Love, femininity and flower gardens were associated throughout the Middle Ages. The champions of garden love were kings, noblemen, monks and nuns, the first two playing in secular love gardens and the last two in sacred ones.

Roses were the great love flowers. They were planted in palace flower gardens to make rosaries, or rose gardens, like the one in the *Romance of the Rose*, where garden games were played as part of the supreme game of love. The most romantic rose gardeners were monks and nuns, especially Benedictines, who gardened as a labour of love, as a pastime and as a game. Their gardens fed and healed their communities, just as household gardens fed and healed families. The monks and nuns devoted a third of their time to hard physical work, and spent much of it in the gardens, making images of the heavenly paradise gardens they hoped to reach after death. They spent a third of their time in prayer, some of it in prayer gardens. These were known as paradises, and were usually at the east end of the monastery church, behind the high altar; little enclosed rosaries where members of the community could pray in peaceful seclusion to the Mystical Rose of Heaven, the Blessed Virgin. The paradise at St Swithun's, Winchester, was called 'Le Joye', and gardens like it, planted with roses and lilies, combined biblical symbolism, prayer and joy. Their model was the 'garden enclosed' of the *Song of Songs*, with its fragrant flowers, fountain of grace, and rose and lily of love. This garden was the inspiration of all the enclosed love gardens of the Middle Ages, just as Eden was of the flowery mead love gardens. The Benedictine Rule assigned the final third of its followers' time to spiritual reading and recreation, both ideal pastimes for gardens.

As well as paradises, there were also monastic orchards, guest house gardens, infirmary gardens, community graveyards and common gardens. Primarily practical, they could still give delight to gardeners and users. Delight was intrinsic in religious gardening.

Plants were used much more variously in the Middle Ages than they are today, and many were beautiful as well as useful, flowers as well as herbs, herbs as well as vegetables. Gardeners with enough time and space made herb gardens like the one in the *Tale of Beryn*, written in about 1400. It was the yard of an inn called the 'Checker of the Hope', looked after by the innkeeper's wife, combining function and delight.

> For many a herb grew, for sew [cookery] and surgery;
> And all the alleys fair pared, railed and maked;

The sage and the hyssop, frethid [tied up] and staked;
And other beds by and by full fresh dight [prepared];
For comers to the host [hostelry], right a sportful sight.

This was a typical medieval herb garden: small, with little beds neatly laid out and tended between sanded paths, bordered with aromatic and sweet smelling herbs. Herb gardens were almost always in sunny, south facing positions, and on hot summer days their intoxicating perfume fed visiting bees and delighted visiting Medievals beyond their hearts' desires. The little twelfth-century infirmary garden at the Augustinian Priory of St Edburg's, Bicester, was called the 'Trimles', a name derived from the Old English trimble, or trumble, meaning to walk unsteadily. Old and sick monks trimbled a few convalescent steps in the scented air. Such herb gardens were the gentlest of playgrounds, their care the gentlest of gardening games.

For the Carthusians, who came to England in the twelfth century, gardening was the only game. They had none of the different kinds of Benedictine gardens. The monks lived alone in little individual cells, with gardens attached. Each monk could do as he liked with his garden, and excavations show that most of them put pentises along the inner and dividing walls, making covered walks for wet weather. Each garden had a stream running through it at its outer end, where a few monks made themselves seats, tanks, even toilets. Most gardens were probably simple prayer walks, with the occasional tree or bush to attract birds and squirrels, and the occasional clump of flowers or herbs to brighten it up. The Carthusians were never a great success in England. They were too austere for the playful English, who liked 'to make him both game and glee' [Sir Thopas].

As time passed, most monastic brethren indulged in a wider variety of recreational activities. In Benedictine houses, a walk once a week became customary rather than exceptional, and extended to the countryside outside the monastic walls. By the fifteenth century it was customary to take walks alone as well as in groups. One monk from Ulverscroft Priory, Leicestershire, used to 'ramble about in the woods and copses . . . looking for the nests of birds and catching other creatures of the wood', just like a country gentleman.

By the late Middle Ages, most big monasteries, like most big houses, had holiday homes. There was a rest home at Redburn for the monks of St Alban's Abbey from the earliest times, and in 1335 Abbot Richard Wallingford wrote out new constitutions for it which allowed three monks at a time to go there twice a year for a holiday. They were to say the Office together and take the morning air in the fields, but not succumb to the temptation to hunt or vault the hedges. A century later, Abbot John Amundesham's constitutions dealt with much bigger numbers, and forbade late nights. Redburn had become a hostel for vacation reading parties, which often went on until all hours.

Reading parties were favourite games of the late medieval aristocracy, especially women; as fewer of them could read, they liked listening. The favourite reading topics were romances and heroic epics. Stories like the Alexander and Arthur romances, which were romantic and heroic at once, were exceedingly popular. Upper-class wills and inventories of the fourteenth and fifteenth centuries abound with bequests like 'unum librum de romanse', left by Joan Hilton of Surrey to her sister-in-law, Katherine Cumberworth, in 1432, and 'unum librum de romanse de Septem Sages', which she left to her niece. By Chaucer's time, the old romances were beginning to pall, and they were being replaced by satirical ballads, provincial and dialect stories, and tales of popular heroes like Robin Hood, recorded on paper as well as by oral tradition. Merchants and minor gentlefolk had joined the book-buying public, and read and listened to all kinds of stories.

Lending libraries were founded in increasing numbers. Merchants left books to their parish churches, and bequest libraries were set up in hospitals. Monastic libraries had secular as well as religious books. The one at Peterborough Abbey in the late fifteenth century had some French romances and some books on chess, as well as theology. The Canterbury tales were reproduced in innumerable manuscripts, some of them cheap editions for relatively poor buyers. In the 1390s an inventory taken at the death of two London grocers recorded the possession of 'four libros de romaunc', costing 4/11d. the lot. Despite being described in French, most romances were written in the vernacular, where once they had been written in the courtly languages of Anglo-Norman and Provençal.

For all that, reading romances was still a popular courtly game. When Pandarus found Criseyde and her friends listening to a Theban romance, his first question was 'For God's love, what saith it? Is it of love?' Love reading was part of the courtly game of love. It made a seductive atmosphere in which every story and conversation was charged with possibly romantic significance. It was an innuendo of courtly dalliance. Ladies listened to romances to learn how to dally, as every lady should. The first thing Criseyde asked Pandarus about Troilus was 'Can he speak well of love?' He could, and did. There were St Valentine's Day festivals at which poets competed to deliver the best love poems. Good love talkers coined maxims, told jokes and asked questions and riddles with double meanings.

The Wife of Bath was not a subtle woman, and followed the courtly fashion for asking love riddles, without any of the courtly delight in subtlety: 'I grant thee life, if thou canst tell me What thing it is that women most desire.' This was somewhere between a crude tavern riddle and a university or monastic guessing game, of which there were many in late medieval England, played to while away the sleepy intellectual hours.

> Question: Who was Adam's mother?
> Answer: The earth.
> Question: What thing is it that hath no end?
> Answer: A bowl.
> Question: What thing is it that never was nor ever shall be?
> Answer: Never mouse made her nest in cat's ear.
> > [fifteenth-century scholars' riddle]

The debates which college, school and monastery men played as intellectual games were played by courtiers as exercises in flirtation. Chaucer describes one of these games in his *Legend of Good Women*. The court divided into two factions, one of the Leaf and the other of the Flower. These stood for two kinds of romantic love, and their members debated which was best, bedecking themselves with leaves and flowers, and enacting leafy and flowery masques.

All the favourite games of the late medieval court were dramatic. Allegories and debates were acted out; there were dances and disguising; fortunes were told by picking flowered and coloured love symbols, throwing dice and playing allegorical love chess and Ragman's Roll. This last game was popular, in a plainer form, with the upper and middle as well as the courtly classes, as were many of the love games. Little love verses, often very bawdy ones, and verses giving rude descriptions of character, were written on pieces of paper attached to strings with a piece of wax on the end. The papers were rolled together and each player chose one of the pieces of wax, and with it one of the papers with its verse. He or she then acted or burlesqued the chosen verse, or paid a forfeit for refusing.

This was a typical late medieval parlour game, such as many a housewife played with her friends, in her chamber or in the garden. One fourteenth-century Parisian householder wrote a little treatise on amusements for his wife, in the form of a story about some Roman ladies who feasted and dined and 'took their pleasure after dinner', while their husbands were away. They talked; played Pinch-me, Hot Cockles and Bric, which was like Hot Cockles only played with a little stick; they played cards, sang songs, told fables and tales, and some played hoodman blind in the road. One lady, called Lucrece, sat alone in her chamber in the innermost part of the house, with her book of hours beside her, waiting for her husband to return. This was obviously the lady the writer wanted his wife to imitate.

He was taking a hard line. Devotional literature had shared in the twelfth-century renaissance, and by the thirteenth century was enlivened with legends of saints' lives and dramatic poems akin to secular romances and ballads. But very few people could afford the illuminated editions of these which made reading them enjoyable. Most women preferred to do what the Wife of Bath did: dress up and go

To vigilies and to processions,
To preaching eke and to these pilgrimages,
To plays of miracles and marriages.

Preachers tried to forestall minstrel story tellers by telling good stories in their sermons. John Felton, the famous Oxford preacher, told tales of Guy of Warwick in his sermons; Bromyard and other successful preachers used little moralised anecdotes, humorous stories of married and clerical life, stories with topical and local flavour, and exotic accounts of marvels like falling stars and fabulous birds. Medieval sermons made lively entertainment, and were very popular with women.

Most stories were told by minstrels, but it became fashionable in the later Middle Ages to sing, dance and tell stories late at night as well as at the traditional time between dinner and supper, which was eaten at dusk, and some of these 'rere supper' entertainments were done by amateurs. They performed to their friends in the garden on summer nights, under the moon. Late medieval city women enjoyed a lot of freedom, and were warned by moralists and reformers not to hold rere suppers, sit up late at home drinking ale, or be seen drunk.

Nor were they to succumb to the extravagant fashions that had been all the rage in high society since the reign of Richard II, and had spread to the middle and lower classes by the fifteenth century. Society preachers entertained society women with sermons attacking their hair styles, make-up and clothes.

It is an evil fashion to pluck the brows, front and forehead, to have away the hair . . . to pluck, pop, and paint the visage . . . some women wash in wine and in other things for to make the hair of colour otherwise than God made it . . . it is an evil fashion for a woman to wear a long train, which is like the devil's tail . . . [Bromyard]

But reform was a lost cause. Low-necked dresses, thick make-up, crisped hair and horned head-dresses won the day. Singing and dancing demanded them. Edward III ordered a tunic for Queen Philippa worked with bands of gold, each in a circle of pearls, the whole ground covered with small pearls and silk. It required 38oz. of small pearls and 400 large ones. And that was a mere tunic. Jewellery and *objets-de-luxe* were favourite playthings of the late medieval affluent.

It was a gorgeously visual age. Nobles collected emeralds, rubies, sapphires, diamonds, pearls and gold, alabasters and tapestries, statues, tiles and illuminated manuscripts. Richard II had an ivory looking-glass in a frame set with jewelled and enamelled roses, with an enamel of the Queen on the back. He had richly worked clasps, goblets, ewers and basins. Noblemen kept pace with the King, and their wives kept pace with them. Rich merchants and townsmen kept pace with the aristocracy. Glamour was a social imperative.

Most medieval nuns were from wealthy or upper-class homes, and in the late Middle Ages many of them found it irresistible to keep pace like everyone else. They joined in the fashion game. In 1441 the Bishop of Lincoln reported after his visit to Ankerwyke Priory that 'the Prioress wears golden rings exceeding costly with divers precious stones and also girdles silvered and gilded over and silken veils . . . Also she wears shifts of cloth of Reynes [The Rhineland] which costs 16d. the ell . . . Also she wears kirtles [skirts] laced with silk and tiring [dress] pins of silver and silver gilt and . . . she has round her neck a long cord of silk, hanging below her breast and on it a gold ring with one diamond.'

But she could never keep up with her secular sisters unless she got herself a pet. Pets were the ornaments of social parade. 'Small hounds' were the favourites, and they were of two kinds: lapdogs and chamber dogs that 'bear away the fleas and divers small fawtes [blemishes, bugs]' [Dame Juliana]. They played about in chambers and walked round the house and garden with their owners. [Illustration 44] Nuns were addicted to chamber dogs, having no one else with whom they could legitimately play and dally. In the early fourteenth century, Archbishop Peckham forbade the Abbess of Romsey to keep a 'number of small dogs in her own chamber, while stinting her nuns in food.' He had to make dozens of similar prohibitions, and in the end compromised to the extent of allowing senior nuns 'one humble, self-effacing little dog unlikely to yelp and caper.'

Chamber dogs often did a lot more than that. Hunting hounds were brought into hall as chamber hounds, to lie on the floor and share in the feast after the chase. The best-loved chamber dogs were taken to church, like hawks. When Lady Audley went to stay with the nuns of Langley, Lincolnshire, she had 'a great abundance of dogs, insomuch that whenever she comes to church there follow her twelve dogs, who make a great uproar in church, hindering the nuns in their psalmody and the nuns thereby are terrified.' Ladies commonly attended services with dogs in their laps.

To the disgust of the reformers, lapdogs were frequently pampered into decorative lethargy. 'Pet dogs must be offered the daintiest flesh . . . the first and choice produce of every dish. If, glutted, they refuse it, then, as though they were infirm, there is a wailing over them . . . After luncheon, for the larger hounds whole bread [a whole loaf: about four-and-a-half pounds] is brought in, and these folk break it and offer it to them with their own hands' [Bromyard].

The *Ancren Riwle* [Rule for Anchoresses] was written in the thirteenth century, and allowed those who chose the life of a recluse to have just one pet. 'Ye shall not possess any beast, my dear sisters, except only a cat.' Cats were the traditional pets of recluses. They were the only domestic companions of the early Irish monks in their solitary huts, where they caught mice and kept their masters silent company. For most Medievals, they were no more than mouse-catchers.

Caged birds, especially magpies, known as pies, and jays, were popular household pets, and teaching them to talk and imitate was a chamber hobby. The Knight of La Tour Laundry told a tale about a woman who had a pie in a cage that 'spake and would tell tales that she saw do'. This pie heard the woman tell her maid to kill a large eel which her husband kept as a pet in the pond in the garden, so that they might eat it. When the husband got home, the pie told him what it had heard, and the husband punished his wife, who punished the pie by pulling its feathers out.

Next best after a chattering bird was a singing one, and larks and nightingales were the favourites. Or strangely and brightly coloured birds, like the parrots brought back from the Middle East by Crusaders. The Earl of Derby went to a lot of trouble to get a really flashy one at Treviso, on his way back from Palermo in 1392. Popinjays, as parrots were called, were often very expensively housed. The Earl put his in a cage for which he had paid the huge sum of £6, in Venice, and he bought a cord to hang it, costing 4/2d. Expensive birds in expensive cages were fed on luscious titbits.

And straw their cages fair, and soft as silk,
And give them sugar, honey, bread and milk.

[*Squire's Tale*]

City ladies favoured talking and singing over decorative birds. They took them into the garden and hung their cages from trees in fine weather, and listened to them calling to the free birds in the branches around them.

Caging wild creatures had a special appeal for the Medievals. It represented a victory in their fight for survival with nature. They made pets of rabbits, squirrels and monkeys. The Abbess of Romsey kept monkeys as well as dogs in her chamber, and in 1387 William of Wykeham complained that the nuns there brought with them to church 'birds, rabbits, hounds and such like frivolous things, whereunto they give more heed than to the offices of the church'.

He would have preferred them to give heed in their leisure to embroidery and tapestry making, pastimes which became women of leisure, especially nuns. Those women who could afford to work at these crafts for pleasure rather than a livelihood produced little exquisites. It was part of the monastic work of many nuns to embroider and tapester vestments, but it could also be a hobby. As early as 679 the nuns of Coldingham were reproached for 'setting their looms and needles to garments more suited to earthly than heavenly bridals.' Ladies in secular society did needlework while they waited for their husbands to come home, and while they talked and listened to stories. They made small, brilliantly coloured items like cushions and small curtains, in exotic designs. The ladies of Sir John Pultney's household made curtains and coverlets for his beds, patterned with lions' heads, eagles, fleur-de-lys, violet popinjays and striped applebloom (apple blossom pink). Romances were a favourite theme for embroidery, and if ladies' husbands were away for long periods, the ladies worked together on scenes from the Arthurian romances, or on traditional designs of plants, animals and heraldic emblems.

By the mid fifteenth century, painted wooden panelling became fashionable, with cushions and drapery done in soft shades like lilady (lily), applebloom, mulberry and grey, to show off the bright colours of the paint. Some ladies did their own panel painting as a change from needlework.

By the mid thirteenth-century the hall was no longer the only domestic living room. People spent increasing amounts of time in their increasingly comfortable, decorated chambers. Ladies had flights of stairs from their chambers to the gardens below, and fireplaces and torches to warm and lighten the room for after dark amusements. It was in their chambers that they played chess and all their favourite parlour games, embroidered, made tapestries, painted, played with their pets, sang, read, talked and received visitors. On one occasion Edward II's daughter, Joanna, paid £2/7/2d. for gold thread, silk, pearls and other necessities 'delivered in her chamber for divers works going on there, to do with them at her pleasure'. A lady's chamber was her living room. In 1397 the inspector visiting Nunmonkton convent in Yorkshire reported that the nuns there 'regarded themselves as great ladies . . . the Prioress had John Monckton to feasts in her room . . . he frequently played at tables with the Prioress in her room and served her with drink.'

Babies and small children shared their parents' chambers, then if they came from a well-to-do family, shared one of their own with a nurse, or with their brothers and sisters. From a very young age they were brought up as little adults, the medieval exuberance of their 'evil manners' being punished with exuberant ferocity. The boys in the dormitories at Westminster School were strictly forbidden to tear their companions' beds to pieces, hide the bedclothes, throw shoes and pillows across the room, or do anything else that would throw their communal chamber into disorder.

There was always plenty of crude, slapstick joking in medieval life. Vulgarity was a game in itself. To take just one example, everybody loved jokes about breaking wind, which ranked high as a popular entertainment. The friar and the lord squire in the *Summoner's Tale* discourse at length on how to divide a fart equally between twelve men, with juicy descriptions of a 'belly stiff and taut as any tabour . . . the sound of it . . . and eke [also] the stink.'

The best jokes were crude and wild, like the best tantrums, into which the Medievals flung themselves with courtly ardour. Henry of Lancaster said that when he was angry he was 'out of sense and reason'; he would hit people with fist and knife, and sword and stick, kick people, and tear his own and other peoples' hair and clothes. The next minute he was hugging everyone round the neck, and splitting his sides laughing at their puns, farts, truth telling and forfeit games. He was rather proud of his performances. 'After anger, game' [*Troilus and Criseyde*].

The medieval Englishman had a very different reputation from his modern counterpart; it was for fickleness and emotionalism, dramatic moves in the courtly game of manners. Chaucer's lovesick heroes and heroines express their feelings in all manner of romantic gestures, ranging from the lustily rude, like sticking red hot pokers up arses and farting into faces, to the sublime, like

in suffisaunce, in bliss, and in singings
This Troilus gan all his life to lead.

His prioress played an unusually dainty game, expressing her sentimentality in tears every time she saw a mouse in a trap or one of her 'small hounds' sick or dying. Love, for God, humans or animals, was the supreme chance for self-expression.

Nothing helped the performance on its way better than drinking, which was second only to loving as the favourite medieval pastime. The favourite drinking places were taverns, but wealthy householders kept their own stocks of ale, which both men and women drank in vast quantities. Cases of the English getting dead drunk at home are legion in medieval records. Chaucer gave a sympathetic account of some typical Medievals drinking at home in his *Reeve's Tale*. It is sympathetic because it put the drinking of Simkin the Miller and his family in the hospitable context of the open hearth, the goose for supper, the bread and ale which they offered to their guests.

This was drinking as part of the evening game of entertaining company. Chaucer's description of it is a perfect cameo of a medieval couple having an evening at home, prior to a night playing wickedly at love.

> They supped, and they spoke him to solace,
> And drunk ever strong ale at best.
> About midnight went they to rest
>
> . . . . . .
>
> As any jay she (his wife) light was and jolly;
> So was her whistle well wet
>
> . . . . . .
>
> This miller hath so wisely bibbed ale
> That as an horse he snoreth in his sleep.

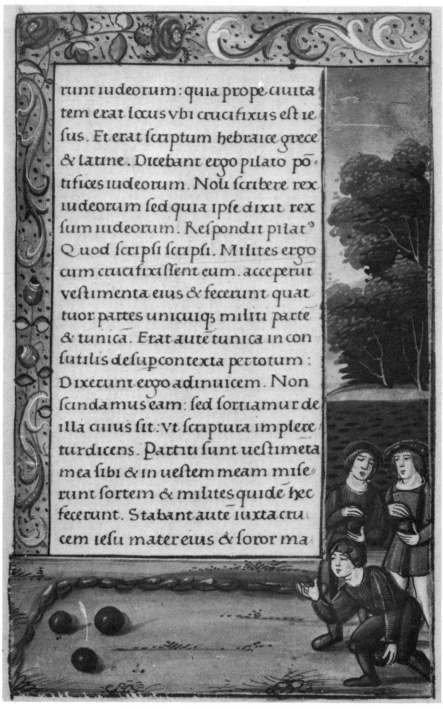

runt iudeorum : quia prope ciuita
tem erat locus vbi crucifixus est ie
sus. Et erat scriptum hebraice grece
& latine. Dicebant ergo pilato pō
tifices iudeorum. Noli scribere rex
iudeorum sed quia ipse dixit. rex
sum iudeorum. Respondit pilat°
Quod scripsi scripsi. Milites ergo
cum crucifixassent eum. acceperut
vestimenta eius & fecerunt quat
tuor partes unicuiq; militi parte
& tunica. Erat aute tunica in con
sutilis desupcontexta pertotum :
Dixerunt ergo adinuicem. Non
scindamus eam : sed sortiamur de
illa cuius sit : vt scriptura implere
tur dicens. partiti sunt uestimeta
mea sibi & in uestem meam mise
runt sortem & milites quide hec
fecerunt. Stabant aute iuxta cru
cem iesu mater eius & soror ma

24 Bowling at a feather target in an alley. *Bodleian Library, Oxford* MS. Douce. 276, fol. 12.

25 A man and his wife playing simple outdoor bowls. *The British Library* Harl 4431, fol. 128.

26 Playing kayles outside a tavern. *The British Museum* MSS. 22494, fol. 42.

27 Tennis played with bound hands, in a wailed court. *The British Library* Harl 4375, fol. 151v.

28 Boys whipping tops. *Bodleian Library, Oxford* MS. Douce. 62, fol. 72v.

29 Stilt walking and fighting. From the Alexander Romance. *Bodleian Library, Oxford MS. Bodl. 264, fol. 123.*

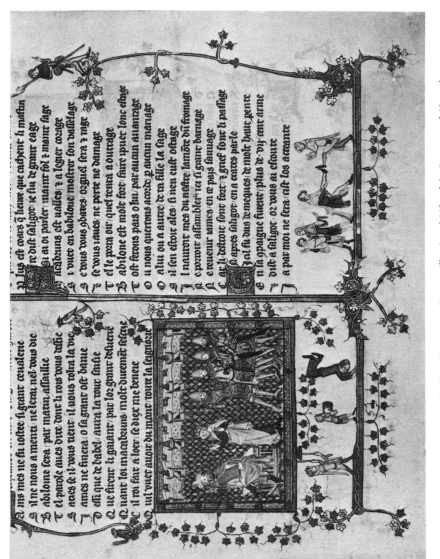

30 Balancing and doing handstands to music. From an illuminated MS. of the Romance of Alexander. *Bodleian Library, Oxford MS. Bodl. 264, fol. 90.*

31 Jumping through the hoop. One of the many acrobatic medieval games. From the Alexander Romance. *Bodleian Library, Oxford MS. Bodl. 264, fol. 64v.*

é a la postoille. cent. E qnt il out den
ma il en fraunce. e prist la fille charl
res le decours de ii ans. morust e fu
regna .viiii. ans e cynk ageis. e cel
mt in escriz. ~. ~.

elberd. Ethelred. e le quart alure

32 Stilt walking. *The British Museum* Royal 14 B v.

ctum ventris tui nobis post hoc exiliu
ostende. O clemens. O pia. O dulcis
maria. Vs? Ora pro nobis sancta dei
genitrix. R. Vt digni efficiamur pro-
missionibus xpi. Oratio.
Mnipotens sempiterne de°
qui gloriose virginis marie
corpus et animam vt dignum filii
tui habitaculum effici mereretur spi-
ritu sancto cooperante preparasti:
da vt cuius commemoratione leta-
mur. eius pia intercessione ab insta
tibus malis et a morte perpetua li
beremur. Per eundem christum dominum nostrum. Amen
Isti tres psalmi sequentes dicuntur
die martis et die veneris. Ad matu-
tinas. An. Specie tua. Psalmus.
Ructauit cor meum verbu
bonum dico ego opera mea
regi

33 A cross between pitch, toss and kick. *Bodleian Library, Oxford* MS. Douce. 276, fol. 63.

34 Game with a swing. From the Alexander Romance. *Bodleian Library, Oxford MS. Bodl. 264, fol. 78v.*

35 A lady bathing naked in a palace pool, watched by the palace owner. *The British Museum* MS. Deposit. 5894.

36 Naked boys being taught to swim. *The British Museum* 38126 fol. 7.

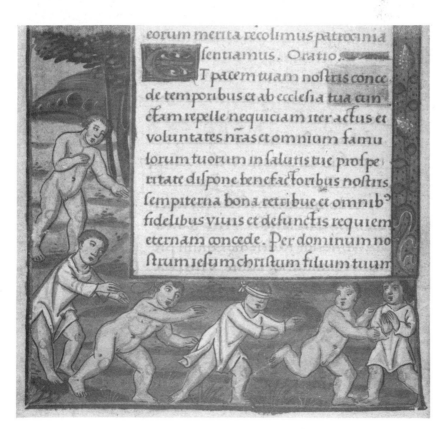

eorum merita recolimus patrocinia
sentiamus. Oratio,
T pacem tuam nostris conce
de temporibus et ab ecclesia tua cun
ctam repelle nequiciam iter actus et
voluntates nras et omnium famu
lorum tuorum in salutis tue prospe
ritate dispone benefactoribus nostris
sempiterna bona retribue et omnib̄ꝰ
fidelibus viuis et defunctis requiem
eternam concede. Per dominum no
strum iesum christum filium tuum

37 Blind Man's Buff, medieval style. *Bodleian Library, Oxford* MS. Douce, 276, fol. 49v.

ancti iohannes & paule. ora
ancti cosma et damiane. ora
ancti geruasi et prothasi. ora
mnes sancti martyres. ora
ancte siluester. ora
ancte gregori. ora
ancte martine. ora
ancte augustine. ora
ancte ambrosi. ora
ancte iheronime. ora
ancte nicolae. ora
ancte ludouice. ora
mnes sancti pontifices et con
fessores dei. ora
mnes sancti doctores. ora
ancte benedicte. ora
ancte francisce. ora
ancte anthoni. ora
ancte dominice. ora
mnes sancti monachi et here
mite. Orate pro nobis.

38 Sixteenth-century hat-fight. *Bodleian Library, Oxford* MS. Douce. 276, fol. 83.

39 Butterfly-chasing in the margins of a falconry scene. July depicted in a sixteenth-century calendar. *The British Library* Add. MS. 24098, fol. 24b.

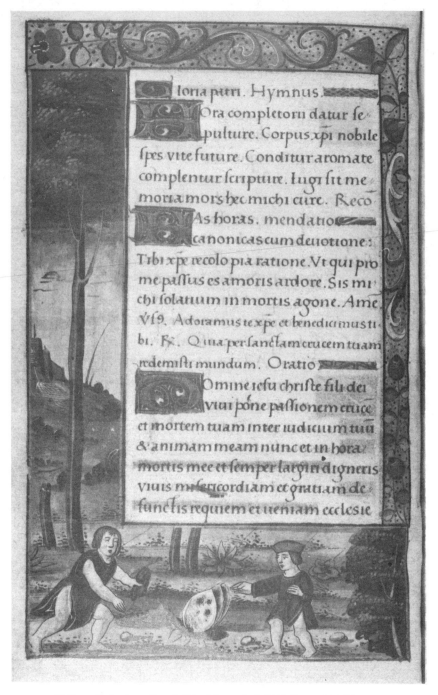

loria patri. Hymnus.
Ora completorii datur se
pulture. Corpus xpi nobile
spes vite future. Conditur aromate
complentur scripture. lugi sit me
moria mors hec michi cure. Reco
As horas. mendatio
canonicas cum deuotione:
Tibi xpe recolo pia ratione. Vt qui pro
me passus es amoris ardore. Sis mi
chi solatium in mortis agone. Ame
Vig. Adoramus te xpe et benedicimus ti
bi. R̄. Q̄ ma per sanctam crucem tuam
redemisti mundum. Oratio
Omine iesu christe fili dei
viui pone passionem cruce
et mortem tuam inter iudicium tuu
& animam meam nunc et in hora
mortis mee et semper largiri digneris
viuis misericordiam et gratiam de
functis requiem et ueniam ecclesie

40 Boys chasing butterflies. *Bodleian Library, Oxford* MS. Douce. 276, fol. 61v.

41 Girls catching butterflies in their hoods. From the Alexander Romance. *Bodleian Library, Oxford. MS—Bodl. 264.*

etiam queda qur opumitatis auribus tanq̃ Vlysses aliter Carmni cantatur: ut poete fabuĺ
pretterebie. —Sed ut euagum tamdem desinat oratio. Enarrationes hac nostras a te Senis
ſpatio expertatas accipies: Merulamq̃ tuam amabis. Vale

42 A reading party in a flower-garden. From the Alexander Romance. *Bodleian Library, Oxford* MS. Bodl.
264. Holkham 324, fol. 159.

43 A formal garden in the making. Note the marginal game of rattles. March depicted in a sixteenth-century calendar. *The British Library* Add. MS. 24098, fol. 20b.

44 April lovers in a garden. Note the bat and ball game played in the margin. From the sixteenth-century calendar. *The British Library* Add. MS. 24098, fol. 21b.

Within the illustration, the manuscript text reads:

r̃ vous conterous de la grant rente
que le grant cam a chascun an en
rette cite de quinsay. et es apartena
tes. si vous conteray primerenit du
sel pour ce que moult vault de ren
te. Sachiez que le sel rent chascun an a somme
xx
iiij. couimans d'or. et chascun coumant est lxx
sages d'or volez pois si que les iiij. couimans du
oij outent. v.m milliers. et vj.c milliers de pois.
d'or. doutt chascun pois d'or vault plus de i. florin

45 Playing chess in a little pleasure garden. From an English MS. of Marco Polo's *Travels*, *c.* 1400.
Bodleian Library, Oxford MS. Bodl. 264, fol. 258.

CHAPTER SIX

Board, Table and Dice Games

Racing, chasing and fighting are three of the most basic human activities, and games representing them have always been the favourite board games. Almost all board games with long histories are representations of these three activities, and to some extent they developed, like the activities, chronologically. Though this was not a clear process, racing games often developed into chasing games and chasing games into battle games.

The last of these developments took place in the Middle Ages, and gave Europe the game that has been supreme among board games ever since: chess, and the game that has been supreme among table games: cards. There were all sorts of less spectacular developments: games dying out and changing, games appearing for the first time, and games using all sorts of equipment, but they all began with simple games and developed from there.

One of the simplest and most fundamental games was dicing, which was also a component of many of the more sophisticated and developing medieval games. Dicing had been popular since ancient times. At first it was played with rolled bones, then with cubic dice, which became popular in about the seventh century B.C. Bone play survived into the medieval period and beyond, played according to various sets of rules and condemned alike by reformers, serious gamblers and public authorities. Dicing was always considered the crude end of gambling, and was associated with seedy taverns and late-night quarrels over the money lost in play.

In one typical case, three Londoners were charged in 1339 with being 'addicted to playing knuckle-bones at night, leading apprentices into gambling habits, and using threats against citizens and strangers.'

People liked dicing because it put them irretrievably at the mercy of chance, which was just why the anti-gamblers disliked it. The twelfth-century bishop John of Salisbury spoke for many when he called dicing 'the damnable art'. With fascinated horror he listed ten dice games which he saw being made by an ivory carver in Kirkudbrightshire. A few of them were race games; many of them simply had names that meant they were dice games, like senio (Latin for dice).

The clergy loved dicing, and were incessantly and ineffectually forbidden to indulge in it all through the Middle Ages. Many played games involving three dice, like the one Christ's tormentors play in the Towneley play of the Crucifixion. 'Raffle' was another three dice game, in which the winner was the one who threw all three dice alike or, if neither player managed that, threw the highest pair. Some preferred two dice games; some played on boards; some threw with cups; some played double games; some kept tally of their throws with counters.

Dicing was usually one against one or pair against pair, which is why it was so cut-throat, and so popular. The most popular dice game of all, and the one which provoked the most bloodshed, cheating and hostility, was hasard. It was a two dice game and its rules were complicated by arbitrary additions, but it was always simple, volatile and deliciously disreputable.

> In Flanders whylon [once] was a company
> Of young folk, that haunted folly,
> As riot, hasard, stews [brothels] and taverns,
> Whereas, with harps, lutes and gitterns,
> They daunce and play at dice both night and day.
>
> [*Pardoner's Tale*]

More than any other dice game, hasard was played in taverns, and played crookedly. Among the countless convictions recorded in the court rolls for playing with false dice, enticing strangers into taverns to defraud them of their money, and dicing by night to the nuisance of the neighbours, are many like this one, from the City of London in 1368:

> William Ludrington and John Oliver foreswear playing
> at dice . . . and other fraudulent games. They have told

the court that William at Wode and Cok of Greenwich are hasardous like themselves and have been associated with them in deceiving people.

Guilty parties were usually taken to the nearest pillory, often to an accompaniment of pipes and trumpets, and installed there with their false dice around their necks. The game was so compulsive, and the tactics used to keep victims playing it so seductive and strongarm, that huge sums of money were extorted. One Stephen Lalleford, a smith by trade and a 'common gamester', cheated a victim of the huge sum of £17 on the night of December 5th, 1375.

The stakes were just as high, and the play just as ruthless, between friends. Throwers bet against each other and against onlookers, who bet between themselves and encouraged the player of their choice with bloodthirsty advice. Men diced away purses, hoods and clothes.

> And the higher he is of estate,
> The more he is holden desolate.
>
> *[Pardoner's Tale]*

The Earl of Derby spent a good many nights on his long sea voyage trying to win back at dice the money he had lost at other games on previous nights.

> Paid to John Walker at Calais, for games there, 5½ florins. . . . For dice games in the ship to Prussia 33/4d. . . . For a dice game bought to order, 8 nobles (£2/13/4d.) . . . For money given for dice at Danzig 30/- . . . For playing with John Rye for two nights 42 marks (£28).

Among humbler dicers none were keener than apprentices, who were constantly being forbidden to play games that might lead them into bad company, fighting, debt or drink, all of them close companions of dicing.

Apprentices and boys played a variant of dicing known as cross and pile, which was considered less of a threat to their good behaviour. It was coin tossing, and got its name from the cross imprinted on one side of farthings in Edward I's reign; the reverse side was known as the pile. It was a simple amusement enjoyed by everyone. King Edward himself played it with his domestic servants; one year he borrowed five shillings from his barber, and an unspecified amount from his chamber usher, to play it, and lost that, plus a further 8d., to one Robert Waterville.

Chequers offered still more scope for loss. It was a relative of dicing, played with pebbles which were thrown or rolled on to a chequered board, the players and onlookers betting on whether each pebble would land on a black or a white square. It was commonly known as queek rather than chequerboard, hence queek or quek rather than chequers. In 1382 William Soys, an embroiderer of the parish of All Hallows in the Ropery, London, was convicted of

> having a false chequer board called a 'queek', in which all the white points [squares] in different quarters there of were depressed lower than the black points; while in the other quarters the black points were depressed, and lower than the white points in the same; so that all those who played with the said board . . . were maliciously and deceitfully deprived of their property . . . He had won of his complainant 27/4d. . . . from Walter Bigod, squire, 34/4d. on this same day . . . and from his servant, Thomas, 15/-. . . .

William and his false boards were put in the Newgate pillory for an hour a day for the next three days.

In 1477 Edward IV prohibited queek alongside closh, kayles, hand-in and hand-out. Played with crude force, it could be as much a throwing as a board game. A lot of the chequers and chequer boards that appear in medieval records probably belonged to queek rather than chess, and when it was played within a time limit, with one section of the board as the target area, it was almost like one of the race games popular among the Medievals under the name 'tables'.

Tables was the general name for a group of everyday games

played with the basic equipment of a board and counters or pebbles, named after the Latin *tabulae*, meaning counters or little pieces. The name was also used to refer specifically to the basic medieval race game, which has remained popular in England, in an altered form, right up to the present day. This game of tables required skill as well as luck, and was therefore considered more worthwhile than mere games of chance. Tables is the name for the medieval ancestor of backgammon, and in its medieval prime it was a universal favourite.

It had been popular much longer than that. Boards, dice and pieces for a race game of this sort have been discovered in the ancient royal cemeteries of Ur and Egyptian cities. It was played by the Greeks and Romans, who carved tables for it in the courtyards of their villas. They played it under three names, which suggest its stages of development: *alea* (dice), a primitive dice game; *tabulae* (tables), a race game, and *ludus duodecim scriptorum* (the twelve line game), a sophisticated race game involving chase and capture.

All these were basically the same racing game, in which two players used three dice to move fifteen men each over a board with three sets of twelve points. In *alea* the course was just two sets of twelve points, and the game was known in this form in Anglo-Saxon England, where it was probably brought by Roman legionaries. A board for *alea* was found at the Roman potteries and works depot of Holt in Denbighshire.

But it does not figure large in English records until after the first crusade, and then in Arabic as well as Roman form. It had become popular with the Arab aristocracy despite, or perhaps because of, being condemned in the Koran as a form of gambling. It was known in the Middle East as nard, the Persian word for a block or cylinder, and was only different from alea in using two instead of three dice. Persian tradition ascribes the twelve divisions of its board to the twelve months of the year, and the fifteen light and fifteen dark pieces to the fifteen moonlit and fifteen moonless nights of each month. From Persia it moved along what was to become a familiar route of cultural transmission. The Arabs took it to Spain, and possibly Sicily. It had reached France by the eleventh century, and was being played for high stakes at the

English court in the twelfth century, by Richard the Lion-heart and his brother John.

Tables boards were square, and sometimes hinged with chess or merels boards, which means it was considered superior to simple race and dice games. The boards were big, to accommodate the big pieces favoured by the Medievals, made of bone, antler, slate, stone, wood and ivory, some plain, others carved and decorated. The rich had rich sets, the poor had plain ones. One William Fornyvale, who found himself in debt in 1445 to the tune of £120, had an inventory taken of his goods by the City of London authorities, and was in possession of a humble set of 'tables and men 4d., and four trussing coffers 12d.' (These were little boxes for things like jewellery and gaming pieces.) The friar in Chaucer's *Summoner's Tale* had a flashier 'pair of tables all of ivory'. There is a tables board cut into one of the flat stones at Norwich Castle.

Carved into one of the stones next to it is a much more primitive race game, something like the modern game of steeplechase, with a long spiral track punctuated by eight-three holes. Simple games like this must have existed in abundance in medieval England, but no one wrote about them, and we have few records of their existence. Tables existed in about twenty-five forms in medieval Europe, and was substantially documented. It inspired followings, begat schools of play, and was publicised in books of instructions. By the fourteenth century it was at the peak of its popularity, and a treatise was written about it explaining all its forms and styles of play to the English, and examining about eighty problems of play.

The terms used in this treatise will make sense to backgammon players: *domus* (home), *egressus* (the way out), *homo* (a man), *homo vagans* (a wandering man), single piece or blot.

The most popular form of play in England was the long game, which was unique to England and included ways of winning with the uniquely English names of limpolding and lurching. Both these involved blocking all five of the opponent's *egressi* with a *unire duo*, or two men on one point, so that he could not get off. This was refined play, and was sometimes further refined by variations such as starting with two pieces off the board, or with two dice and the option of adding a third. Most tables was played in the Roman way, with three dice, though the third one was often left permanently as a six. If only two dice were used, they could be made into three by duplicating the higher (*majoret*) or the lower (*minoret*) of the throws.

Next most popular after the long game was *paumcarie*, more primitively racing, and playable on the whole or half of the board. *Emperador*, in which the pieces were laid out along three points, was popular in both Spain and England, where it was played in variations known as Half-Emperador and Provincial.

If players agreed to play tables *ad fallum*, inability to use a throw meant immediate loss of the game. There were so many different ways of playing that quarrelling was as rife as gambling on tables. When the Earl of Derby tired of dicing at sea, he bought a couple of expensive 'tablers', one costing 43/4d., the other double that. He then lost 'to a Lord in the galley for his game at tables, playing with a Gascon, three ducats [twenty-seven shillings]'. In one disastrous night he lost £4 at tables to someone called Thomas Cotas, and no less than £26/13/4d. to him at dice. For all its sophisticated possibilities, tables had a primitive appeal, and was often played like dicing. In 1482 the Abbot of Wenlock was dismissed from office for fathering illegitimate children and spending his time 'playing at tables and other games the whole day and night with buffoons and other such persons.'

But more often tables was classed with chess, of which it was the after dinner partner in upper- and middle-class Europe.

'They dauncen, and they play at chess and tables.' [*Franklin's Tale*] Really simple games were never mentioned in the same breath as chess, if they were mentioned at all. Many of them, like the one carved into the stone at Norwich Castle, had only make-shift boards and were played with pieces made of stones, nuts and pips. Or, like the game for which a London fishmonger in 1454 had 'a bag of counters, value 1d.' (court inventory), they were too humbly equipped to establish a lasting identity,

It was the aristocrats of race games that developed variations, like tables, and the most common development was towards alignment, quickly followed by the development of capture to stop the opponent getting his pieces aligned. Games of this sort were known in the romance languages as merels, from the Latin *merellus*, meaning a small coin, counter or token.

Merels was the basic alignment game of medieval Europe. Almost every local English dialect had its own version of the word merels: marls in Dorset, merry-holes in Lincolnshire and Northamptonshire, miracles in Cheshire, and over most of the country the version that eventually supplanted them all: morris.

Like tables, merels is still played today, and like tables, it has always existed in a lot of different forms. The simplest medieval form was nine holes, for which boards were often carved on the cloister benches of monasteries, and on the pews and porches of parish churches. Like all board games, it was a favourite with the monastic clergy, who whiled away their recreation periods playing it. And it was a favourite with everyone who had a few counters and a bit of time to spare. Its simplicity was the secret of its success.

Players had three pieces each, which they put down alternately, trying to get three in a row, like noughts and crosses, which is a paper and pencil version of the same game. Sometimes the points were joined up by lines, in which case the game was called the smaller merels, or three men's morris. The pieces could easily be moved along the lines to neighbouring empty points, to make a row of three. Merels was easy, harmless, and capable of countless variations, such as the one hinted at on the merels board in Norwich Cathedral cloisters, which has an extra large centre hole, or on some of the boards in the Westminster cloisters, which only have a horizontal line on one side. [Illustration 46]

The most popular development in merels was capture. In five or six men's morris, played on an expanded board which made room for capture, the opponent's pieces could be landed on and captured after they had formed a row. If all ten or twelve pieces were on the board, they were moved along the points alternately, on to enemy points, and the first player to be reduced to two pieces was the loser.

Once capture was introduced, no one could get enough of it, and by the late fourteenth century this version of merels had been completely superseded by a bigger and more aggressive one, known as the larger merels, or nine men's morris. Boards for this were scratched on slate boulders and doorsteps, on the chapter-house steps and cloister seats of monasteries, on tombstones and castle walls all over Britain, and everywhere the British have lived, from the early Christian settlements on the Isle of Man to the crusader castles in Palestine.

In about 1400 diagonal lines were added to the board and the number of pieces increased to eleven or twelve per player. By now, the larger merels was considered a sufficiently sophisticated game to be combined with chess in hinged boards. Its essential elements, chasing, blocking and capturing, were combined to make up a board version of the favourite medieval sport of hunting. Five smaller merels boards were joined together to form a cross, on which a set of pieces, usually thirteen in number, hunted a single piece belonging to the opponent. The hunter was usually known as the fox and the hunted as the geese. Fox-and-geese was a huge success, especially with countrymen, who took a vengeful delight in defeating the fox. But it did not stop at countrymen. Edward IV ordered 'two foxes and fourty-six hounds of silver over-gilt to form two sets of merelles', enough for a double game with some to spare; there were never more than seventeen geese and one fox in a game. The fox captured the geese by jumping over them, and won the game if he took enough of them to stop them hemming him in. The geese could only move one point at a time, and won if they hemmed the fox in. The geese had a hard time of it, and their number was often increased from thirteen to seventeen to make the contest more equal.

There was one medieval chase and capture game, probably related to fox-and-geese, which deserves a mention because in the early Middle Ages it was pretty well supreme among board games, before it died out in the thirteenth century. The game is called 'hnefatafl', and it was robbed, first of its supremacy, then of its very existence, by chess. But before chess came to western Europe, hnefatafl had the same high status chess had later, and in some remote areas of Europe it was preferred to chess for centuries.

Like fox-and-geese, it was a hunt game with a solitary quarry. One of the old Icelandic names for it is *hala tafl*, the tail game, i.e. the game of the creature with a tail, the fox. But it was commonly known as tafl, the table game or just the game, and as hnefatafl, the king's game. The Greeks had played a similar game with cities (*petteia*) and the Romans with soldiers (*Ludus latrunculorum*). Pieces moved backwards and forwards, to left and right, over and odd number of squares, anything from seven by seven to nineteen by nineteen. Judging from the number of boards for *ludus latrunculorum* found on the sites of Roman camps along Hadrian's Wall, it was very popular with the cold and bored legionaries on the northern frontiers.

The Irish had their own Celtic version of this hunt game in the tenth century, under the name *fidchell*, and the Welsh under the name *gwyddbwyll*, the pieces representing men and women instead of cities and soldiers. The Norsemen popularised the game as hnefatafl. They used pieces made of horses' teeth or bone, usually a red one for the king and white ones for his attackers. Like the fox in fox-and-geese, the king started at the centre, but unlike the fox, he usually lost the game, and as time went on, had to develop a team of courtiers or defenders to help him against his attackers, who were grouped round the edge of the board.

The numbers in the game, and the size of the boards, were increased over the years, to increase the element of battle. Most games underwent this kind of increase, for this kind of reason. Capture in hnefatafl was by a method similar to the fox-and-geese method, by sandwiching an opponent's piece between two of one's own pieces. When there was no other escape open to the king, he could move over a square between two attackers to a free square beyond, in answer to his opponent's warning 'Watch your king!'

And it was a kingly game. Under its other Welsh name, *tawlbwrrd*, it was played at the Welsh court. When the Welsh chancellor was admitted to office, he received a golden ring, a harp and a tawlbwrrd from the king, and was expected to keep them as marks of honour all his life. Courtiers used tawlbwrrds as pledges, and a youngest son had the right to inherit his father's tawlbwrrd, harp and coulter. The Welsh king's own set had the same high price as his harp and his cloak: 6 score pence, itemised in the royal accounts as 30d. for the king piece, 30d. for his eight defenders, and 60d. for his sixteen attackers. There is no mention of the board, which was separate. Pieces and boards were made of exotic substances like walrus ivory, whalebone, hart's antler and bullock's horn. Away from court, humbler players used sets made of bone or wood.

The fatal game played between Cnut and Earl Ulf in 1027, which ended with the earl upturning the board and Cnut murdering him in revenge a few days later, is always referred to by later chroniclers and historians as chess, but they have mistaken the heir for the king. Chess had not yet succeeded tafl in northern Europe, and the game must have been tafl, which features in all the early Scandinavian chronicles.

'I am strong at tafl play', Earl Rognwald of Orkney began the list of his accomplishments in 1125. But less than a century later, tafl was little more than a memory in most of Europe, surviving only in pockets. It was still being played in Wales in 1587, and in Lapland in 1732, where the pieces were called Swedes and Muscovites.

The chances are that it was never really popular. Few could play it well enough to make a good hunt of it, and the fact that it existed in so many different forms may have meant that none of them was satisfactory rather than that it was universally popular. It was a status symbol at court, not an everyday amusement. There is a scrap of written evidence for tafl which indicates just that. It comes from an Irish gospel book of the twelfth century in which the scribe has inserted a couple of pages about a game he calls *alea evangelii* (the gospel dice game). It is obviously a kind of tafl, and he says that it was unfamiliar to most people. It was, he goes on, 'brought away from the king of the English, from the house of King Athelstan, by Dubinsi, Bishop of Bangor [d. 951]'. It was played on a large board, between dukes and counts, and the scribe's description of play is cryptic and imprecise. It may well be that he was one of the many at court who, by his own account, were ignorant of play. 'There is a citadel and a city', he says, 'with nine steps twice over . . .' His description develops into a tafl-gospel cryptogram: 'The square . . . has four sides because there are four evangelists . . . the primary man signifies the one purpose of Matthew, Mark, Luke and John, and the unity of the Trinity.' [Illustration 47]

But the game and the message were lost on the readers of the gospel book, and tafl disappeared from history, along with other Irish games with enticingly mysterious names like Conchobar's forehead, brandub, branfach and cenuchaen. It was only natural that later continental writers of Celtic romances should substitute chess for this unfamiliar game, though some later Welsh translators of these romances re-substituted tawlbwrdd for chess. They were in a minority. Chess swept the board.

No other medieval game aroused the same passions as chess, and no other game was anywhere near as popular; it was in a class of its own. In particular, it offered the battle satisfaction that tafl lacked. The early medieval Persians, from whom the Arabs, thence the Europeans, learnt it, listed ten advantages of chess; the first was that it nourished the mind; the last that it combined war with sport. These two alone would have been enough to guarantee it success in courtly Europe, and courtiers played it as if their lives depended on it, as indeed they sometimes did. More than one chess player died for the sake of checkmate.

The Normans brought chess to Britain in the twelfth century, after it had crossed into France from Muslim Spain, at the end of the Muslim games route from India, where chess probably originated. Reginald of Durham met a carver in the mid twelfth century who made 'combs, tablemen, chessmen, dice, spigots and other such articles of bone and horn'. It was already keenly played in England by that time, and there is a poem about it from that date, written in Winchester, which calls the pieces by their standard medieval names, all of them derived from middle Persian via Arabic, testimonies of its Islamic origins. The piece now known as the queen began its medieval life as the fers, from the Arabic *firz* or *firzàn*, a wise man or counsellor, and from the Persian *ferzēn*. By the twelfth century the fers had started to change into the queen, perhaps as a result of moving away from Islamic countries to Christian ones at the height of the twelfth-century romantic renaissance; the Troubadours, unlike the Arabs, preferred queens to counsellors; they wanted some femininity in their battles.

The piece now known as the bishop was known as the fil, from the Arabic *fil*, meaning elephant, and from the Persian *pil*. In the twelfth century it started to turn into an old man or bishop, a more European symbol of strength than the elephant. The modern rook was a roc in the Middle Ages, from the Arabic *rukkh*, and from the Persian *rukh*, meaning a chariot. But it was taken as what it sounded like, and quickly came to be a rock whence, towards the end of the period, a castle. The word chess comes from the Latin *scacci*, which comes from the Arabic and Persian word *shah*, meaning a ruler; in Europe a king. Check comes from the same root word, and mate from the Arabic and Persian *mat*, meaning dead, so that check mate, *shah mat*, means the ruler, or king, is dead.

Because Islam forbids the representation of the human form, Muslim pieces were basically just blocks with little distinguishing embellishments carved on them. They remained in use in Europe after the development of European figure pieces, and have survived in far greater numbers than figure pieces, but this may be because the latter were kept, and lost, in collections rather than individually. Muslim pieces were used in England as late as the fourteenth century, but those who could afford good sets, preferred figured pieces. By the eleventh century, stylised Muslim pieces were carved with elaborate relief work and developing almost figurative features, like the dome-shaped top of the fil and the head-like projection of the *faras* (horse or horseman), which developed into the bishop's mitre and the knight's head. The human pieces were given eyes. [Illustration 48]

European chess pieces were a microcosm of the courtly society that adopted them as its favourite game: a king, a queen, a bishop, a knight, a castle and a band of retainers. Chess was a courtly game; it required leisure, of which knights and barons before the thirteenth century, locked up in their remote castles, had more than enough. It required strategic thinking, in which they were trained, and specially made pieces, on one possession of which they prided themselves. Chess skill and a fine set of chessmen were the hallmarks of a superior knight or gentleman.

When Guy of Warwick was not fighting duels, he was playing chess with anyone who would take him on: fellow knights, noble enemies and noble ladies. Because chess was a pastime of chivalry, it was a passport to ladies' chambers, a game of courtly love.

> Then down was the checker laid
> And before the maiden's bed displayed.
>> [Guy of Warwick]

A lot of medieval illustrations show chess being played by noble men and women, often kings and queens, in chambers, halls and gardens. Aristocratic children learnt to play chess as they learnt to ride, hunt and hawk. Some household retainers learnt it too; Guy of Warwick beat the Emperor of Germany's steward at chess twice running, but in general it was an upper-class game, at least until the late fourteenth century, and anyone who played it was suspected of belonging to the aristocracy.

Except for the clergy. They loved chess from the first moment they encountered it, and played it irrespective of class. Chess was the perfect game for monks: its excitement broke up the routine of cloistered life; serious-minded brethren played it as an intellectual, even a philosophical, exercise. Archbishop Peckham was horrified to find 'chess and other scurrilous games' being played by the Augustinian canons of Coxford, Norfolk, when he visited it in 1281, and the Cistercian General Chapter nine years later ordered punishment for any brethren found playing chess. But Peckham was notoriously unplayful, and the Cistercians notoriously austere. The Church's early scruples about chess as a dangerous addiction likely to cause arguments, anger and obsessive time wasting, gave way to enthusiasm for it as an unbeatable game and an intriguing philosophical allegory.

'The world resembles a chessboard which is chequered black and white, the colours showing the two conditions of life and death, or praise and blame,' began one twelfth-century 'morality' sermon on chess. 'In this game the devil says "check!" when a man falls into sin, and unless he quickly covers the check by turning to repentance the devil says "mate!" and carries him off to hell, whence there is no escape.' As chess spread to the middle classes, chess sermons, featuring death as the unavoidable checkmate, and life as a chess game between man and the devil for man's soul, were preached in vivid detail to fashionable congregations.

Yet the Church's early scruples about chess were not unfounded. It was an extraordinarily violent game, in play and in the passions it aroused. Victory was either by checkmate or 'bare king', the taking of all the opponent's pieces, and either way it was secured quickly and violently. Medieval chess knew no mercy. According to the chroniclers, Henry II's younger son, John, quarrelled at chess with Fulk Guarine, a Shropshire nobleman, and broke the board over his head. Guarine nearly killed John in return, and as a result was kept from his rightful inheritance of Whittington Castle when John became king years later. Victory in a serious chess game like this one was a point of honour. Like any other honourable tournament, chess attracted spectators, who kept the pressure on the players with a stream of advice and abuse, keen to see a quick victory.

Chess was forever being speeded up. At first it was too slow; it had too much introduction and not enough action. So players used dice for the opening moves, or extended the board to give greater freedom of movement, or re-arranged the pieces. The king, queen and pawns were allowed to open by moving to the third square, and a system of play from more advanced positions, known as the short assize, became very popular.

But the best way to speed up play was to change the moves of the pieces themselves, and the assize the English liked best was the long assize, which favoured move rather than position changes. At first the queen could only move one square at a time, diagonally, keeping close to the king, who could only take straight, not diagonally, to block rook checks. Pawns reaching the other end could only be turned into queens, no other pieces, and pawns' play was despised by the Medievals as inconsequential, the more so as other pieces improved their moves.

Even when pawns were given their modern opening move and power to take in passing, they were played as little as possible, like the stay-at-home queens and crafty bishops, who could leap an adjacent diagonal square into one beyond, and were nicknamed spies, or thieves, because they took people by surprise. They gave up this vaulting move, but remained unpopular. It was rooks and knights the Medievals really liked, because they had the freest moves and combined well to make 'bare king' victory. The king was allowed to jump to safety, to avoid this and make the struggle for it all the more tense, a move the English called 'ward making' because it got the king to the safety of a ward, or hut.

The heart of a good chess game was king, knight and rook in mortal combat. Romance writers rated a corner checkmate by a rook the most skilful of all: 'after check for the rook were sore the mate' [*Audelay Poems* 1426]. But the English had a soft spot for knights, and for checkmate in the centre of the board which was so popular in the thirteenth and fourteenth centuries that writers called it the 'guy cotidian' (daily game).

> Therewith Fortune said 'Check here!'
> And 'Mate!' at the mid-point of the checker,
> With a pawn errant, alas!
> Full craftier to play she was.

Such was the lament of the knight in Chaucer's *Book of the Duchess*, about his loss in a game he played against fortune for the prize of love.

Life and love were popular stakes with the romantic poets, but in fact chess was one of the very few medieval games that was so absorbing in its own right that gambling was not a vital part of it. There certainly was chess gambling; John of Brabant used to put a couple of shillings on his Christmas games, but like most people he really played for honour, and for fun. The universities forbade their students all knightly games, such as jousting, hunting, hawking and games of chance, but they made an exception in favour of chess on Sundays and feast-days, providing the stakes were only eatables and drinkables.

By the fourteenth century chess had spread to the minor nobility, gentry and townsfolk, who could afford the time and equipment to play. Expenses could be kept low, but if the players wanted to cut a dash, they played with gorgeous sets like the ones used at court, with ivory and ebony pieces carved in flamboyant shapes, moving over ivory boards inlaid with mother-of-pearl, silver and gold.

Most ivory pieces were red and white, red and black or red and green; sometimes, but less often, they were black and white. Boards were plain at first, with squares outlined on them, but soon became chequered, usually in black and white. [Illustration 49]

Both the pieces and the boards were often very big, too big to pack up and carry or store, which is why so few of them have been preserved. Boards were often a yard long, and hung on iron pins on the wall. Some sets were double, with tables on the reverse side; some folded in the middle, and some had little boxes inset to hold the pieces, which became more and more elaborate.

By the later Middle Ages chess was popular with tradesmen and shopkeepers, who kept their wooden and bone pieces in canvas bags or wooden boxes. But many did their best to have a 'show' set as well as an everyday one, and these became status symbols. In 1378 Alice Perrers had, in one of her manors near Ruislip, 'a table with chessmen worth 12d.' for private play, and 'a set of chessmen with boards of ivory worth 3/4d.' for social play.

Those who did not have a show set had to rely on their play to make an impression. By the fourteenth century there were vernacular treatises on chess, which added practical advice to the mythology and theorising of earlier works in Latin. But they were 'show' treatises, to go with show sets, and their advice was pretty elementary. One of these treatises, from the late fourteenth century, shows the fashionable French influence on English chess. It lists games with titles like *fol si prent* ('he is a fool if he takes'), *sans array* (battle without array), *le guy covenant* (the covenant game, in which players agreed that one should not take, and the other should not move, a particular piece). But on the whole, European interest in the theories of chess was superficial, compared with Muslim interest. Europeans preferred playing it to studying it; it was a game, not a heritage, for them.

By the fifteenth century it had spread to all classes and was a popular tavern game. Wyclif berated the clergy for playing in taverns, many of which had names like 'The Checker of the

Hope', and were dens of gaming. Chess became crude as well as strategic, supreme not just among battle games but among all board games. At the hour when wealthy merchants were finishing their after-dinner games on their gorgeous new boards, labourers and gameful friars were sitting down in their local taverns to play chess on boards that doubled for quek and chess.

The only other battle game played on any scale, and it was nothing like the scale of chess, was a derivative of chess, and only worthy of mention alongside it when chess was at its most debased: 'the checker . . . the draughts, the dice, and other dregh [dreary, tedious] games' [*The Destruction of Troy*, 1400].

Draughts were originally called 'ferses' because the game began as a game for chess queens, moving in their original chess style, one square at a time, over a chequered board. In France today draughts are still called dames, a diminutive version of *jeu-des-dames* (the queens' or ladies' game). Draughts probably got their principles of alignment from merels, but they were more closely related to chess; the ferses, or queens, were promoted into kings when they reached the other end of the board.

Taking only became compulsory, under pain of huffing, after about 1535, and the game with optional capture (*jeu plaisant*) continued to be played alongside the huffing game (*jeu forcé*) in rural England until the late seventeenth century.

Draughts probably originated in the south of France in the twelfth century; it had established itself in England by the late fourteenth century, but never approached chess in popularity. Unlike the ubiquitous chess, draughts only appears about five times in English literature, and only very occasionally in art, between 1200 and 1500. In Chaucer's *Book of the Duchess*, the duchess replies to the knight that his grief at losing his fers in a game against fortune is excessive, and would have been so 'though he had lost the ferses twelve'. The game she had in mind was obviously draughts. But the game the knight had in mind was obviously chess, and he did not understand her complacency: 'Thou knowest full little what thou meanest; I have lost more than thou wenest [thinkest].' [Illustration 50]

No knight would have played draughts when he could play chess. Still less would he have played, or thought of playing, rithmomathy, which, like draughts, originated in France in about the twelfth century, and was played with counters on a chequered board. But there the resemblance ends, not just to draughts but to any other board game, medieval or modern. Rithmomathy is the most obscure of all medieval board games, little played, and derived not from any game but from the Greek theory of numbers, which is why the Greeks called their earlier version of it the philosophers' game, and why hardly anyone ever played it. If it was played at all in medieval Europe, it was by a tiny élite of mathematical scholars. The only mention of it in English is in a late fifteenth-century treatise on games written by John Shirwood, Bishop of Durham, for his patron, George Neville.

The first stage in the game was to capture the opponent's king, by ludicrously complex arithmetical gymnastics, and then to move over the board, which was usually a double chess board, of eight by sixteen squares, in all directions by means of number systems called *equaliter* – adding, subtracting, multiplying and dividing. There were three final triumphs, each of them a mathematical progression arranged in a row.

Understanding how to play rithmomathy at all was a triumph. It was a severe mental test, a battle game in the learning as well as the playing, and there is no evidence that the Medievals thought it a battle worth fighting. They had more playful things to do with their time.

Fifteenth-century England was swept by a craze for a new game, which offered race, chase and battle, while requiring neither board nor pieces. The game was cards, and it became the favourite table game of late medieval Europe.

Like tables, cards is a name for several different games, and like chess, cards came to Europe along the Muslim games route from India. 'In the year 1379 there was introduced at Viterbo the game of cards, which comes from the country of the Saracens, and is called by the latter *naib*,' wrote the Italian chronicler Nicholas de Covelluzo, in the first formal reference to cards in Europe. *Naib* was the Indian word for king, and for the game of cards. Cards came with the Saracens to southern Italy and Spain, whence to northern Europe, which thus got its second game of military and hierarchical strategy the same way it had got its first one three centuries earlier.

Cards were probably known in Spain and France a little earlier than Covelluzo says; by about 1340, when they were still in their earliest form, that of the tarot, with its fortune telling suit of triumphs as well as the four strategic suits of swords or pikes, cups, clubs and money. The twenty-two triumph cards were marked with figures and given European identities, just as chess pieces had been: emperor, hermit, death, love, squire and others, of which only the fool survived the disappearance from common use of the tarot pack; it still exists in modern packs as the jester.

The triumphs became known as trumps, and within a century had been dropped from the pack because they did not contribute to the battle the Europeans enjoyed so much. Only their name was retained, as the name for the suit that overcame all suits, as fortune overcame all the strategies of men. *Triumfo*, known in England and France as trump, or ruff, was one of the earliest card games in existence, and passed on its trump power to its modern descendant, whist. Like all the most popular medieval card games, it was a battle game, and like chess, it was played primarily with a view to massacring the enemy. Court cards, like the courtier pieces at chess, were valued above the rest.

The earliest European card games were Spanish, and though many of their rules are lost today, their names betray their masculine and military character. *Ombre*, for instance, was a pool-winning game played with only forty cards, the eights, nines and tens removed from the pack; the 'ombre' was the man who won the pool. *Primera*, a northern and more feminine version of a Spanish game called *primero*, may have been derived from *ombre*. It was very fashionable in England in the sixteenth century, and huge sums were bet on it. *Piquet*, the only game still in existence, has a directly battling name, derived from the French name for a pikesman, just as *lansquenet*, another medieval favourite, was the French name for the light-armed German troops employed by the fifteenth-century French kings.

As cards moved away from Islam towards France and Spain, they developed a more feminine element. Spanish packs had horsemen (*caballos*) between their kings and their knaves, and like the ferses in chess, these were changed into queens by the chivalrous French and Italians. Every country had its own version of the suits, and England's were descended from those of Spain, via France. The Spanish *espadas*, French *piques*, became first pikes then spades in England. The Spanish *copas*, or cups, sharpened their shape and became diamonds. The Spanish *bastones*, or clubs, became first clubs shaped for battle, then the clubs of today, shaped like the French trefoils. The Spanish *oros*, or pieces of money, became hearts. [Illustration 51]

The court cards, which led these packs into battle, were identified as favourite military heroes. The king of spades was usually represented as David, and the king of clubs as Alexander. But these heroes too acquired national characters. The English and French represented the knave of clubs as Lancelot, their favourite knightly hero. They all fought with late medieval weapons in their hands, and dressed in late medieval clothes, as they have done ever since. The knaves in modern packs are dressed just like Chaucer's squire, with the addition of a fifteenth-century cap. Their favourite colours, and those of all the medieval court cards and chess pieces, were green and red. By 1440 the knaves of hearts and spades were always shown in profile, as they are today.

One of the queens they championed became supreme over all the suits. She was Henry VII's wife, Elizabeth of York, who is still the queen of every suit today. There is a picture of her, painted during her lifetime, which shows her in the dress she wears on cards today, holding the white rose of York in her hands. Her marriage to the Lancastrian Henry Tudor, Henry VII, ended the Wars of the Roses, and she was commemorated by the English on their cards as the queen of peace, the beautiful young darling of the late medieval court.

Until the invention of printing, cards were hand painted on ivory, vellum or parchment, or engraved in outline on wood, and the colours filled in by hand later. In 1392 Charles VI, the mad king of France, paid fifty-six *soles Parisi* (about £1) for the painting of three packs of cards. Card making became a craft in its own right, and it was centred at Nuremberg, whence cards were exported to all the European courts, packed in small casks.

The earliest known woodcut for a card was made at Augsburg in 1423, and has St Christopher as one of the court card models. After about 1450, cards were produced more locally, as the local demand for them rose, but German cards remained the most popular, and some found their way to England, with their picturesque suits: columbines (spades), hares (clubs), pinks (diamonds) and roses (hearts).

By 1463 there were card makers in England; Edward IV passed a law protecting them from foreign competition, 'that no merchant shall bring, send nor convey . . . chessmen nor playing cards.'

For the first 150 years of their existence, playing cards were restricted to the courtly and the wealthy; then, like chess, they spread downwards through society. In 1464 Sir John Howard and the Duke of Norfolk whiled away winter evenings in the King's service in Wales playing cards with the Duke's steward, who won 4 marks (£2/13/4d.) off his master. But these were trifles compared with the duke's usual gambling losses, and anti-gambling campaigners never thought cards worth attacking in the same way as dicing and games of pure chance. Like chess, cards had skill in their favour, and skill exercised players to the exclusion of distractions like gambling.

By the early sixteenth century cards had won over all opposition. In 1527 Latimer galvanised the Protestant university of Cambridge with a Christmas sermon 'concerning his playing at cards', an activity he would never have indulged in had he thought it ungodly or disreputable. He drew his similes from primera and trump, which were currently the talk of the town. He 'dealt out an exposition of Christian precepts . . . I purpose to deal unto you another card . . . heart is trump.' Buckingham, the Prior of the Cambridge Dominicans, gave a Catholic reply using dicing similes. He told his congregation to confound Lutheranism by throwing a four, standing for the four doctors of the Church, and a five, standing for five New Testament passages. But it was not a success; cards won the day.

They were both respectable and playful, and perhaps the best comment on them is the last mention of them in the medieval records. It does not attempt to describe whether the nature of their play was gambling, battling or anything else, but just makes it clear that it was good fun. The entry comes from the Privy Purse expenses of the Queen of cards, Elizabeth of York. Just before she died, she was given an allowance 'to the Queen's grace, for her disport at court this Christmas, to spend at cards'.

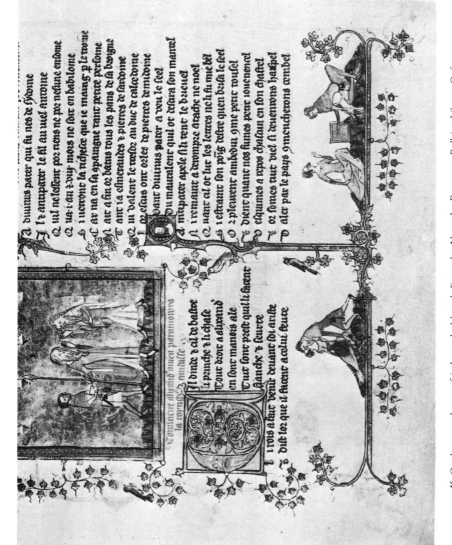

46 Outdoor merels on a faintly marked board. From the Alexander Romance. *Bodleian Library, Oxford*, MS. Bodl. 264, fol. 76v.

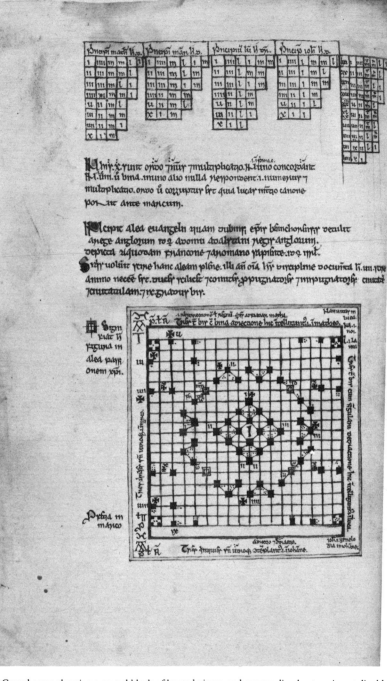

47 The Gospel game showing a central block of hunted pieces, and surrounding hunters, in a stylised layout. *Bodleian Library, Oxford* MS. CCC. D. 122, fol. 5v.

asſis nous a ia ſes engiens fait ðreðjier
eour en poes loſt gtre ual oel uergier
a vos ij neueus mandail auantier
Q uains iiij ioas venroit entoz oes murs lanðj
v alles diſt eaſſamus naics ſoing deſinaier
Q uen noſtre ſecors uient alixanð ðaðer
ſont en ſa opaigne x mille ðheualier

48 Game of chess. From the Alexander Romance. *Bodleian Library, Oxford* MS. Bodl. 264, fol. 112.

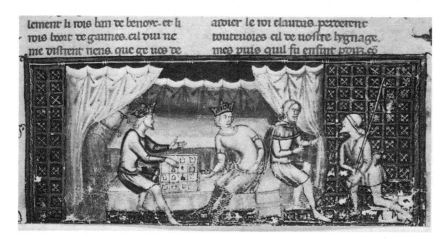

lement li rois hin ðe benoye et li   arðier le roi claunus perðerent
rois boot ðe gaunes cil ðui ne   toureuoies cil ðe noſtre hygnage
me ðiſtrent riens que ge nos ðe   mes puis quil fu enfint poiz eð

49 A fourteenth-century chess game, showing a small board and crude pieces. Add. 12228, fol. 236.

50 Board games, one of which may be draughts, with a form of merels on the right. From the Alexander Romance. *Bodleian Library, Oxford* MS. Bodl. 264, fol. 60.

51 A late medieval game of cards. *The British Library* Add. 12228, fol. 313v.

CHAPTER SEVEN

Glee: Medieval Music, Singing and Dancing

Music means the art of the muse, and the medieval muse sang, danced and played musical instruments. Until at least 1400, music, song and dance were indissolubly linked, and each of them included a wealth of playful activities. Together they constituted glee, which was the heart of medieval happiness.

Glee meant entertainment, play or sport, generally musical, in the midst of rejoicing. An insight into glee is an insight into the workings of the medieval heart. It is the key to the playful Middle Ages. Its story begins in Anglo-Saxon England, where glee was the work of gleemen, and ends in England at the accession of the Tudors, when glee was the work of singers, versifiers, dancers, musicians, acrobats and illusionists.

The early gleeman's stage was the world, which he travelled far and wide to bring song and dance to its audiences. Descended from the Roman *mimus*, a bawdy slapstick artist who held the day after the condemnation of theatrical *spectacula* by the early Church, and from the Teutonic *scop* (literally 'a maker', i.e. a creative artist, a bard or poet), the Anglo-Saxon gleeman was an all-round entertainer. He might be a disreputable or a highly reputed figure, or both at once. If his performances were strongly mimic, he was condemned by Churchmen and despised by connoisseurs; if they were more in the story-telling tradition, and the story was clean, Christian, or both, he was honourably treated, though some strict Churchmen disapproved of all secular entertainers throughout the medieval period.

The earliest English heroic poem, and possibly the earliest English poem of any sort, is *Widsith* (Anglo-Saxon for the far traveller). It is the story of a gleeman of that name who has travelled the courts of Europe 'singing and saying' a story, in return for generous tips. The heart of his performance was story telling or singing, the heart of his music a harp. Beowulf often tells of 'the noise of the harp, the clear song of the poet . . . his wood of joy was touched, his song was often sung.' He and others like him were patronised in mead-halls and monasteries alike.

Some time between 658 and 679, during an evening of amateur story-telling in a lordly mead-hall somewhere in Yorkshire, a herdsman called Caedmon found himself unable to sing when his turn came, and withdrew from the hall. He fell asleep and dreamt that a stranger commanded him to 'sing of the beginning of created things', and told him verses which he remembered when he woke up, and was able to add to with more of his own. He was taken before Hilda, Abbess of the nearby double monastery of Whitby, who decided that he had received the gift of poetry from heaven, and kept him there as a monk, versifying passages of scriptural history which the learned brethren recited to him. Many of his Genesis sequences, which have titles like *The Troubled Girl* and *The Old Woman Bertha*, are just like secular songs. Medieval Christendom seldom took the trouble to make distinctions between the sacred and the secular, since everything good came from God and returned to God in the end. It was much more concerned to distinguish the good, in entertainment terms the art of the scop, from the bad, the art of the *scurra* (bawd, coarse comedian).

But this distinction was abandoned before the Normans got to England, as gleemen began to accompany their stories with music and dance, or with tricks and acrobatics, or with hired help to make their performances into variety shows. By the Conquest, scops and *mimi*, or *scurri*, had given way to story tellers, tumblers, leapers, hoppers, dancers and a host of other performers who went under the general title of minstrels. Some, such as Edward the Confessor's minstrel, Berdic, who was given three villas in Gloucestershire, were highly thought of. Others, like the dwarf minstrel kept by Edward's stepmother, a bawdy little grotesque, were not. But as distinctions between different types of minstrels multiplied, simple divisions into good and scandalous blurred, and attitudes became as diverse as minstrelsy.

Immediately after the Conquest the story teller held the place of honour, and in many peoples' hearts he continued to do so throughout the period.

Some story tellers recited jests, rude stories, satires and dialogues as well as the standard romances and saints' lives. Those who could not speak the language of their new Norman lords told stories of Hereward and Old English heroes and saints, by the roadside and at shrines and on pilgrimages.

There was no reason to stop at vocal performances. The thirteenth century history of Fulk Fitzwarine described how John de Raunpaygne 'knew enough of tabor, harp, flute, fiddle, citole [a small-headed, long-handled predecessor of the lute] and jugglery; and attired himself very richly, like an earl or a baron, and caused his hair and all his body to be entirely dyed as black as jet, so that nothing was white except his teeth. And he hung round his neck a very handsome tabor, and then, mounting a handsome palfrey, rode through the town of Shrewsbury to the gate of the castle . . . he told the king he was an Ethiop minstrel, and made great minstrelsy of tabor and other instruments, . . . and played for Sir Ardulf in his chamber.'

He caught the royal favour, and was a huge success. Reformers denounced minstrels like him as 'bawders showing bawdful words and many japes . . . harlots, flatterers and glossers.' With credentials like that, they could not fail, and in the thirteenth century St Thomas Aquinas broke through Church reserve by arguing that minstrelsy was not in itself sinful, indeed it was good, since it was for the solace of humanity.

By the early years of the century the Franciscans and their lay orders and fraternities were powerful patrons of everything they considered to be respectable entertainment. St Francis urged his followers to become God's gleemen. They preached with love songs about Our Lady, 'the woman clothed in the sun with the moon under her feet.' They wrote songs and meditations, especially for Christmas and the Epiphany, about Christ the lover of the world. They recruited the carol, that most characteristic medieval combination of song and dance, into their sacred entertainments.

Both earthly and clerical repertoires were basically heroic and romantic, and had expanded by the thirteenth century to include lighter fables, anecdotes, satirical sketches, especially about the clergy, and riddles. Thirteenth-century story tellers numbered in their ranks rhymers and versifiers, jesters (tellers of heroic 'gestes', and, increasingly, rude tales and jokes), *conteurs* (prose story tellers) and *menteurs* (tellers of fabulous stories and elaborate lies). Almost all their stories were sung, and the harp remained the favourite instrument of accompaniment. Chaucer's friar was a model of the new breed of story tellers, in the tradition of John of Raunpaygne, who used all sorts of trickery and devices to embellish their performances. The friar affected a lisp

> To make his English sweet upon his tongue,
> And in his harping, when that he had sung,
> His eyes twinkled in his head aright . . . . . .
> And certainly he had a merry note,
> Well could he sing and play on a rote

(a small cello with an extended handle, mostly used to accompany lays). Music was still inseparable from song, and both had gone a long way beyond their original role of simple accompaniment to long stories. From about 1200 onwards, English song writers wrote more and more love lyrics, sacred and secular, in Norman French and English. They wrote little seasonal songs, some courtly, some popular, like *Sumer is icumen in* (*c.* 1240), which has a canon and repeated bass that suggest it was the work of a Churchman, though enjoyed as a carol by everyone. Some clerics wrote songs, some sang them directly to their congregations or in taverns, like Chaucer's friar, and many hired minstrels to play for them in their private apartments. Music was the most professional of the major minstrel arts. [Illustration 52]

The golden age of the harp ended when bardic story-telling gave way to more versatile minstrelsy, though the harp remained popular and highly esteemed throughout the period. The little six-stringed harp, which early medieval minstrels carried with them from hall to hall and tavern to tavern, was beginning to decline by about 1300. The big harp lasted longer, and was nearly always played by professionals. In Celtic areas of Britain, where bardic mintrelsy survived longest, the only medieval rival to the harp was the crowd, or crwth, which had various forms but was basically a kind of lyre, played with fingers and bow. Its stopped strings played a melody which matched the singer's voice, while its bowed ones gave a low background burden. It was popular a long time in Wales, where Sir Tristan, according to thirteenth-century romance writers, played it well. It was joint ancestor of the violin, together with the vielle, which developed in the same way from a plucked to a bowed instrument, and from about 1300 onwards, as minstrels used it more and more, to a free ranging instrument capable of producing elaborate tones.

The rote, gigue and rebec, usually known as the rubeb, were other violin type instruments which flourished in the thirteenth century as drone accompaniment instruments like the monocord and chorus died out.

The fiddle kept similar pace with musical development. Originally it was oval shaped, and played with the bow near the neck, so that only one string was touched at a time. In the late twelfth century minstrels incurved the sides of their fiddles and the true viol, with its greater playing freedom, made its appearance. So did the plucked guitar-fiddle, best known in England in its fig shaped form, as the cittern or citole, the early prototype of the gittern, guitar and lute.

By the early thirteenth century, solitary minstrels were fewer than minstrel bands, which often incorporated dancers and tumblers, very often a singer, sometimes a dancing animal, in their performances. Minstrels who regarded themselves as the aristocrats of their profession gave pure musical performances before sophisticated listeners who regarded themselves as the aristocrats of pure minstrel patronage. In 1289–1290 Bishop Swinfield stayed at Reading Abbey, and while there 'paid Bennett, a violin player of London three shillings, Lord Randolph Pippard, citharist, two shillings, and Master Henry, harper of Lord Edward of Mortimer, 12d.' These were the noble minstrels of noble lords, used to playing solo in lordly chambers. When Swinfield was in remote and unfashionable Monkton, in Pembrokeshire, he contented himself with performances by groups of nameless local musicians costing 2d. a day each. [Illustrations 53, 54]

There was no shortage of patrons for humble minstrels like

these. Connoisseurs and crude addicts alike often felt like a dose of rustic minstrelsy, to the sound of bagpipes, which men like Chaucer's crude old miller played; timbrel, a little jangly tambourine, usually played by women; tabor, a little double-headed drum often used in conjunction with a pipe to beat out dance rhythms and rolls for acrobats and jugglers; clappers; cymbals; bells or triangles, and some kind of pipe, like a cornetto, a double-whistle flute or a shawm. A vigorous rattle of percussion, accompanying dancing girls, acrobats, balancers and jugglers, delighted many a lord bored with finer music and many a labourer bored with the sound of scythe or hammer.

The Minorite chronicles tell how a couple of friars arrived at the Benedictine grange at Abingdon in 1224 and were mistaken for minstrels by the porter, who 'welcomed them with unbecoming glee . . . and when the error was discovered, turned them out with contumely.' They were mistaken for minstrels when they must have looked tatty from travelling. There were far more poor minstrels wandering from village to town and house to hall, with meagre costumes and equipment, than the records suggest.

That does not mean they were all what the disapproving preachers called 'japers'. Many were simple musicians without the accessories or companions to make japes. The contrast between well-established minstrels who travelled circuits between aristocratic households, and poor ones who travelled the highways in summertime, looking for patronage, was not a simple one of quality. Even if performing skills tended to divide that way, audience tastes did not.

In 1306 Edward Prince of Wales was twenty-two, and his father staged a magnificent festival at Westminster to celebrate the occasion of his becoming a knight. About three hundred young noblemen were knighted with him, each accompanied by one groom, one minstrel, and a host of guests. They were entertained by what the royal accounts describe as a 'multitude of minstrels', 175 in number, many of whom were itinerant, about fifty-three permanent members of household troupes, lent for the occasion, and twenty-seven members of the royal household. Some of these last held the rank of squire; all held the same high rank as the royal falconers and huntsmen. They were paid

7½d. or 4½d. a day, according to rank, plus three meals a day, while they were on duty, and a summer and a winter robe and a pair of shoes each year. They included harpers, stringed instrument players, horn and trumpet players and pipe and percussion players. The whole multitude of minstrels was paid a standard wage of five shillings or 40d., according to rank. Nothing shows better than this occasion how diverse medieval minstrelsy was, and how catholic the tastes of its audiences.

There were trumpeters, who acted as the king's personal announcers, and played in partnership with nakerers, as they did when they went with the king on campaign. 'Nakers' were pairs of kettle drums, slung from the waist or strapped to the back, and almost always played in partnership with trumpets, or clarions, as the Medievals often called them. Other than on royal occasions, they were most commonly played at tournaments, and became very fashionable after the 1306 celebrations.

There were horn-blowers, who blew the night watch at the palace, just as municipal horn-blowers did at city gates. They called people to banquets, at which they blew fanfares to introduce each new course. At one of the Westminster festival meals a whole throng of minstrels brought two swans before the King with music, dancing and tumbling, as he sat at table.

There were stringed instrument players, who played during meals while others sang and danced, and who played in private chambers, alone or with a singer. Dominant among them were harpers, who played and sang the chivalrous songs King Edward loved.

There were three German gigue players, Heinrich, Conrad and an unnamed one, who came to display their art to the English court and stayed for seven years.

There was William, the Queen's psaltery player, who sang hymns and little virtuoso pieces to the clear, sharp sound of his instrument. He was a court minstrel for twenty-five years and psaltery player to three queens. Psalters were much respected and enjoyed. They had biblical associations, and were played on the knees, often by women, who also enjoyed listening to them; they made pure and gentle minstrel music.

She laid a psalter on her knee,
Thereon she played full lovesomely.

[Robert Mannyng, *c.* 1300]

There was Nagary, the King's crowther, whose name comes from the Breton *hagar*, meaning 'the good'. Being an Arthurian enthusiast, Edward was very fond of the crowth, the traditional instrument of the Celtic courts, and it is typical of him to have had a Celtic crowther in his household.

There was little William the organist, whom Edward borrowed from the Countess of Hereford for the occasion. He would have played one of the little portative organs that were so popular at the time. They had tiny pipes and built-in bellows, which were worked by one hand while the keys were played with the other. There were few big organs, and they were all in churches, to which people flocked on feast days to hear their 'iron voice'. Just as organs were modified and improved in the fourteenth century, so hurdy-gurdies, which came to Europe in the twelfth century as five- or six-foot-long instruments played by two seated men, one stopping the rods and the other turning the crank, were modified into small, easily worked instruments of popular music. [Illustration 55]

There was a lutanist, a citoler and a guitarist among the 1306 minstrels. There was a taborist, an estive (small bagpipes) player and someone called *menestral oue les cloches*, the minstrel with the bells, to provide some ringing good dance music. Hand and chime bells were great popular favourites, and every well equipped dance band could accompany its dancers with ringing, tinkling, clashing and jingling. Dancers and players often wore little bells attached to their clothes, arms and legs.

It is impossible to tell how much dancing there was at the 1306 festival. Many of the minstrels, especially those who came from other noble households for the occasion, were simply called by their personal names in the accounts, with no descriptive titles. Many had stage names, like Lion de Normanville, suggesting their place of origin, or like Merlin, a very popular romantic stage name.

Some had pet names, like Bolthead and Pearl-in-the-Eye, an

affectionate term for a mote or cataract in the eye. But there are no details of their minstrelsy. All that is certain is that even the most distinguished minstrelsy had a lot of japing about it.

The disreputable associates-in-glee of music and song, japes were professional spectaculars. Music was often played professionally; japes always were. They were feats of circus minstrelsy: juggling, performing with animals, balancing and acrobatic dancing of all sorts. Some very well-established minstrels went in for japes, as can be seen from the 1306 accounts. But more often it was itinerant all-rounders, whose tricks were as crude as they were flashy.

The minstrel in *Piers Plowman* attributed his lack of success to the fact that

> . . . I can neither taber, ne trumpe, ne tell no gestes,
> Fartin ne fislen [wander idly about, tell idle tales], at
>   feasts, ne harpen;
> Jape, ne juggle, ne gently pipe,
> Ne neither saylen (leap) ne saute (jump), ne sing to the
>   gittern,
> I have no good gifts to please the great lords.

Nothing pleased great lords better than fools. Villages had their clowns; courts had their fools, who were later called by the name originally given to story telling minstrels: jesters. Fools kept their masters consoled, amused and playfully attended. In return, lords paid and clothed their fools generously, and provided for them in their old age. Lots of medieval illustrations show kings attended by their fools, who had affectionate nick-names like John le Fool, John Stultum (Latin for stupid), John Fatuus, Skip our Fool and Robert the Fool. Fools fooled on formal state occasions as well as festive and leisurely ones. [Illustrations 56, 57]

Independent as well as household fools danced, pranced and somersaulted at the head of processions and pageants, and on tables in taverns and noble halls. One, called Martinet of Gascony, used to 'play before the Lord Edward', son of Edward I. Another, called Bernard, used to provide more adult entertainment for the Lord Edward's father, on one occasion coming with fifty-four companions 'naked before the King, with dancing and revelry.' But this was closer to bawdry than buffoonery.

Fools wore suits of patchwork colours, most often green and yellow, which symbolised eternal youth and gaiety. They wore pointed or flat-topped, double-horned hoods which, like their suits, were skin tight, and often adorned with bells. Many of them, especially in the later Middle Ages, carried little puppet fools on sticks. Some were dwarves themselves.

Most were generously tipped by their audiences. Worcester Priory had a household fool in the later Middle Ages, for whom the priors went out in person to buy 'a motley', which they sent to the laundry for the best cleaning. Foolish japes won their way straight to the medieval heart.

Jugglery, being the most disreputable of japes, won its acclaim most easily of all. It had been popular since Anglo-Saxon times, but did not reach its heyday as an entertainment in its own right until the mid fourteenth century. Until then it was closely associated with animal tricks. Part of its appeal and disreputability seems to have lain in a certain animal quality, which had a roguish sex appeal. *The Juggler and the Baron's Daughter* was a popular song in which a jolly juggler juggles himself a horse out of nothing, which he rides to a lady's tower. There he and his horse dance their way into the lady's heart, and after some juggling in the baronial hall, he into the lady's bed. 'God and Our Lady and sweet St John,' ends the song, 'Send every giglot of this town such another leman [lover, sweetheart], Even as he was.'

But balancing was a more certain means of winning entry into a noble household than seduction. Dangerous as it was, balancing was safer. Swords and knives were the favourite balancing and juggling accessories. Both arts were performed, with fearless panache, to music. Quite often they were performed by women, who combined them with contortionism, acrobatics and dancing. Most japes, in fact, were forms of acrobatic dancing.

Medieval dancing was so closely associated with acrobatics, when performed by professionals, that the seventh-century Anglo-Saxon translators of St Mark's gospel described Salome as jumping and leaping, rather than dancing, before Herod. This connection lasted throughout the period. 'Saylen', which Piers

Plowman's minstrel could not do, comes from the Anglo-Saxon salio, to leap or dance, and was a chief skill of Anglo-Saxon gleemaidens. The only woman on the 1306 payroll was a saltatrix, or leaping dance-girl, with the delightful name of Matilda Makejoy. She was not a court minstrel, but performed at the royal court now and again for at least fourteen years. Her performances, and those of minstrels like her, were mostly given before small households, city corporations and companies on procession days, and villages on summer evenings. Once, when Edward I was passing through Surfleet, Lincolnshire, he was entertained by one 'William the Saltimbanque' and some companions, who 'made their leaps before the King', then returned to the anonymity whence they came. [Illustration 58]

Fourteenth-century illustrations show both men and women tumbling, in all sorts of costumes, and often naked, and in all sorts of japing combinations and positions, some of them very gymnastic. Tumbling was popular because it was spectacular, either gymnastically or buffoonishly. Edward II kept tumblers, one of whom used to amuse him by falling off his horse, for the handsome fee of twenty shillings a time.

Woman tumblers, by contrast, made a specialist art of keeping their balance. Sometimes they balanced on tight-ropes, sometimes on the shoulders of men partners, often alone, to the sound of drums and pipes and the jingling of the little bells attached to their costumes. Illustrators often show them in miraculously adherent long dresses, but they are more likely to have worn short, close-fitting tunics and coloured leggings, their hair tucked into sequined nets or plaits. On the stone floors of baronial halls they danced their elegant contortions and balances in and out of the flickering firelight.

When Richard of Cornwall visited the court of Frederick II of Sicily in the early thirteenth century, he saw two Saracen girls dance while balanced on two balls, singing and playing the cymbals. It went to his head so much that the first thing he did when he got home was tell the chronicler Matthew Paris about it, lest it should go unrecorded. In the wake of the Crusades, the sinuous Saracen style of dancing became all the rage, and as late as 1380 Richard II paid a Venetian dancer £6/13/4d. for 'playing and dancing before him'. To earn such a huge fee, she must have performed every trick she knew, some of them doubtless learnt from middle eastern dancers visiting Venice.

Tambourine dancing was a favourite trick. Performers balanced their tambourines on their sides and used them as vehicles for jingling hand-walks. Contortionism was another favourite trick, performed to music. Dances on ropes and stilts were done with the help of snakes and swords, on hands and on one foot. A few minstrels extended the use of their swords into a kind of fencing ballet, combining the movements of swordmanship with the flamboyant acrobatics of dance. In 1306 a pair of minstrel fencers, Walter le Skirmisour and his brother, received £3 each for entertaining King Edward's court, a big enough fee to imply that their swords were sharp enough to earn them danger money. Mock sword fights had been a traditional minstrel entertainment since Anglo-Saxon times, and the 'gladiatores' who performed them were generally regarded as the roughest of rough japers. [Illustration 59]

Sword dancing belonged to villages as much as to minstrels; it could be amateur or professional, and was more often amateur, part of the amateur treasury of folk dancing that enriched medieval life so much that in all the Germanic languages the words for dance and play are the same.

Amateur dancing was basically either processional or round. Both types probably originated in pagan spring and winter festivals, and were regarded by the Christian Church with the same ambivalence as all the pre-Christian games: on the one hand with distrust and suspicion of devilishness; on the other hand, with enthusiasm, as potential recruits to gleeful Christianity.

Bishops in the early Church were called *praesules* or dance leaders, and their clergy kept peoples' attention during vigils by organising hymn and psalm singing, processing and round dancing, in churchyards. The early Church councils drew the line at dancing in church, where it was only allowed in the form of religious processions. Whether the religious element preceded or followed the folk, or was even separated from it, the fact is that by the twelfth century the Church had lost its battle to keep control of folk dancing, and was condemning its most popular form, that of the carol, as a 'circle of which the centre is the devil, and all turn to the left.'

The carol was a singing round dance, and one of the top medieval games. Carolling was an intoxicating delight. It was mirthful, sexy and compulsive. Until St Francis and his religious gleemen began its appropriation to the Church, it was the Church's pet hate.

It was performed by a chain of dancers, sometimes open but usually closed to form a circle, who held hands or linked arms. They took three steps to the left, perhaps originally towards the sunset, while their leader, who usually stood in the middle of the circle, but might be a member of it, sang a lyrical stanza. Then they marked time with a rhythmic tread during the singing of a chorus, or burden, in which they all joined. Endless variations of carol dancing and singing developed during the Middle Ages, but this was the basic pattern of them all.

People of every class and calling carolled, and in the early part of the period carolling was synonymous with round dancing. The legend of the cursed carollers of Kölbigk (Saxony), who were condemned to carol ceaselessly for a year because they had carolled in the churchyard during mass in defiance of their parish priest, was itself one of the most popular medieval carols. It was written down, like many carols that were semi-learned in origin, though popular in performance. Others were folk in origin as well as destination, and were transmitted solely by song and dance.

Sometimes they were just sung. Women sang carols while they did their needlework. These were often narrative carols, feminine versions of the gestes sung by men, with a leader singing the narrative stanzas and the rest of the group joining in with lyrical refrains. It seems likely that a lot of the early English carols were heroic, telling stories like the exploits of Hereward the Wake. Women had a monopoly of carolling until the twelfth century. That was partly why the Church distrusted it; it was too seductive by half. One thirteenth-century sermon threatened damnation to any high-society girl who 'walketh about in meads and fair places leading dancing and singing, as it were showing herself to lose her maidenhood.'

Carols like the early fourteenth-century *Maiden in the Mor*

Lay were based on pre-Christian traditions of water sprites and moor maidens, and were performed out in the fields in the summer season of love. The dancers acted out a mime of the verses, offering their maiden leader in the centre of the circle wine to drink, primroses and violets to eat, a bed of flowers to lie on, and so on as the words of the carol indicated. Many carols may have been acted out in this way, which must have greatly added to the fun of romantic carolling, especially when it was performed by men and women jointly, as it usually was from the late twelfth century onwards.

The third theme of carols, after heroism and romance, was religion, which became a popular theme about 1300. Verses answered by a repeated refrain have always been characteristic of the Christian liturgy, and it is even possible that this was the source from which carols were derived. Most early carols were composed in the metre of the early Latin hymns, especially those of the Ambrosian office, with their eight-syllable lines. The Church was the obvious source of choral musical inspiration.

It was the direct source of the coundute, Latin *conductus*, a two-, three- or four-part piece, some of the parts vocal and others instrumental, which accompanied the liturgical and processional celebrant's changes of position. It developed a distinctive tenor melody and was the origin of most part songs, such as rotes and motets. Together with the 'lead singing' of folk music, it may have been the origin of the polyphonic dance music which Britain alone developed.

In the late twelfth century Gerald of Wales wrote that the Welsh 'do not sing in unison like the inhabitants of other countries but in many different parts . . . as many different parts and voices as there are performers, who all at length unite, with organic melody, in one consonance . . .' Polyphonic, part, round and carol singing were all, at least in part, originally liturgical. One of the first English popular songs, a topical one about St Thomas Becket, was directly derived from the liturgical celebration of his feast.

It is not surprising that in the twelfth century the Church began to claim its share of the gleeful profits of its contribution to music and dance; it is only surprising that it took so long to see that this was the thing to do. It was impossible to tell vernacular religious songs, known as *laudae*, from the secular songs they rivalled in popularity. Sacred and secular were united in celebration of God's creation, through loving song. In 1325 an English Franciscan, William Herbet, wrote some pious love songs which became popular carols. They had three-line external refrains after each stanza, and were irresistibly catchy. The great age of the carol, especially the religious carol, had come. The early carols were almost all joyful. The word carol was commonly used to mean general rejoicing, and carols were always talked about in this spirit.

> Merry time it is in May
> Damsels carols leadeth.
>
> [*Arthur and Merlin*]

Churchyards were the favourite carolling grounds, despite the efforts of their priests to reserve them for religious activities. Sometimes carolling danced its way right into the Church. In 1308 Bishop Baldock of London issued a decree to the people of Barking, rebuking them for 'dancing, wrestling and doing lascivious sports not only in the cemetery but even in parochial and conventual churches.'

When carolling was done by both men and women, to the jingling of tambourines or the music of drums and pipes, it became fast-moving to the point of frenzy. In 1313 a small group of Cambridgeshire men, led by a chaplain called William de Scorborough, were found guilty by the St Ives court of carolling at the fair there on May 6th 'to the terror of the fair and the great damage of the merchants.' The medieval Church was quite right to regard the effects of dancing, especially carolling, as something in the nature of possession.

Winter carolling was confined to indoors where, in the great hall, carols were danced between meals and between the courses of meals. The trestle tables were swept away and the feet of the dancers picked a way between the greyhounds and lap-dogs, the hems of the ladies' dresses trailing through the spilt food and drink. Or everything was swept off the tables, they were pushed together, and the carollers climbed up and danced on them. In November 1379 John of Gaunt ordered 'fourty little oak spars to be made into rails for under the great chamber tables in Kenilworth Priory; to cover and repair these rails and tables and dance on them on this coming feast of Christmas.' On any feastday, on any ordinary day, in towns and palaces, in gardens and on village greens, in churchyards and fields, dancers danced their carols. [Illustration 60]

The words were usually simple but the music, and with it the dancing, became increasingly elaborate from the thirteenth century onwards. Musical minstrelsy still honoured the harp and the story telling it accompanied, but in more elaborate settings than before. The old rhyming couplet was still the favourite metre for tale-telling, but Chaucer and his contemporaries used a whole variety of metres to tell a whole variety of tales. Some were in the old heroic and romantic traditions, and were told by fableurs, who accompanied themselves on the harp. But by Chaucer's time such performances were dated, and his audiences listened to them restively, waiting for one of the new burlesques, lively little moralities, satires or ballads.

There were popular 'bowrds' (bawdy tales) like the *Tale of the Basin*, a crude burlesque of an Arthurian romance, pious tales like the *Mourning of the Hare*, which lamented in colourful detail the tragedy of a hare hunted to death by hunters too keen on their sport to stop for mass, and tales about yeoman heroes like Robin Hood. There were political poems criticising the government. Every class had its own minstrel style, and by the later Middle Ages its own range of minstrelsy to display it in all its specific detail and variety. Many fableurs took to speaking rather than singing tales like the Robin Hood ones, often in concert with quite different kinds of minstrels, and harpers took to jesting, acting and fooling, also often in concert with other minstrels.

The fourteenth-century Priors of Durham enjoyed the full range of story telling and harping available to them. In the 1330s the Prior often listened to itinerant harpers, and also had a household harper called Thomas, for whom he bought a harp costing three shillings in 1335. In 1357 he paid a blind harper called

William two shillings for a Christmas performance; three years later he paid Lord William of Dalton's Welsh harper 3/4d. for some traditional bardic playing, and two years after that he paid five shillings to the Bishop of Norwich's harper on the feast of the Translation of St Cuthbert (September 4th) for a performance as an actor (*histrio*) harper.

The traditional harper survived, and made some profit out of the nostalgia for the past in late medieval households. Henry V and his Queen, Catherine of Valois, not only patronised harpers but also learnt their art for themselves. They paid £8/13/4d. for two harps to play on. Middle-class patrons followed their example, and payments to harp makers become ever more frequent in late fifteenth-century records. Small harps were made for household use and entertainment, and big ones for export to the continent, where harps were popular as the instruments of old Britain.

On the first Sunday in Lent, 1323, a crowther called Roger Wade showed his London audience just how adaptable a player of a conservative instrument like his could be. He 'solemnly celebrated his own internment, as though he had been dead, and had masses sung for his soul, both he himself and others in his company making offering so that many persons marvelled thereat.' Roger was a typical late medieval harper: he mimed and acted, sang, and ran a company.

But by the late fourteenth century a solo minstrel was rare enough to give rise to comment. In January 1380 John of Gaunt paid 3/3¾d. to 'a strange minstrel without companion.' As well as spending 'all the day in fables', the young Lydgate played 'on sundry instruments, on harp, lute and on gittern.' These three instruments kept close company in the fifteenth century, providing the dance and song music for poetic forms like ballads, which took over from heroic gestes as the favourites of courtly audiences.

With a heroic story to tell, the metre of a village dance and the form of a stanza, often accompanied by a carol refrain, the ballad was the liveliest of lyrical games. It could be a song, a dance or both.

There were three ravens sat on a tree,
Down a down, hay down, hay down.

Ballad carolling brought folk music to court.

They were as black as they might be.
With a down derry, derry, down, down.

Long-ballads and narrative poems were often recited serially, after dinner, hunting or Vespers, and over suppers of spiced cakes and wine. Like the music that accompanied them, they were more widely performed by amateurs in the late Middle Ages, leaving minstrels to capture audiences with more dramatic arts. From about 1300 onwards, singing began to be played more often as a gleeful game separate from dancing. The Knight of La Tour Laundry described how in 1371 he was inspired by the sound of birdsong in his garden to 'make for her [his wife] love songs . . . ballads, roundels [rondeaux: carol like songs with refrains within the stanzas], viralles [virelays: ditties in short lined couplets of seven or eight syllables with a refrain] and divers new things in the best wise that I could.' It is clear from late medieval writers like Lydgate and Henry of Lancaster that 'making' songs meant singing and playing as well as writing them. Musicians like them favoured harps, lutes and gitterns, to play 'letters and songs' like ballads, roundelays and virelays.

The gittern was ideal for stylish amateurs. It was relatively simple to play, having only four strings, and was plucked by a plectrum, so it gave a strongly vibrating sound. It was quaintly ornamental, with a long tail-piece and carved end-button. In 1404 John Bount, the son of a Bristol burgess, and a man keen to cut a figure as the musical man-about-town, left his business partner 'forty shillings, my new statutes, my swords ornamented with silver, my great harp and my cittern [gittern] with a girl's face on it.' The less closely music accompanied song and dance, the more closely it was accompanied by elaborate display.

'Fine harps' and all sorts of expensive instruments, and books of 'pricksongs', or songs written with notation as well as words, increased greatly in number in the fifteenth century. Men and women bought and used them for fashionable performances. Henry IV's first wife, the Countess of Derby, accompanied her songs on a guitar for which a new set of strings cost eight shillings. She had a pricksong book for which she bought a new, smart, parchment cover. Minstrels found new ways of making money, tuning and mending musical instruments, touching up old ones, selling their own, and teaching music.

Women were the keenest pupils. They all wanted to be able to present that most delightful of late medieval spectacles: a pretty woman making a pretty tune. Chaucer's Wife of Bath boasted that

> Well could I dance to a harp small,
> And sing, y-wis [certainly], as any nightingale,
> When I had drunk a draught of sweet wine.

St Cecilia was revered as the patron saint of music from the early fourteenth century onwards, and was the model of domestic glee, be it robust like the Wife of Bath's or languorous like that of more leisured ladies.

Humble musicians played cheaper versions of the instruments their fashionable betters played; they sang country or tavern versions of the same songs, and drew more attention to their dancing and drinking than their clothes and accessories. Not having gleeful settings, their songs and dances were not set pieces but gleeful exhibitions. In Chaucer's *Cook's Tale*, Perkyn the Reveller could play dice better than any other apprentice, 'hop and sing and make much disport', and play the gittern and ribible (*rebec*: a sort of pear shaped lyre, plainer than the gittern, mainly used to accompany dance music). His songs would have included traditional ballads, war songs, love and marriage songs, most of them very coarse, stories of marvels and calamities, and wood, stream and spring songs.

Clerks like the ones described by Chaucer in his *Miller's Tale* were among the best amateur gleemen, and richly expanded the late medieval repertoire of both sacred and secular songs, especially carols. 'Those who ought to be found at vespers are to be found at the dances,' complained Bromyard. Oxford clerks who went to Magdalen, Corpus or All Souls, were given permission to sing in hall after supper on religious holidays, because this was a 'respectable amusement'.

The fourteenth- and fifteenth-century public was more musically and poetically sophisticated than it had ever been before. In such an age there was no necessary antipathy between professional and amateur minstrelsy; both could flourish. Minstrels added to their performances, which became spectacularly versatile. Well-to-do householders kept resident companies of minstrels and hired itinerant ones, to entertain them and their guests.

The staple task of household minstrels was mealtime entertainment, and it was far from being an easy one. Meals and their minstrelsy became more spectacular. There were more courses, which were more exotic and required more exotic accompaniment from minstrels. By the late Middle Ages food was a performance in itself. There were subtleties – a supreme medieval misnoma – marzipan and sugared paste sculptures of fantastic birds, castles, pageants and mottoes, painted bright colours and carried or wheeled in by brightly dressed wafer and dessert minstrels known as waferers, to the sound of drums and trumpets. The Earl of Derby took a clerk of the kitchen to the Holy Land with him 'for painting various foods'. There were wildfires, ancestors of our burning Christmas puddings but on a vast and vastly more dramatic scale; blazing landscapes of gaudy food. There was course after course of meat, fish, game, pies and tarts, all dramatically presented and garishly coloured and glazed, and eaten with plate-fuls of starchy soup and bread.

After piping the courses in, the minstrels played and sang while they were eaten, including in their performance some pieces of background accompaniment so that guests who felt like it could do their own singing between mouthfuls. Towards the end of the period it became fashionable to play in the minstrel gallery at the back of the hall, but more often play was on the floor in the centre of the hall, surrounded by the feasting. If a guest wanted an individual performance, the harper, or whoever gave it, might get up on the table and play in front of whoever wanted it. A sizeable household band would comprise about six minstrels.

Wind instruments like doucets (a kind of flute) and reed pipes became popular in England in the fourteenth century. Bagpipes developed from the rustic to the fashionable, and by the mid thirteenth century were being made with drones. Edward III sent his household piper, Barbor, to 'visit minstrels' schools overseas', to learn the best way of playing the best pipes.

Trumpets remained basically percussive and heraldic, and were used at meals to announce entrances and new courses, and to beat out brassy dance rhythms. Edward III had five trumpeters in his household band. They usually played in a separate group from the other minstrels, solo, or with drummers. By the fifteenth century clarions had developed an almost S shape, which was accentuated still more to become a double sliding pipe, the ancestor of the modern trombone.

Recorders only appeared in England in the very late fifteenth century. Henry VII left a collection of seventy-five of them, made of box, walnut and ivory, which he used to hire a child to play to him. The 'pipes' Chaucer often referred to, and which featured in almost every late medieval band, were hornpipes, originally a Cornish speciality, cornettos, flutes and flageolets, both these last often in double form.

For the most part, pipers remained apart from chamber players. There was at least one piper in most bands, specialising in solos. The pipe took over from the harp as the top solo instrument, and was occasionally used, like the harp, to accompany singing. The shepherd playing his pipe 'as have these little herd grooms' became a model for the accomplished courtier.

No medieval band was complete without drummers. They provided the background for jingling, clashing and piping, in individual and in concert performances. The Prior of Durham had a pair of minstrels who performed in his chamber now and again, and a pair described in his accounts as husband and wife; both were probably taboreter and taborette.

It was mainly the feasters who did the dancing at feasts, but in the fifteenth century there was a fashion for 'commoning', i.e. for minstrels to lead the feasters in a musical, dancing procession round the hall.

Singing was more of a group art, but it only figured as such, separately from music, at the very end of the period. Usually the audience sang while the minstrels played, but sometimes a whole minstrel troupe sang. In 1432 the treasurer of Bicester Priory gave six minstrels four shillings for singing a legend about the seven sleepers, in the refectory on the feast of the Epiphany. But there are few surviving details of minstrel singing. Sometimes local amateur troupes did performances before landlords in return for a feast and a modest fee. It was a social obligation on late medieval householders to open their doors to local song-and-dance troupes, particularly at Christmas, when carol singers sang, and usually danced, their carols in the great hall. Minstrels very seldom, if ever, performed carols.

Apart from the occasional local performances, the only professional group singing was that done by chapel choirs like the one set up by John Howard at Stoke Nayland in the 1480s. Only courtiers as eminent as he – he was a close associate of the King, admiral, treasurer and a senior diplomat – established such choirs, and only at the very end of the period. Household chapel choirs date from the late fifteenth century, when minstrels had either become actors or japers, or formed themselves into dance bands, and serious choral music such as English composers were beginning to write, under continental influence, required separate patronage.

The best Burgundian musicians, like Dufay, incorporated the *contenance angloise* (English style; a very expressive one) of John Dunstable, Henry V's protégé, into their best works. From the fourteenth-century on, attention began to be paid to the distinction between loud and soft music, to possibilities of complex combinations of music and voice. Priority was given to instruments that could move from the loud to the soft and play several notes at once. In England this taste for the polyphonic and harmonic extended to song, and the part singing Gerald of Wales described in the twelfth century was developed in monastic schools like the one at Worcester Priory in the fourteenth century. It found a voice in the descant singing which England exported to the Continent, and with which it so impressed visitors, in the fifteenth century.

Richard III was a bountiful patron of English musicians and singers. He further endowed the already splendid Chapel Royal, and commissioned one of its members, John Melynek, to 'take and seize for the King' any children who showed promise at singing and also 'all such singing men expert in the science of music . . . within all the palaces of the realm, as well cathedral churches, colleges, chapels, houses of religion . . . or elsewhere.'

John Howard and early Tudor courtiers with similar tastes had talent scouts like these. Howard listened to music wherever he went, and brought singers from London back to Essex to school his choir, which consisted of at least four children whom he fed, clothed, paid, and boarded with a local priest. He took a personal interest in their welfare, and referred to them all by name in his accounts: Dyke, Edward, Harry and 'Little Richard', who seems to have been his favourite and was taken on an outing to London, perhaps to hear the choirs there, by the duke's wife.

She was as fond of music as her husband was. She chose new shoes for the choir children on Easter Day 1484, having already bought them stockings and bought the men singers sumptuous gowns. She bought handsome song-books to record the songs they learnt. She had her son taught the horn; she herself played the lute, and may have had an organ of her own, as well as the one in the chapel.

Generally speaking, the organ remained a church instrument throughout the Middle Ages, and became more popular with the increased vogue for polyphonic music, played in churches, in the fifteenth century. By 1400 organs were being made with big reed pipes, pedal keyboards and solostops, so that they covered three octaves instead of their original one. They became fully chromatic, and church and chapel owners delighted in maintaining them at their best.

The fifteenth century was the polyphonic age for the keyboard. As early as 1360 the English had tried to develop a stringed instrument that would give the keyboard sound without the problems of keyboard maintenance. The echiquier, which a contemporary described as 'like an organ that sounds with strings', was not a success, despite royal encouragement. But the work that had gone into it helped to produce the chromatic organ and the versatile late medieval lute, with its eight frets and eleven strings. At the same time the psalter developed into the dulcimer which, with its bridged metal strings and little striking hammer, was the medieval ancestor of the piano.

Minstrel bands playing these instruments wore a colourful version of their masters' livery, and often won tips of caps, gowns and stockings as if, complained Bromyard bitterly, they were lapdogs or prostitutes. A lot of late medieval bands belonged to town corporations, not individual householders, and wore their town livery, in colours like verdulet (bluish green), rayed plunket (striped woollen cloth, usually light grey) and russet motley. They were known as waits, and sometimes played for private households on big occasions. Henry IV had thirteen minstrels and a wait, who had made a name for himself as a singer of Christmas carols, in his household band. The London waits were so good that John Howard used to go and listen to them whenever he was in London.

In the early years of their existence they were watchmen at the city gates, and used to blow the hours of the night on shalms. They continued in this capacity until the thirteenth century, some of them throughout the period. But the development of urban and corporate life had made minstrels of most of them by 1400. In 1423 Coventry had four 'city minstrels', and levied a tax of one penny on every house with a hall, and a halfpenny on every cottage, for their maintenance. They were the gleeful part of civic pageantry just as household minstrels were of household display, and their profession, like that of household minstrels, was an all year round one, earning them a steady salary.

Naturally they wanted to protect it from trespass by itinerant minstrels who, they complained to the king in 1315, stayed on after their performances in wealthy households, as hangers on. They formed themselves into gilds to organise and safeguard the practice of their arts, each little gild under the direction of a King of Minstrels. In 1380 John of Gaunt ordered his King of Minstrels to arrest all the minstrels in his home honour of Tutbury who refused to do their service and minstrelsy. The next year he set up a minstrel court at Tutbury, with legal jurisdiction over the minstrels of the five neighbouring counties. Like all household servants, minstrels had to be kept on the job.

The more so as their job did not have a fixed structure.

Comparatively formal though household minstrels were in their glee, they often went on visits to nearby towns and households, while minstrels from other households or from itinerant troupes performed in their place. They followed their masters to war and on pilgrimage. They split up to give individual shows, and sometimes even moved to a different household if they were better suited to its demands. Royal minstrels were particularly peripatetic, partly because there were so many of them that some could always be spared to perform away from court, and partly because the royal court itself was so peripatetic.

Minstrel performances were as varied as their locations. Glee was always variety entertainment, and even when music, song and dance grew into distinct arts, there were other arts to keep up the variety. Audiences provided more and more music, song and dance for themselves, so minstrels presented theirs in dramatic and acrobatic scenes. They acted out carols, songs and stories, and masked and disguised band performances. Late medieval household accounts record payments to minstrels, players and *histriones*, and the purchase of costumes and 'disguising stuffs' to embellish their performances. Minstrels provided the music, and often some japing and miming, for the late medieval gild plays. A good household band could always make a living; if it could do some japing and acting as well, it could make a better one. Still, many late medieval solo musicians earnt extra tips from chamber performances, which were a welcome change for house-holders who had withdrawn into their curtained privacy, away from the noise and conviviality of concerts in the great hall.

John of Gaunt always referred to his chamber musicians by their personal names in his accounts, and most of their names are affectionate diminutives: Rollekyn, Peterkyn and so on. In December 1381 he gave his 'much loved minstrel John Cliff of Coventry, a minstrel's collar, a silver eschucon [escutcheon] and a pair of nackers'.

Like solo music in its percussive intimacy, japing in its fun and audacity was always welcome to private audiences. While John of Gaunt was giving his favourite minstrel drum and drum-sticks, the Prior of Durham was paying one of Lord Neville's minstrels and a leaper 6/8d. to perform before him in his chamber at Beaurepaire, his week-end home. He gave some more of Lord Neville's minstrels 3/4d. for performing there together with six shillings' worth of presents, which he described as 'silks and knives for the boys'.

For all that, most travelling minstrels found life hard. They were at the mercy of porters, gate-keepers and the weather. They might arrive at a household after it had been closed for the night, or a company offering the same sort of entertainment had just been admitted, or the household had left for business or pleasure elsewhere. In winter, when every household, town and village welcomed gleeful diversion, it was often impossible to travel. Many touring artists stayed in the nearest big city all winter, hoping to find odd jobs to earn them food and shelter until the spring travelling season. As one French minstrel put it in one of his songs, 'Chill are my loins when the east wind blows . . . in summer I sing, and in winter I make lament.' If the performers had animals, a winter base was essential, and it is no wonder travelling minstrels had the reputation of being flatterers and fawners. Even the least 'japish' of travelling minstrels were credited to some degree with the roguish flirtatiousness traditionally associated with jugglers.

A fourteenth-century Prioress of St Michael's Priory, Stanford, in Lincolnshire, reported that one of her nuns, Sister Agnes, 'has gone away into apostasy cleaving to a harp player, and they dwell together, as it is said, in Newcastle-upon-Tyne.' Having a reputation for this kind of thing might help as much as hinder a minstrel's career, and even in the little extract just quoted here is a hint of delight, or at least fascination, at the adventures of Sister Agnes in distant Newcastle. There is no way of telling whether the harper she ran off with normally travelled such long distances on tour, or whether he did so in this case to get safely away from the priory.

As for Sister Agnes, she may have felt that her sin would be gently judged. The twelfth-century renaissance began a tradition that minstrels were under the special protection of the Virgin Mary, a tradition spread through the story of the *Tumbler of Our Lady*, which gave 'japing' a romantic aura that no amount of reforming disapproval could diminish. The story gives an idea of the spectacularly acrobatic nature of medieval tumbling.

It tells of a tumbler who entered the monastery of Clairvaux, some time in the twelfth century. The monks there were Cistercian, which means they had a special devotion to Our Lady, in honour of whose purity they wore white robes. It also means that they were exceptionally austere, and the tumbler found himself unable to join in the singing of the monastic offices, having lived only to 'tumble, to turn somersaults, to spring and to dance', and hard put to it to endure the gleeless silence. He decided to honour the Virgin Mary in the only way he knew. While the other monks went into church to sing the office, he went down to her chapel, took off his clothes and laid them by her altar, and began to tumble before her statue, dressed 'so that his body would not be uncovered (implying that it normally would be) . . . in a clinging and close fitting tunic.' He tumbled, leapt, turned high and low, backwards and forwards somersaults, and seven different kinds of somersaults from different parts of Europe, like the somersault of Metz. Eventually the abbot found out about his activities, and was watching him in secret one day when he saw the statue of the Virgin come to life and minister to him because he had tumbled himself into an exhausted faint. The abbot was so impressed that he allowed him to go on with his tumbling prayers, and the story ends with a gleeful little message: 'Thus died the minstrel. Cheerfully did he tumble, and cheerfully did he serve, for the which he merited great honour, and none there was to compare with him.'

There were one or two who compared with him in England. In 1334 Edward III paid a tumbler five shillings for 'doing his minstrelsy before the image of the Blessed Virgin Mary in Veltam [Feltham], in the presence of the King.' But the most common way to tumble for Our Lady was to accompany a procession to one of her altars or shrines with acrobatic dancing. In early fifteenth-century Leicester, to take just one of countless examples, there was a Martinmas procession each year at which twelve gildsmen, dressed as apostles, each with his apostle's name stuck in his cap, carried statues of the Virgin and St Martin through the streets 'to the accompaniment of much music and singing'.

Any talented amateur could provide these, and individual minstrels did best to specialise in the spectacular, such as only they could provide. At events like gild feasts, there were 'jesters' bawds . . . and gitterners' glee', magic shows, leapers and tumblers, juggling and tricks with animals. Minstrels did histrionic goading of animals; they baited, wrestled and danced with them. They put on masks and danced with costumed dogs, apes and horses. They imitated drunks, fools, cats and asses.

'Sciences by which men delude the eye with divers appearances' [Chaucer] were the most spectacular minstrel tricks of all. The artists of illusionism were known as tregetours, and they held the audiences of late medieval Europe spellbound with delight. Their japes were too amazing to be true, and Chaucer described them with a mixture of fascination and uneasy disapproval. They could be done in miniature.

> There saw I Colle tregetour [the most famous of his day]
> Upon a table of sycamour
> Play an uncouth thing to tall;
> I saw him carving a wind-mill
> Under a walsh-nut shale [walnut shell].
>
> [*House of Fame*]

But they were mostly done on the grand scale, using fantastic props, full supporting cast, and perhaps a touch of hypnotism, to produce effects like the ones described in the *Squire's Tale*. Chaucer only says he 'heard tell' of these effects, which were probably far humbler in real life than the wonders hearsay made of them. They were somewhere between conjuring tricks and masques, and the effects in the *Squire's Tale* included the turning of great halls into lakes with barges rowed up and down on them, and the sudden appearance of grim lions, flowery meads, vines and castles, which disappeared as suddenly and inexplicably as they had appeared.

When Chaucer wrote, tregetours were at the height of their popularity. By the fifteenth century they had lost pride of place to 'sleight of hand' jugglers, whose tricks were easier to stage. Their speciality was a combination of knife and sword juggling with acrobatic balancing. When Prior More of Worcester wanted some good tricky japes to entertain him in the early autumn of 1519, he hired a group of the 'king's minstrels with shambulls [stools or benches]', a group of the Queen's players led by a man with the suggestively sleightish name of John Slye, and one of the King's jugglers, called John Brandon, whom he hired again eight years later to give a one-man show at his country house in Grimley. Brandon did 3/4d. worth of juggling and his child did eightpence worth of tumbling.

Prior More's was a typical late fifteenth- or early sixteenth-century household of entertainments. His accounts show the overlap between amateur and professional song and dance in the mixed minstrelsy of the late Middle Ages. Singing appears frequently in the accounts, performed by local choirs in festive seasons, particularly Christmas, when carol singers sang almost daily before the Prior, between Christmas Eve and the Epiphany. By the time the accounts were written, carols were as much festive songs as round dances.

Their favourite theme was the old folk one of the struggle between the sexes, or between two opposing parties, such as the holly and the ivy. The burden at the end of each verse often told some piece of proverbial wisdom, such as

Pride is out, and pride is in,
And pride is the root of every sin.

There were carols on marriage, childhood, money, mourning, politics, women, vices and virtues. But from the early fourteenth century on, when the Franciscan reconciliation of song and dance with Christianity began to bear fruit, religious carols began to dominate. 'The Holy Ghost maketh his chosen sing in their hearts the sweet songs of heaven,' wrote the Ayenbite poet in about 1340, and by the fifteenth century carols were the gleeful heart of Christmas.

Man, be glad in hall and bower;
This time was born our Saviour.
                                        [Fifteenth-century carol]

The secular was subsumed into the sacred, drink, sex, paganism and all, and the nativity story gave it an overwhelmingly successful focus. Old number chants were thinly Christianised into carols like the seven joys of Mary. One of the most popular refrains in religious carols was 'Hail!', meaning hale or health, and derived from the drinking toast 'Wassail!' The French equivalent, *Noël*, appeared in a few English carols in the late fifteenth and early sixteenth centuries.

The emotional devotion of the Franciscans and the ever growing cult of the Virgin gave birth to lullaby carols of passionate sensitivity.

> I saw a fair maiden sit and sing;
> She lullayd a little child, a sweet lording.
> Lullay, mine liking, my dear son, my sweeting,
> Lullay my dear heart, mine own dear darling.

Carols were popular in church as well as hall, and were sung before the crib, where scenes from the nativity story were acted out. The favourite way of telling this story was a ballad carol, with the central message repeated within the verses and in the refrain. Such a carol had the high colour characteristic of all carols and the tenderness of romantic ballads, many of which were sung elaborately by minstrels as well as plainly by singers at home and in taverns. Ballads were the major festival songs of the late Middle Ages, and were so popular that the word ballad was used for all narrative, festive, dialogue and even lyrical love songs.

The love lyric in all its many forms, sacred and secular, was distinguished in England by a sardonic humour that delighted in mixing the sublime with the frivolous. English lyrics in the fifteenth century included dialogues between opposites, light aphoristic touches, understatement and ambiguity, all of them welcome reliefs when lyrics seventy verses long were commonplace.

But the ultimate gleeful addiction was one which never dated or palled, and was above fashion. There were no less than three officially acknowledged forms of medieval dancing mania: St Vitus's Dance, St John's Dance and St Guy's Dance. Unofficial forms including hopping, which was done ever more widely by all kinds of people, and masked dancing, which always got completely out of hand. The masters and scholars of Oxford University were forbidden to dance 'with mask or any noise whatsoever in the churches or in the streets, in garlands or crowns woven of leaves.'

There was a vogue for the leafy and the pastoral in late medieval courtly society. In the late fifteenth-century courtly poem, the *Flower and Leaf*, the courtiers divide into flower and leaf factions to debate their respective merits. Pastoral dances were the first of many pastoral games to become fashionable at court, and were to reach a dazzling peak of popularity in the pastorally devoted Tudor court.

The galliard was a courtly version of the Morris dance, and became very popular at the end of the Middle Ages. It was based on a simple movement of steps followed by a spring into the air, like the circling steps and spot treading of a carol. In the early sixteenth century it developed, like the round dances, towards elaboration and fragmentation. Round dance circles were broken up for their members to dance in pairs.

There is a contemporary description of festive dancing in a little known Scottish poem of the late fifteenth century called *Colkebie Sow*, which is a satire on the pastoral cult at court. It describes a feast at which a band of shepherds make fools of themselves by trying to dance all kinds of exotic dances, just as courtiers made fools of themselves by trying to dance shepherd dances. 'The sun shone in the south . . . they danced a dandy . . . danced Overfoot, Orleance, Rustybull' and a whole litany of other dances based on fashionable dances of the time.

After trying a lot of these 'dances at leisure', or virtuoso display pieces, they got into a ring and danced *My dear darling*, obviously a carol, but dramatised by the shepherds with a little solo sequence, 'without knowledge, so they merely pranced'.

They were accompanied by bagpipes, such as accompanied farandols and crib dances in real life. These last were developments of folk dancing, the first a popular late medieval shepherd dance which was an elaborate procession, the second a dramatised Christmas worship dance.

The Colkebie shepherds then 'clumsily danced the *Base*', which their landlords had developed into a dance 'beyond the reach of all their plain poor thoughts'. Before the landowning class began dancing it, it was a type of farandol, and it underwent the same process of elaboration and dramatisation as many shepherd dances in the late Middle Ages. The Colkebie shepherds did leaping and hopping dances, ballads and pair dances, and dramatic re-enactments of the visit of the shepherds to the stable crib.

As the number of households with halls big enough to accommodate dances increased, their owners copied courtly dance styles, and evolved dances that would show off their halls, clothes and minstrels. Dances with brilliant patterns of pairs and small groups, brilliantly costumed and involving stylised steps, were late medieval bourgeois imitations of courtly dances.

The galliard did not become really popular until the Tudor period, but its roots lay in medieval sword and Morris dancing. In Tudor times it fragmented from a dance round the room in couples to one in which the partners danced their steps before each other in individual display, before joining hands to go and repeat the display at the other end of the room. This was the dancing equivalent of playing a lute solo; it was gleeful personal display.

The basse dance, so called because it was performed on the ground, without springing in the air, was another late medieval refinement of a folk dance, in this case the processional dancing and 'open' carolling which had already been refined into the farandol. In Tudor times the basse developed individual display sections, like the galliard, but in the late Middle Ages it was still basically a courtly folk procession, performed slowly and elegantly in couples, punctuated by bows, courtsies and decorative side-steps.

The pavane was a fast-moving basse dance with quite elaborate displays of steps, but much more elaborate costumes. So gorgeous were the long trained dresses of the ladies, and the dress cloaks of the gentlemen, hung over their outthrust swords, that the name pavane may have come from the Latin *parvo*, meaning peacock, though it may come from the name Pavia, the town where the dance probably originated, and where it was certainly popular in the late fifteenth century.

The Italian-Burgundian style of display dancing became all the rage in late medieval England. Dance became a game to play by watching as well as performing, and the Italian dance manuals which gave the early Tudor court its rules of dance constantly reminded the performers to have their spectators in mind. The reason Chaucer's miller admired the clerk Nicholas's dancing was that it had twenty manners of display.

Dancing everywhere became more dramatic. Disguising gave added significance to dances in the courtly game of love, and professional dancers acted out allegories as well as dancing acrobatically. The most spectacular of these was the Dance of Death, which was staged after pageants and feasts, to remind their participants of their approaching end, and as a scene in some of the early morality plays.

The 'Dancing Day' carol was more concerned with life, in particular with its irresistibly gleeful theme of love. It used the Old Testament allegory of the love between human lovers for the love between God and man to tell the story of the Redemption. It told of the love between a man and a woman, and at least officially, the man was Jesus. It must have been a dancing carol, though it has survived to the present day as a sung Christmas carol only. Every verse ends with the word dance. It could have been performed equally successfully by amateurs and professionals, indoors and outdoors. It is a late medieval model of the reconciliation of the sacred and the secular, of the song, the dance and the romantic lyric. Its first verse is an epitaph for medieval glee, and there could be no better or lovelier one.

> Tomorrow shall be my dancing day,
> I would my true love did so chance
> To see the legend of my play,
> To call my true love to the dance.
> Sing, O my love, O my love, my love, my love;
> This have I done for my true love.

52 A tonsured clerk hymns the greatest Lord with the aid of hired minstrels. Initial of Psalm 80 Exultate Deo in the Bromholm Priory Psalter, *c*. 1325. *Bodleian Library, Oxford* MS. Ashmole. 1523, fol. 99.

53 Musicians. Initial of Psalm 80 in the psalter of Robert of Ormesby, monk of Norwich Cathedral Priory, *c*. 1325. *Bodleian Library, Oxford* MS. Douce. 366. fol. 109.

ezonas enfera / parce z reueftue
Qui a noftre roi eft / de marit atendue
Car li uertus damozs / qui toute autre efuertue
De fortune z de dzoit / dont pas ne fui tenue
Eftoit a fon aius / ens ou roi contenue
Car bien mouftra quamozs / eft dedens li efmue
Fortune fait que tout / autre poor feftiue

54 Musicians. Left to right: bagpipe, hurdy-gurdy, cornet or recorder, portative organ, kettle drums, From the Alexander Romance. *Bodleian Library, Oxford* MS. Bodl. 264, fol. 180v.

55 A costumed jester before his employer. *Bodleian Library, Oxford* MS. Douce. 18, fol. 113v.

56 The Court of Mirth from the *Roman de la Rose*. By Robinet Testard for Charles d'Orleans and Louise de Savoie. c. 1490. *Bodleian Library, Oxford* MS. Douce. 195, fol. 7.

57 Contortionist performing. *Bodleian Library, Oxford* MS. Douce. 5, fol. 18.

58 Disreputable japes. From the Alexander Romance. *Bodleian Library, Oxford* MS. Bodl. 264, fol. 74.

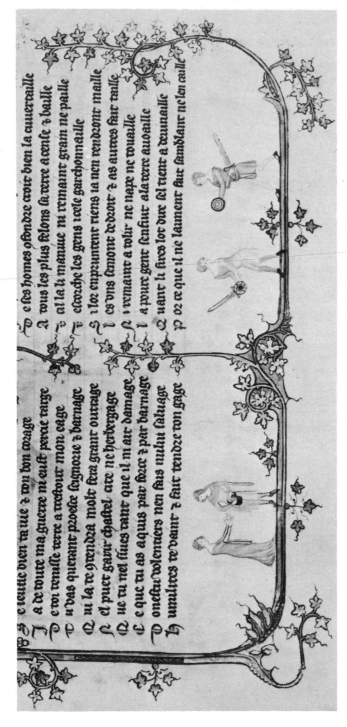

59 Gladiatores performing a stylised Sword Dance. *The British Library Royal 4 E III fol. 89.*

fait la damoisele sachies q̃ w̃ le
raures ains temain eure de disn̄.
Oie iuoist dont fait la wine q̃
se temain ne deust venenir. il
m̃ alast huy par mon congier.
Er il montre ꝛ la damoisele ausi
si se parrent de lauens sans autre
compaignie fors dun seul escuier
qui auoer la damoisele estoir ue
nus . Et n̄r il st̃ pũ de canuae
lor si cheuauchent tant q̃l sont
uenu ala forest. si se misent ou
gr̃t chemin upe errerent tant
qũl uinrent en une ualee . Er
lors uoient deuant aus au tra
uers dun kemin une abeie de
nonnains. ꝛ la damoisele tour
ne cele pt̃ / si tost c̃omeil sont p̃.
Er qn̄t il sont uenu ala poite si
a parle li escuiers / ꝛ on li ouure
si entre ens . qn̄t il forent q̃ lanc
estoir uenus / chil de lauens li fi

la ueille de la pentecou
ste qn̄t tour li compaig
non de la table reonde fu
rent uenu a camaelor ꝛ il eorent
on le seruice / il fisent mettre les ta
bles . a eure de noune entre en la

q̃ w̃ en f[
saunt ꝛ l[
biautes[
quil ne[
ge il eur[
plaist n[
iont as[
str̃ ne lo[
wlentes[
uorleur[
uolons[
mam . i[
fait enf[
nuit tre[
toure la[
leglize .[
me le fil[
ses espe[
apies li[
douna[
le frst̃ p[
ꝛ nauo[

60 A king entertaining his guests with music and a story during a meal. *The British Museum* Royal 14 E
III fol. 89.

CHAPTER EIGHT

Medieval Drama

The oldest play in the world is probably the sword dance. It evokes the creative magic of the new year, with its hope of spring and plenty, against the winter and scarcity of the old year. Every European country has this dance somewhere in its dramatic history. Strictly speaking, it is not itself dramatic because it lacks dialogue, but medieval drama was not strictly spoken. It included dramatic dances like the sword dance, folk plays, processions and pageants, mimes and mummings, masques and mockeries, as well as the strictly dramatic trio of mystery, miracle and morality plays.

These last were the glory of medieval England, but they began as simple dramatic dances which developed into folk plays, thence full stage plays. The sword dance was the most popular of these basic dramatic dances, performed at midsummer to ensure fertility and at midwinter to look forward to it. The dancers began to enact little episodes, and turned their dances into mummers' plays. [Illustration 61]

The mummers' play was introduced by a request for room to perform a duel, after which the wounded loser of the duel was revived by a doctor, and the chorus ended with a romp, a song and a collection of money. The symbolic associations with seasonal death and rebirth were clearly shown in the costumes and mummings, though all the players were masked. There was a cheeky little devil who joined the fool and the grotesques at the end in a bawdy dance, and was always the favourite with the audience; in the Midlands Plough Monday play he was christened Little Devil Doubt and treated to extra generous tips.

By the fifteenth century, if not before, the hero of the sword dances and Pascal (Pace Egg) plays was firmly identified with St George. There is no record of any St George plays being performed before this date, but that does not mean they did not exist. Some sort of St George 'passion' existed in Europe in the fifth century, and during the crusades St George emerged as the ideal of saintly knighthood. In England his opponent was usually a Turk. Parishes celebrated his feast day, April 23rd, with 'ridings' consisting of processions and mock combats with the devil, dragon or infidel. At St Margaret's riding in Norwich, St George fought with a dragon, in a wood outside the town. Some ridings remained dumb pageants; others became part of mumming or miracle plays; still others combined elements of both and became masked mimes with spoken introductions known as devices, and sometimes dialogues to accompany the performance.

The most primitive masked mimes or 'disguisings' were really just elaborate dramatic dances, and often amounted to little more than rowdy street parties. City councils repeatedly passed prohibitions like the one issued in London in 1418 against 'any manner mumming, plays, interludes, or any other disguisings with any fained beards, painted visers, deformed or coloured visages in any wise.' But games like these continued to be played, especially at Christmas time, the miming and mumming season. The beheading game in *Sir Gawain and the Green Knight*, which may have had some connection with the ritual killing of the old year, is described in that romance simply as 'a Christmas game'. It probably involved miming or masking of some kind.

Morris dancing was a gentler, more stylised version of sword dancing, identifying the old enemy as the Moor, hence its name. It became popular in England just when the reconquest of Spain from the Moors was being completed in the late fourteenth century, and there was a fashion for all things Morish all over Europe. Morris dancers decorated the defeat of the Moorish devils with white costumes, silver streamers and silver-belled shoes. They also had a traditional man/woman in their dance, with a bias in favour of femininity, as suggested by the title they gave her: the Betsy.

Courtiers played elaborate Christmas disguising games. For the royal games at Otford in 1348 the clerk of the wardrobe ordered 'twelve men's heads, each surmounted with a lion's head', twelve surmounted with elephants' heads, twelve with bats' wings, twelve with wildmen's heads, seventeen with girls' heads, fourteen with tunics of red worsted and fourteen with tunics of green worsted, lined with gold. As tournaments declined from the chivalrous to the histrionic, so mummings developed from silent to spoken mimes, with lavish scenic devices, including mobile stages which could be removed to make room for dancing. They were indoor tournament pageants, the forerunners of the extravagant masques of the Tudor period. [Illustration 62]

Special effects as well as words were added to fifteenth-century mummings, which were then called by the more accurate name of disguisings. Duke John of Norfolk paid some one called Gerard of Sudbury 21/0½d. for 'some stuffs' for one of his Christmas disguisings. The stuffs included 'gold paper and silver, rough and clear and green', gold foil, 'arssowde' (rattles), 'sursuphuryfe' (cymbals) and 'callis' (chalices), glue, thread and gunpowder. He also paid a couple of local musicians half a mark (6/8d.) each to provide music, and possibly dancing as well, at the performance.

As time passed, folk disguisings developed the same fondness for props and effects. In Canterbury every year on July 6th a cart was drawn through the streets bearing a boy dressed as Becket who was struck down before an altar by 'four other boys dressed as knights, beneath the device of an angel and with a leather bag for the blood.' The old folk processions adopted the heroes and images of Christianity, with spectacular results.

The music was often provided for them by waits and minstrels; the spectacles were part riding, part procession, part pageant. Pageants were corporate dramatics in the medieval style, vast and vulgar. In the later Middle Ages they reached epic proportions. Financed by city gilds and corporations, they glorified their patrons, entertained the citizens, and absorbed dangerous political energy. By the late fourteenth century there were countless civic processions, celebrating the feast days of gilds and churches, and the election of gild and city officials, especially the mayor. By the mid fifteenth century the Lord Mayor's procession in London was a glittering showpiece, and the gilds fought each other for the right to precedence in the state progress by barge down the Thames, from the Gildhall to Westminster.

But the most glorious pageantry of all was royal. Richard II's coronation in 1377 was marked by the most spectacular pageant yet seen in England, and over the next century the Lancastrian kings made great play with pageants in London to glorify their kingship, until in 1432 Henry VI was welcomed back from his coronation in Paris as King of France with one that excelled all others of the Middle Ages. It was dramatic display at its most brilliantly visual, sparing no device or contrivance. The poet Lydgate wrote a verse commentary for it, explaining its epic symbolism. Everything about it was heaven sent, even the weather.

> . . . the merry sun
> Upon a Thursday shed his beams bright
> Upon London, to make him glad and bright.

The Mayor and aldermen, 'each one well horsed', were dressed in sumptuous crimson and scarlet, the leading craftsmen in white, symbolising, said Lydgate, the purity of their loyalty.

The route was from Cornhill to Cheapside, and such was the number and complexity of the tableaux, and of the minstrels accompanying the procession, not to mention the press of the crowds, the showmen, beggars, animals and refreshment stalls and sellers, that it took the King five hours to get to St Paul's. At the little conduit next to St Paul's there was a pageant representing the Trinity, with a multitude of angels singing and playing on various instruments. A procession of churchmen came down the steps of St Paul's to greet the King and take him into the service, to the sound of massed choirs and pealing bells, after which they accompanied him and the city dignitaries to Westminster for a Te Deum in the Abbey.

Cheap was one of the widest streets in medieval London, and a favourite tournament, fair and market ground, 'a lusty place, a place of all delights'. [Lydgate] On this occasion its fountain ran with wine and was surrounded by a paradise of artificial trees tended by the prophets Enoch and Elias.

Stage management had found the ultimate challenge in this pageant. Earth, heaven and hell were depicted in three-storey scaffolds.

The top storeys were roofed and backed with painted sky,

stars, moon, sun and clouds. The middle storeys, representing earth, had mountains, arbours, gardens, fountains, castles and ships, usually modelled, occasionally painted or embroidered on a backcloth. The lower storeys were hellishly dark, with the odd painted or masked devil, and machine-made or painted wildfire.

The scenery was in a class by itself, but its tableaux characters were procession and pageant regulars; virgins and angels, devils and dragons. Folk pageants preferred wild men to the more sophisticated political enemies that threatened Henry VI in the pageant, and often featured giants played by men on stilts or on each others' shoulders. When Edward IV's queen, Elizabeth Woodville, visited Norwich in 1469, she was greeted by a pageant guarded by two splendid giants made of wood and Hungarian leather, stuffed with hay, wearing crests of gold and silver leaf. They were mounted on a stage covered with red and green worsted, and adorned with angels and escutcheons.

Village mummings, with different resources, developed differently, towards the less spectacular and more truly dramatic form of the folk play. By the thirteenth century, New Year dances and May games included not only wooing songs and dialogues but also plots and symbolic characters. The traditional shepherd and shepherdess of French *pastourelles*, Robin and Marion, may have come into English from French May games in the late Middle Ages, by way of minstrel songs, and merged with the yeoman hero who was becoming popular in the late fourteenth century: Robin Hood. Whatever its origins, the Robin Hood and Maid Marian play was the dominant folk drama in England by the end of the period, and combined pastoral songs and dances with episodes and characters from the Robin Hood ballads. Maid Marian is an idealised version of the typical shepherdess, and a refined version of the Morris dancers' Betsy. She was usually called Malkyn, until the very end of the period. Robin was often called Wat.

One of the very few folk plays other than Robin Hood recorded from this period appears by chance in the ecclesiastical court rolls of Wistow, Yorkshire, for the year 1469. There was a summer festival there every year, financed by offerings made at one of the church candles. The chief witness to the assault case of which the games were a cause was a man called John Gaferer, who stressed how 'honest' they were, and reported with bland innocence that another of the players, one Thomas Barker, got married the Sunday after them, having played the Wistow King opposite a woman called Margaret More, who played the Wistow Queen.

Most folk festivals were organised under kings and queens, just as court festivals were under a Master of Revels or a Lord of Misrule. The Wistow festival games sound like a typical mixture of song, dance, drama and fun. The players were led by a 'mime or actor with a club,' who may have joined in the acting, or just japed and fooled. The games were held in a barn next to the churchyard, known as the 'somer [summer] -house'. Margaret More stayed at the games from mid-day Sunday until after sunset, 'listening to the play and playing in it herself.' A man played the king's steward, another his butler, and two men played knights who waited upon the queen. There were at least a hundred people present, but it is impossible to tell how many were listening to the play and how many were playing in it.

If the games were anything like the Robin Hood plays that were becoming popular at the time, most people did both. A complete set of accounts survive for one of these Robin Hood plays: the one done on Mayday each year by the parishioners of Kingston-upon-Thames in the late fifteenth and early sixteenth-centuries. The accounts were kept by the churchwardens, who got the profits of the play for church use, and itemised the expenses. By this time, the folk play was a parish play and pageant, employing professional help for its costuming and music.

The accounts are under the overall heading of 'Robin Hood and May Game', and their first item, for the year 1507, is a payment of 4d. 'to a minstrel on Mayday.' The Morris dancers, with whom the play was always closely associated, were supplied with bells and gowns, Robin Hood with a banner, his lady with a dress costing eight shillings. The next year Robin Hood and Friar Tuck got coats, and Maid Marian was clothed in a kendal huke (a hooded cape or cloak made of green wool), trimmed with Cyprus satin. She and Robin Hood got a pair of gloves each.

Over the next few years there were purchases of arrows, shoes and coats for Robin Hood, and shoes and 'gold skins' for the Morris dancers.

In 1513 the play went on tour to Croydon, where it brought in 9/4d. to add to the £2/13/4d. it had made at the Kingston 'gathering' (collection). The local gentry were expected to contribute to these 'gatherings', and open their doors to their local troupe of folk players, just as they did to their local troupes of folk singers and dancers. Prior More of Worcester's accounts are full of payments to 'the Robin Hood box'. Troupes from other villages and parishes in the neighbourhood got together to rival those of other regions, taking their plays round manor houses, taverns and village greens. The Kingston players seem to have restricted themselves to Kingston and Croydon, and devoted the money they saved on travel expenses to improving their costumes and hiring the best minstrels.

In 1536 their dancers were given hats and purses, their fool a new coat made of 4 yards of cloth, their leading characters double soled shoes, Maid Marian a worsted kirtle costing 6/8d., and their minstrel the substantial fee of 10/8d. There was also a well-paid taborer, and a local piper, who accompanied the play to Croydon, but they seem to have been amateurs, like the actors. Robin Hood's coat was kept at its best by being 'sponged and brushed' at a cost of 2d. This was an elaborate, expensive, highly organised refinement of the original folk play, itself a late medieval characterisation of basic folk drama. It became the highpoint of the summer festival, in Kingston and in towns and villages all over England.

The winter highpoint was a unique dramatic celebration that was part folk, part ecclesiastical: folk in its attachment to the ruling principle of turning everything upside-down; ecclesiastical in being performed at a church festival, in monasteries and cathedrals, by members of church communities, in partnership with a few of their young parishioners. It was the Feast of Fools, and more particularly the Feast of the Boy Bishop, which was the form it came to take in England.

The original Feast of Fools came into existence in France in the late twelfth century, and was common over most European countries two centuries later, despite condemnation by the Church hierarchy. It was basically a Christmas burlesque of religious dignity and ceremonial, and was very popular with secular canons serving cathedrals. They elected one of their number head of the cathedral chapter for the period between St Stephen's Day (December 26th) and the Circumcision (January 1st); they played dice on the altar, sang filthy songs in the choir stalls, burlesqued the sacred ceremonies by preaching mad sermons and getting fools to jangle the altar bells ceaselessly, made incense out of stinking shoes, and held grotesque processions to install their head, mounted on an ass, in office.

The feast was never popular in England, and had died out in all but two places by the late fourteenth century. One of the reasons for its failure was probably that there was already a strong tradition of Christmas merry-making among the lower clergy, and the new feast was superfluous. It found a fresh focus, which enabled it to survive, in the Boy Bishop. He became the leader of the Christmas games, just as Robin Hood became the leader of the May games. Peasant, middle- and upper-class congregations, including clergy of all ranks, crowded into the cathedrals to hear his nonsense sermons.

They were never really irreverent, like the games in the Feast of Fools. The Boy Bishop's festivities had a kind of gleeful dignity about them. On the feast of St Nicholas, the patron saint of schoolboys (December 6th), a local boy 'sufficiently handsome in person' (York Cathedral statutes, 1367) was elected by the clergy in cathedrals, religious houses, colleges and schools. On the Feast of St John (December 27th), he was solemnly installed in office, and for the next couple of days, often longer, he was in sole charge, and all was fun and games, if not chaos. The thirteenth-century Bishop of St Paul's had a white mitre embroidered with flowers, an ornate pastoral staff, and ornate vestments to match. His attendants, who were also boys, mostly choirboys, had expensive copes.

Many Boy Bishops stayed in office, at least unofficially, from Christmas to Candlemas, and did frequent *quêtes* (request songs) asking for entrance to halls, and fund raising journeys, to help pay for their increasingly expensive costumes, regalia and attendants. In 1348 the Bishop of Exeter condemned the Order of Brothelyngham (brothel was the medieval word for a scoundrel, and the name was a satire on the Order of Sempringham) and the 'crazy lunatic . . . whom they call their Abbot . . . at the sound of a horn instead of a bell they led him not many days since through the streets of . . . Exeter, with a great throng of horse and foot at their heels, in which procession they laid hold of clergy and laiety . . . and extorted from them certain sums of money by way of sacrifice – nay, rather, of sacrilege.'

Fools' feasts were more common in female than male monasteries, and were more severely frowned upon. There was scope for the wrong kind of fooling. But nuns liked to give festive suppers to their altar boys on the Feast of the Innocents, nicknamed Childermas because it was a children's day. Sometimes these suppers developed into games played by the nuns, their altar boys, and other local children of both sexes. In 1441 the monks of St Swithun's paid their customary subsidies for beer, bread and wine 'to the boys of the almonry together with the boys of the chapel of St Elizabeth, dressed up after the manner of girls, dancing, singing and performing plays before the Abbess and nuns of St Mary's Abbey in their hall on the Feast of the Innocents.'

The reforming party disapproved of all fools' festivals, and the Protestant reformers suppressed them as soon as they came to power. A Boy Bishop was elected for the first time since the Reformation in the Shropshire village of Bucknell on St Nicholas's Day, 1978, but even the most puritanical of reformers could not have objected to his festivities, so pious and proper were they. The boys from the village school received his blessing in the parish church of St Mary's. He gave them some sweets and there was a service conducted by the vicar. English religion has a long way to go before it recaptures its medieval glee.

Each of the great medieval play types had gleeful origins in religious ceremonies. The central religious ceremony of Christianity is a drama in itself, and it is from this ceremony that medieval drama was derived. The mass was overhauled and embellished by the Benedictines in the ninth century, and one of their most dramatic additions to it was the trope, an introductory explanation of each day's mass theme, which they sang in choir as a dialogue. Soon tropes were being acted as well as sung. The Easter Sunday *Quem Quaeritis* (Whom Do You Seek?) trope was being presented 'in imitation of the angel seated in the tomb and the women coming with spices to anoint the body of Jesus' in the tenth century, when the *Regularis Concordia*, a summary of the Benedictine rule at that time, from which this trope description is taken, was compiled.

It was not long before a couple more scenes were added: the approach of Peter and John to the tomb, and the appearance of the risen Saviour to Mary Magdalen. Details too were added: Peter lagged behind John with a limp, Christ held a resurrection banner in his hand, the women bought spices on their way to the tomb. By the late twelfth century, the *Quem Quaeritis* was a regular Easter cathedral drama, performed before the morning mass. Easter was the dramatic heart of Christianity.

During the Easter season the mass itself contains dramatic episodes, like the washing of the feet on Maundy Thursday, and the Good Friday veneration of the Cross. Many small churches that did not have tropes dramatised these ceremonies further by burying the sacred host, altar cross and crucifix on Good Friday in a specially made 'sepulchre' near the altar, and keeping watch over them until Easter Sunday, when they dug them up in time for the dawn mass.

The late fifteenth- and early sixteenth-century churchwardens of St Mary-at-Hill in London kept records of their 'sepulchre' plays. The centre of their performances was the sepulchre, which was erected beside the altar and covered with a painted cloth. In 1426–1427 a joiner called Thomas was paid four shillings for making a sepulchre, plus 9½d. for nails, wire and glue, the wood being already provided. It was dismantled after Easter and mended before being used again the next year. It may have been quite grand, belonging as it did to an important church.

It was 'watched' faithfully through Good Friday and Holy Saturday night, with praying, singing, dancing and drinking, under the supervision of the parish clerk and his assistant, a man called Paris. For the two years 1479 and 1480 the clerk and Paris were paid 23d. 'for meat and drink, for watching of the sepulchre'.

Three years later Paris was on his own, deprived of meat but compensated with ale. It was he who took the sepulchre to bits after Easter and stored it in what was obviously a damp and dirty cupboard: in 1527 the wardens spent 12d. on 'an ell of linen cloth to amend the sepulchre cloth whereat it was eaten by rats . . . and 12d. to a bedmaker for mending and sewing the same.' They also paid someone called Mr Wolf five shillings for 'painting and renewing the images in the same cloth.'

The other Easter drama at St Mary-at-Hill was the *Prophetae*, which was part of the Palm Sunday procession. A wooden platform was erected over the north door of the church for the prophets to stand on and deliver little plays to the Palm Sunday processors on their way out into the churchyard, and possibly also on their way back in to the church. The prophets' stint was demanding enough for them to be given 1½d. worth of bread and drink to sustain them through it. There were two of them, and they wore costumes, wigs and beards provided by the churchwardens.

The Palm Sunday procession they addressed was one of the most important in the liturgical year, and also one of the most dramatic. It re-enacted Christ's progress through Jerusalem, through crowds waving and strewing palms. It was a simple and powerfully dramatic occasion, and as early as the tenth century elaborate rituals had been evolved to embellish it: the blessing of the palms, and dialogue singing between the procession priest and his processors. But being basically a part of the liturgy, it did not develop as much dramatically as decoratively.

In the later Middle Ages, St Mary-at-Hill was decorated on Palm Sunday with box, symbolic, like all evergreens, of lasting fidelity, St John's wort and orpin. The pews were strewn with fresh, sweet smelling rushes, and the floor with rush carpets. As the processors returned to the church, they sometimes got a shower of flowers and 'obleyes' (little cakes and biscuits) from the Prophets above the north porch.

Dramatic tropes were quickly developed for Palm Sunday and the passion gospels read in the week before Easter. From Passion Sunday a week before Easter to Easter Sunday itself became part of a dramatic Easter season, with tropes extending over topics from Old Testament prophecies to the New Testament resurrection accounts. The season was later expanded still more, to last until Pentecost.

The Ascension was a dramatic tour de force, enacted with the help of holes cut in the church roof. These provided exits for Assumption and Pentecost dramas too. The St Paul's Pentecost drama was celebrated with the opening of the roof hole during the singing of the *Veni Creator Spiritus*, to let in the Pentecostal symbols of a dove, a fiery globe, tongues of fire made of bits of burning tow, a censer, and the festive extras of flowers and flaky pastry.

Special effects men, who were to do such spectacular work in the late medieval theatre, were apprenticed to their craft in the late twelfth and early thirteenth centuries. Likewise stage managers, as plays expanded beyond their liturgical foundations and moved out of churches into church porches and yards, which could accommodate them better. Semi-liturgical dramas, like the raising of Lazarus and Herod's banquets, began to appear, as well as miracle and saints' plays, based on sermons and local saints' legends.

Miracle plays were single episodes, taken from the lives of gospel figures or local saints, and unlike mystery plays, they were not joined together to make liturgical cycles. Saints' plays featured some standard saints: the Virgin Mary, St Nicholas and St George were popular everywhere, and some local favourites: St Mary Magdalene was especially popular in Norfolk, St Thomas Becket in Canterbury and King's Lynn, St Christina in Kent.

But most plays were liturgical or semi-liturgical, part of the ever expanding cycle of Easter, and to a lesser extent, Christmas. Until the thirteenth century Christmas was very much the poor relation of Easter. Christmas tropes were choral celebrations of the Introit, not dramatic introductions. Perhaps the growing popularity of the crib forestalled any demand for Christmas drama. One of the few plays that did emerge was the shepherds' play, the Pastores, which featured Mary's midwives, angelic messengers and an ox and an ass, as well as the shepherds. Sometimes the Holy Family was represented by statues in a crib; sometimes all the parts were acted.

Plays related to Christmas were more popular than plays of Christmas itself. The prophets and the Magi, leading up to the birth of Christ, gave plenty of scope for dramatic expression. The prophets consigned people to fiery furnaces made of burning cloth and oakum fibre; Balaam rode in on an ass. The magi, in their *Tres Reges* (Three Kings) play, appeared by the light of stars in the sky, wearing magnificent costumes and crowns. In fourteenth-century Lincoln there was not only a *Tres Reges* play but also a more unusual one called the *Salutatio*, about the Visitation. The props for it included a star, a dove, and gloves for Mary, Elizabeth and the angel.

As the plays expanded, they needed more actors, space, props and costumes. The Beverley Resurrection play of 1220 was performed out of doors, probably in the churchyard, and had such a big audience that one member of it, a boy who could not see over peoples' heads, climbed up inside the church to one of the top windows. He fell off and lay as if dead, but was apparently miraculously restored to life by the play.

What finally made the miracle plays into a complete cycle, and moved them out of churches and into 'the city streets or in graveyards . . . where folks are glad to come' [William of Waddington] was the establishment of Corpus Christi as a universal feast in 1311. This gave the plays a summer focus, joined the Easter and Christmas cycles together, and finally made them into one self-contained cycle, performed at Corpus Christi, the first Thursday after Trinity Sunday. In the Catholic Church, it is a celebration of the ever present body of Christ, a dynamic feast tied only to the date of Pentecost, belonging to midsummer, and in the Middle Ages, to resplendent celebration. The Corpus Christi procession was led by a priest in his festive best: a silk cope, a rose garland on his head, the sacred host, fixed in a cross, carried in his covered hands beneath an elaborate canopy held up on staves by four acolytes.

In big churches like St Mary-at-Hill all the processing clergy wore garlands of red and white roses; there were garlands on the processional crosses and on all the statues in the church, which was hung with hawthorn and birch boughs and sweet woodruff.

The procession was flanked by torch and flag bearers, and washed down afterwards with wine and ale.

Sometimes the Corpus Christi plays were performed on the feast day; sometimes they were moved; at Chester they were moved to Pentecost, but still called the Corpus Christi cycle. Sometimes they were performed during the procession, when it paused for rest on the way round the town; sometimes afterwards. They were performed on pageants, or stages, which were either on wheels and followed the procession round, or built at 'stations' where the procession stopped to rest. By the late fourteenth-century the actors in the plays rode behind the procession, advertising the drama that would take place at the various processional 'stations'.

By this time mystery and miracle plays were town plays, written by local Benedictine monks or gild priests, performed by the citizens in churchyards, market-places and streets, and produced and financed by the gilds.

Nearly a hundred English towns and villages, some of them quite small, performed plays in the late thirteenth, fourteenth and fifteenth centuries. The tropes had been written in liturgical Latin, but the plays were written in racy, dialect English, understandable to everyone.

That is why the reforming and preaching friars were against them: the plays' colloquial techniques were pirated from them and the plays' dramatic techniques outdid those of the friars.

The most dramatic preachers preached outside from scaffold pulpits set up in churchyards, but now there were more dramatic stages. Procession sermons were taken over and made into plays. Lazarus's address in the Towneley play of that name is an almost word for word repeat of Bromyard's sermon on the fate of the dead. The four great mystery cycles, those of York, Chester, Beverley and Wakefield, the latter known as the Towneley plays, all had close affinities with verse homilies that had become popular literature, like the *Cursor Mundi* and *South England Legendary* stories.

Miracle plays aroused more hostility than mystery plays because 'players in the play which is commonly called a miracle use masks . . . Thus do the demons whose game is to destroy souls and lure them by sin.' [Bromyard] The Benedictines, from whose liturgy the plays had developed, and the parish clergy, in whose churchyards they were often performed, had a more sympathetic attitude than the reforming friars. They wrote and advised on the plays; they supported them as preferable to secular games and plays.

Plays were commonly performed by religious gilds, who had the necessary theatrical and financial resources. The number of religious gilds increased greatly in the fourteenth century, especially after 1311, when Corpus Christi gilds were founded all over the country. With clerical help, they were the intermediaries between clerical and secular, Latin and vernacular productions of the cycles. In 1300 the London gild of St Nicholas, whose members were parish clerks, performed miracle plays, probably about the local saint, Bartholomew, in the open, at Clerkenwell. The Abbot of Clerkenwell Abbey complained about the damage done to his fields and crops by crowds going to the plays, but they continued, and in 1348 the chroniclers reported elaborate performances of plays there, from four to seven days long, covering the whole Christian story from creation to judgement. To stage performances on this scale, trade and craft gilds joined with, then took over from, the religious gilds.

The gilds had a ceremonial image to keep up, and by the late fourteenth century had begun to do so by staging the plays. Minor and single plays continued to be performed in many places by informal groups and religious gilds, but cycle plays like the Beverley ones were performed by craft gilds and 'mysteries' (from the French *métier*, a craft, from which the name for this type of play may be derived).

Each gild was assigned a play appropriate to its craft. The water leaders and drawers in Dee, for instance, did the deluge; the Wakefield listers (dyers) did Pharoah because they could use their dyes to make the Red Sea red. There were some delightfully whimsical assignations: the Chester inkeepers and cooks did the harrowing of hell because they could use their pots and pans to make an infernal din.

As time passed, the number of plays increased and the cycles grew. When the Chester cycle was first produced outside, in about 1375, it was as one long, stationary play. By 1422 individual gilds were performing the plays separately. By 1429 the fishmongers were using a pageant wagon for their play, which meant that the plays were being performed processionally. By 1467 there were at least eighteen gilds there producing plays; by 1500 there were twenty-six.

York gave all its plays in one day, starting at 4.30 a.m. Some of them had to be shortened, and some dropped, to fit them in before dark, and the Corpus Christi procession itself was moved to the next day. The Beverley and Wakefield plays took three or four days, and completely overshadowed the procession that served as their vehicle. In smaller towns that did not have enough gilds for each to do a play, certain stations were used as stock sets such as heaven, hell and Nazareth, and adapted for others by the wheeling on of extra pieces of scenery, such as Noah's ark. Whenever possible, gilds shared pageants. In Chester the painters, coopers and skinners shared a pageant because they all needed one with a hill, and they performed on the first, second and third days of the festival respectively.

Stock stations and pageants were often placed close together so that the actors could move from one to another, say from Rome to Jerusalem, without much trouble. Moving pageants too were placed close together, to compress time and space. When they were not in use, they were stored in pageant houses, whence they could be wheeled out on occasions of display, such as civic pageants. At York they were stored in a line of buildings at Toft, backing on to the inner moat of the city walls, where they rotted away and got so infested with rats that the buildings became known as 'Ratton Rowe'.

They were two-storey carts, or wheeled houses, the top storey used for performance, the bottom one for changing. They were pulled by gangs of men, sometimes with horses to help. They were roofed, partly to protect them from the weather and partly because overhead effects were sometimes required, such as lightning or descending angels. The storeys were curtained, the bottom one to hide the off-stage actors, the top one to open and close scenes at need.

The scaffold actors on the upper storey often exchanged a

dialogue with the actors on the ground, the distance between them representing the difference between their stations in life. Streets, buildings, market-places, bridges and any other natural extensions to the sets were used to the full, and there were ladders giving easy movement from the heights to the depths, from the surrounds to the pageants.

Cramped sets made for ingenious scenery and special effects, provided by machinery. The Cornish plays used moving, working scenery, including 'two fair trees . . . and an apple upon the tree and some other fruit upon the other . . . a fountain and fine flowers . . . and fish of diverse sorts and certain beasts', to depict paradise.

Productions aimed to provide their audiences with 'figures', or working models. There were fire-making kits, to make lively figures of hell. Hell's mouth in the Coventry Domesday play required 'starch to make the storm, a barrell for the earthquake, a link [torch made of tow and pitch] to set the world on fire, and payment for setting it on fire, 5d.'

Christ's death was 'figured' with actual crucifixions, the actors in the York and Coventry plays being roped to a cross and hauled up on high. Props, like scenery, came to life when the figures demanded it. In the Towneley Cain and Abel play, Cain entered ploughing, and when he made his offerings a double blast of smoke issued from his fire. Oxen, asses, doves and ravens were common members of casts, but the camels and horses for the magi were a bit too ambitious, and were usually made of hoops, lathes and painted canvas. The magi were splendid enough without their animals. They borrowed finery from local nobles, and wore their crowns all the time; while they travelled and did homage; while they were awake and while they slept.

Headgear was important in every costume. Nothing showed a character's nature better than his hat. The tormentors often wore scarves tied round their heads, knotted at the back, to make them look like Saracens, the traditional enemies of medieval Christianity.

To a lesser extent, gloves too were characteristic. They were worn by the pure and gentle, in particular God, the Blessed Virgin and the angels. Costume as a whole symbolised good and evil.

174

Angels proclaimed their holiness simply by wearing white, sometimes with wings made of feathers and 'golden skins' (Coventry drapers). God dressed in white, sometimes with 'six skins of whiteled' (white leather; Coventry smiths 1451). Adam and Eve may also have worn the white of innocence: tight-fitting tunics that made them look as if they were naked, though in the Chester plays they did not bother. Instructions for the paradise play there included 'Then Adam and Eve shall stand naked and shall not be ashamed.'

Costuming evil characters was much more fun. The devil was a familiar figure in the medieval consciousness, and an old faithful in the mystery plays. He appeared as anything from the comic mischief-maker to the terrifying power of evil incarnate. He had as many names as forms, from Beelzebub to Satan, and as many costumes. To tempt Adam and Eve he, or rather she, dressed as a serpent, or worm, as the Medievals called it, often with an 'adder's coat' (Chester) on the bottom half and a 'virgin face and yellow hair upon her head' (Cornish). Occasionally he was feathered like a bird. Most commonly he wore the standard devil's uniform of a black leather tunic, black hair and a black mask. The devil was always masked, a grotesque figure from the ancient world of mime, the accursed outcast from heaven who dared not show his face before God and his angels, some of whom sometimes wore white masks to emphasise the contrast between them and their fallen associates.

There is a surviving list of stage properties, probably the earliest of all the surviving lists, for the Beverley play of 1391, which captures in a few words the importance and simplicity of medieval costume symbolism and the devices that accompanied it. These are the items the Beverley players required to stage the paradise and fall play:

> one car for the angel to descend from heaven,
> eight hasps, eighteen staples to fasten the gates of para-
> dise when Adam and Eve are driven out by the angel,
> two visers (masks),
> two wings angeli,
> one furspar (tree of knowledge),

one worm,
two pairs of shirts,
two pairs of linen stockings,
one sword.

for Adam and Eve,
when driven out.

The list is paradisical and simple. The mystery plays display more clearly than anything else from the Middle Ages the fusion of the natural and the supernatural, the simple and the sublime, that gave the period its essential unity. The plays are full of heavenly homeliness. When the exalted came down to earth, it did so with easy familiarity. The Chester shepherds approached the Christ-child with awe and terror, but as soon as they saw him lying in the manger, watched over by Joseph with his

beard like a bush of briars,
with a pound of hair about his face or more,

they relaxed and brought out their gifts: a bell, a flask, a pottage spoon and a cape. The lad Trowle offered a pair of his wife's old hose; four boys offered a bottle, a hood, a pipe and a nut-hook.

They talked about their flocks being in the fields near Chester. Locality is familiar in all but the York plays, and of all the localised characters the shepherds are the most at home and the most familiar. They are, in fact, real medieval shepherds transferred on to the stage. One of the main dramatic devices used to secure this effect was language. 'Hail, little tiny mop!' is one of the Towneley shepherds' greetings to the Christ child. Mak, the sheep stealer, talks about his wife bringing forth 'ilk year . . . a lakan [baby] – and some years two.' He and his companions argued about the weather, grazing rights and the evil state of the world, their own poverty in particular.

The shepherds were immediately recognisable because they sang, and singing was a traditional shepherds' art. In the same way, God always spoke majestically:

Methought I showed man love when I made him to be
All angels above like to the trinity;
And now in great reproof full low lies he.

[Towneley *Noah*]

Noah always spoke like a henpecked husband.

> As muck upon mould
> I wither away.

Noah's wife was always the henpecking wife, abusing and hitting her husband. Like Noah, she became a prototype: she of the shrewish wife, he of the henpecked husband; nagging women were called 'Noah's wife'; henpecked men were called 'old Noah'.

It was impossible to overact a prototype because whatever he or she did only strengthened his or her identity. Joseph was the prototype of the jealous husband, grumbling at having to leave home and trail all the way to Egypt, disbelieving the angel who tells him that Mary has conceived by the Holy Ghost, and moaning all the time about the trials of marriage to a paragon, and fatherhood of a child prodigy, and a strong-willed prodigy at that.

The fourth and final prototype gave the same relief that the comic devils gave from the deadly ones. Herod personified the raging tyrant. Sometimes his cruelty and tyranny were composed and calculating, sometimes frenzied and incoherent. When the latter was the case, the audience could relax and laugh at him because his excesses made him comic. Producers gave him plenty of scope for excess. He was always magnificently arrayed, so his rantings would be all the more degrading. Herod tearing his silver, gold and green finery to shreds, and breaking his glittering sceptre to bits in his fury was one of the highpoints of the Coventry cycle. The more he did it, the more his audience loved him, and hated him when he became coldly cruel.

His costume was always being repaired. In 1490 his rantings in Coventry earned him 3/4d. which was 1/4d. more than God, two shillings more than Peter and Malkus, and more than anyone else in the cycle except Pilate. Herod was a star part. He was probably played by different actors in the different plays in which he figured. Every gild wanted to produce a better Herod, Noah, God and any other major character than the next gild. The York cycle used twenty-four Christs in their plays of Christ's adult life alone.

It was tempting for actors to hire themselves out to as many companies as would take them. In 1476 the York city council imposed a fine of forty shillings on anyone who acted in more than two performances in one day. There was competition to get good parts. The council appointed 'four of the most conning, discreet and able players within the city, to search, hear and examine all the players and plays and pageants.' The actors were locals well known to the audience, who made heroes or fools of them, and with them their plays and gilds, on the strength of their performances.

By the late fifteenth century, standards were high and the acting business very efficiently run. Pageant masters were appointed to manage the plays. They hired actors and technicians, and supervised rehearsals and production. In 1391 a rope-maker called John of Arras became master of the full pageant in Beverley, for life. Good masters, like good actors, were much in demand, and if they were not being used by their own company, might hire themselves out to do a play for a different one. The Coventry smiths once hired the skinners' master, Thomas Coklow, to do their play for them. Hiring technicians and costumers from other companies was good sense and common practice; gloves were hired from glovers, scenery was painted by painters, and so on.

As the number of gilds keen to achieve play producing status increased, extra care was taken to keep up the overall standard, and by the late fifteenth century many of the gilds found the plays more onerous than honourable. They tried to get out of their obligation to stage them, but were forced to continue by the town council, for the sake of civic pride. Like all late medieval dramatics, the plays became more and more spectacular and expensive, and the gilds had to levy a tax of between 1d. and 4d. on all their members, to pay for them. This tax was known as pageant silver, and increased to keep pace with production expenses until some actors were paying a crippling four shillings, as in Beverley in 1490.

Worse, they could be fined if they acted badly. In 1452 a Beverley weaver called Henry Cowper was fined 6/8d. because he did not know his part on Corpus Christi day; 'because he was poor fourpence was taken from him, and the rest excused on condition of not doing it again.' But the disgrace could not be removed or excused.

The plays had become civic showpieces. Scenery, sets and costumes were lavish; banner bearers rode through the streets in advance of the pageants, announcing what would appear. Wealthy citizens watched from platforms raised above the streets, where most people stood to watch, or bid for the right to have a station fixed near their house, so they could watch from their windows or balconies. Watching became part of the performance. In 1457 Coventry scored a huge success when Queen Margaret of Anjou brought a retinue of lords and ladies to watch its plays. They stayed with a prominent citizen called Richard Wood, and watched all but the Domesday play from his house, nibbling green ginger, pippins (pippin apples), oranges and 'two coffins of comfits [sweet pastries]', for all to see. This was late medieval play going in style.

Miracle and saints' plays were produced in the same processional way as the mystery plays, and were also written or edited by clerics, who helped decide when farce and comedy had become too strident, and were obscuring the religious purpose of the plays. In 1431 the York masons complained that their play, about a character called Fergus at Our Lady's funeral, caused 'more laughter and clamour than devotion', and they were given Herod to perform instead.

Instruction was simple, to suit the audiences, but it also contained some sophisticated theology for the more sophisticated minority. Some of the scenes in the Chester plays, with their apocalyptic emphasis, were explained by an expositor, whose equivalent in the Coventry plays, the doctor, described his function thus:

To the people not learned I stand as a teacher
And to them that be learned as a ghostly preacher
That in my rehearsal they may have delectation.

The best plays had entertainment in their instruction, and figures for everyone.

Music advertised, brightened and heightened the plays.

Harps and psalteries heralded the entrance of angels; crashing drums and cymbals heralded earthquakes or raging tyrants. In the Chester *Cain and Abel* play, minstrels heightened the drama of the moment before Cain murdered Abel by playing music. Saints' plays contained even more music than mystery plays; when little was known about a saint, a lot was added by way of music, display and dramatic imagination.

Small towns that could not stage a whole cycle did single plays. Lincoln did a little cycle of the Assumption on St Anne's day, but it was more common to move or pick out a single play, and perform it on a saint's day or to mark a royal entry or court festivity. Popular plays might be taken on tour.

It is not known what kinds of theatre there were for their performance. Plays were given in Canterbury in the Gildhall, in Reading in the market-place, in Chelmsford in a 'pit', and in many places in churchyards and unidentified 'theatres of the city', like the one used in Exeter in 1348. The Lincoln cycle was staged in the cathedral nave in 1483, under the direction not of the city council but of the Dean and Chapter, and financed by voluntary subscription. There was as much variety of performance and management as there was of drama. In Leconfield, Leicester, Halstead and Winchester, plays were performed in church right up until the Reformation. The Cornish cycle lasted five days in 1384, a week in 1411, and was performed on local days of devotion, outdoors 'in the round.'

Officials known as stytelers guided and controlled the crowds so that they did not interfere with the drama being enacted in their midst. Town councils tried to help crowd controllers by passing laws against the bringing of weapons to plays, but enthusiasm always bordered on the riotous, and control was minimal.

The Cornish cycle included a number of morality plays, which were more sobering than miracle, mystery and saints' plays, but nonetheless lively and lavish. Where mystery plays were basically liturgical, and told the story of salvation, morality plays were basically homiletic, and told the way to salvation. They were dramatised sermons about the struggle between good and evil, and featured allegorical characters like Death, the World, Envy and Everyman.

The Church regarded the *Pater Noster* as its basic rule of life and the *Credo* as its basic rule of faith, and the first morality plays were based on these two rules, in particular the *Pater Noster*. This was the basis of countless sermons, meditations and instructions, and in the wake of Archbishop John of Thorseby's 1378 preaching campaign in York, was made the subject of the earliest recorded morality play in England: that of the York *Pater Noster*. By 1389 there was a gild of the Lord's Prayer in charge of producing the play, which seems to have developed into a series, if not a cycle. In 1411 there were nearly as many craft gilds in Beverley doing *Pater Noster* as there were doing cycle plays; in 1467 there were more, and the pageant stations assigned to them were the same, with one exception, as those assigned to the cycle plays in 1449.

It was not long before the struggle between the vices and the virtues expanded beyond its *Pater Noster* setting. In 1435, and every tenth year thereafter, a long creed play, written by a local priest, was substituted for the mystery cycle in York. 'Death, God's Messenger' was another morality theme. So was the Dance of Death, in which death danced with a representative of every rank of humanity, from pope to peasant. *Everyman* was a serious play about death and judgement, in a mood of lenten grimness; *Pride of Life* was like the Dance of Death, and described the 'game' played for the human soul by life and death.

But by the late fifteenth-century a reaction had set in against elaborate productions. The fashion was for short plays with few characters and little scenery, that could be played in private houses. In Henry VI's day high society watched the theatre from the streets, as ostentatiously as possible; in Edward IV's day it brought the theatre into its own homes. By the late fifteenth century, plays were part of the minstrelsy of a great hall. In 1465 the Durham monks had a 'player-chamber' at their Finchale cell. But it was more common to watch plays in the household hall.

A board-on-trestle table was set up in the middle of the floor, perhaps with a few bits of scenery. Or a space was cleared and a screen put up to make a backcloth. Or the household ate at tables round the edge of the hall, leaving the dais where they usually ate as a stage. Short plays, or interludes, were performed between meal courses, between meals and drinking parties, and between hunting and meal times.

In the fifteenth century there were more substantial house-holders than ever before, and they were keen to accommodate the new plays. In 1462 the mayor and most of the town council of King's Lynn spent the feast of Corpus Christi not watching a mystery play but 'being in the house of Arnuphe Tixonye . . . to see a certain play . . . three shillings paid for two flagons of wine.' Some of the plays performed by the touring troupe of New Romney and Harling in the fifteenth century were described in the accounts of the towns they visited as interludes, and seem to have been miniatures of mystery and saints' plays. In 1463 a 'play of the interlude of Our Lord's Passion' was performed at New Romney.

Interlude players did not earn much money because they did not do elaborate performances. They had only limited time and place to play in, the little scenery and costume they could carry around with them, and a few people in their troupes. The standard number seems to have been about five; four men and a boy, and if the play required more than that, the actors had to double parts. The Croxton *Sacrament* interlude toured with only six men, who 'play it with ease', though it had twelve parts. Most interludes were about a thousand lines long and lasted about an hour, but could be cut if preferred. Medwall's early sixteenth-century inter-lude, *The Four Elements*, was intended to take one-and-a-half hours 'but if you list you may leave out much of the said matter . . . and then it will not be past ¾hour of length.'

That was quite long enough for most audiences. *The Four Elements* was about the importance of devotion to study, and however fashionable the new renaissance devotion to classical learning, it did not make riveting drama. People who wanted that went to the big public plays. Schools like St Paul's and Eton, the Inns of Court and the Oxford colleges were the homes of learned, often classical, interludes. In 1512 Oxford granted a degree in grammar to one Edward Watson provided he composed a comedy for them.

Private householders preferred less academic entertainment,

and much of their drama included farce and Christmas minstrelsy. The distinction between plays, disguisings, minstrel shows and mimes had virtually disappeared by the end of the Middle Ages. Over Christmas 1427 Henry VI was entertained by the interludes of the Abingdon players and those of Jack Travail and his companions.

The gleeful commerce of the late Middle Ages seems to have benefited the travelling actor player more than the humble travelling minstrel, who responded by extending his repertoire to include some acting and take advantage of the welcome accorded to travelling actors. Sometimes players wrote their own interludes; sometimes they did plays written by members of the households they visited.

The last word on every kind of medieval drama should come from one of its plays; the last play of the Cornish mystery cycle, which covers the Christian story from creation to crucifixion and sums up the medieval enthusiasm for drama. At the end of the cycle, God welcomed the ascended Jesus into heaven, wearing robes the colour of his blood, to sit at his right hand until the end of the world. The cycle ended with these unmistakeably medieval lines:

And now his blessing on you every one.
Now let us all go to the side of home.
Now minstrels, pipe diligently,
That we may go to dance.

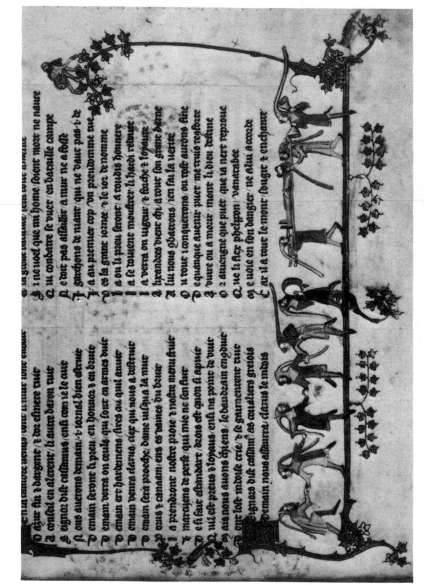

61 Mumming in long-tailed hoods. *Bodleian Library*, Oxford MS. Bodl. 264, fol. 129.

62 Mummers with beast's heads. *Bodleian Library, Oxford MS. Bodl.* 264, fol. 181v.

CHAPTER NINE

Folk Games

Drink was the basic ingredient of most medieval folk games. The English were notoriously fond of drinking, and 'drinking in parties was a universal practice', to the horror of the Norman chronicler, William of Malmesbury; 'in this occupation they pass entire nights as well as days.'

With the help of some good strong ale, most social occasions turned into parties and most meeting-places into drinking houses. Every village had its community drinking parties, which were known as 'ales', and it was only a short step from parish ales to parish festivals of all sorts, which the Church incorporated into its calendar. The Christian year was a round of festivals, rituals and games, with which the Medievals played away the grime of their working lives.

It was a hard-working year, starting with the spring sowings of corn in ground newly ploughed and harrowed after the long frozen winter. The best refuge in these conditions was a fireside and the best resource was drinking. Home and tavern drinking merged. When Reginald was Bishop of Durham in the twelfth century, he went to a drinking party given by one of the priests in his diocese which, he said, lasted most of the night and was attended by most of the parish. All that was needed to make a party like this into a tavern session was a licence to make and sell ale, and clergymen like the one who entertained Reginald were the first to get such licences.

Monasteries such as Canterbury and Gloucester that were big pilgrimage centres opened hostels for their pilgrims, whom they refreshed with monastic ale. Many of these hostels passed into independent ownership, and local women were licensed by their manorial lord or town council as ale and bread wives, running home or hostel refreshment centres. Many ale wives became pole wives, so called because inns were marked by poles or bushy branches hung out above their doors.

Alice the pole-wife, mentioned in the records of Ashton-under-Lyne in 1422, was one of countless medieval pole-wives. She provided a certain amount of lodging space, and a virtually unlimited amount of ale, for the wool merchants who came to the town's famous fair, and for the ever-thirsty locals who inhabited every medieval town. [Illustration 63]

An inn usually offered accommodation as well as drink, an ale-house just drink; a tavern might offer either, and it was the most common name for every sort of drinking place.

If thou hauntest to make thy play
At the tavern on the holiday,

warned Mannyng in his *Handling Sin*, 'It slay ye, either soul or life.'

Drinking in taverns after mass was a regular folk ritual, repeatedly and ineffectively condemned by reformers. Town constables were more realistic, and limited their efforts to preventing taverns from opening until mass was over. Early Sunday and holiday mornings, and after curfew night hours, were the only medieval closing times, and even these were impossible to enforce. Court rolls are full of convictions of 'nightwalkers' (curfew breakers) for haunting taverns after hours, getting drunk and losing their money dicing and hiring prostitutes.

Some of the taverns near Petergate and Goodramgate in fifteenth-century York were brothels specialising in the lesser clergy from the Minster, who appear constantly in the Minster's court rolls convicted of drunkenness, and usually debauchery as well.

All kinds of women drank in taverns. A Bohemian visitor to England in the fifteenth century, Nicholas von Popolan by name, was delighted by the tavern prostitutes he met. 'Their cry,' he wrote, 'is "Dear Master, whatever you desire, that we will gladly do."'

But prostitutes did not have a monopoly among their sex on tavern *bonhomie*. Eminently respectable city businessmen were always telling their wives not to get drunk in taverns. Poor and peasant women like the ones in the fifteenth-century song, *Wives at the Tavern*, thought it 'full good sport' to meet together in taverns and drink.

> Some be at the tavern once in a week;
> And some be every day eke.

Even nuns drank in taverns, though they were not supposed to. In 1489 Archbishop Rotherham wrote to the Prioress of Nunappleton in West Yorkshire 'that none of your sisters use the alehouse nor the waterside, where concourse of strangers daily resorts.' Their masculine brethren, especially friars, were notorious tavern haunters. Secular clergymen drank in taverns like they walked the streets and farmed their land, as part of their everyday parish life. Churchwardens did church business in taverns; the ones at St Mary-at-Hill spent small sums on 'Mr Alderman and others of the parish at the Sun . . . at the hiring of Balthazar the clerk, at the Sun tavern . . .' One of the most famous late medieval taverns was the Cardinal's Hat, which extended the whole way from the end of Lombard Street to Cornhill. Class was no drinking barrier, and in 1491 the St Mary churchwardens spent 17/11d. taking Lord Husey and Lord Bryant to drinks and supper there one evening.

Ale, and in the later Middle Ages beer, were the favourite tavern drinks, followed by cider, mead and, for the wealthier, wine. Most Medievals drank ale with their bread breakfast at dawn, and thought of eight o'clock as a lamentably late start for drinking. Drunkenness was their capital vice and they drank as they ate: enormously and with little variety. In *Piers Plowman* there is a tavern game called *New Fair*, in which a cobbler called Clement offers his cloak for sale, and it is bought by Hikke the hackneyman with his hood, plus a full cup of wine to make up the value of the cloak. Anyone disagreeing with this exchange as unfair was to be fined a gallon of beer. That was what the Medievals considered a drink worth winning. They drank gallons as people today drink pints.

Drinking was part of every medieval festivity, and since most festivals were religious, church ales were many and popular. They were organised by the parish clergy to make money. The priest provided cheap ale, which gave the church a small profit and the parish a good time. Most ales were on feastdays, such as Whitsunday, or on local saints' days. In 1489 the churchwardens of St Michael's, Bishop's Storford, made a big profit, £4/6/8d. from 'two drinkings called May ales'. Eight years later they restricted the drinking to the town's bachelors, and only made 35/4d.

They also held, like most churches, smaller ales for their local festivals and minor needs, either in the church or the churchyard. If the ale was connected with something going on inside the church, it would take place inside. There were no seats or pews in medieval churches until the late fifteenth century. Their empty floors, fringed with side chapels, altars, statues and pictures, made ideal drinking grounds. In 1491 there was a church ale, 'made to the use of the tabernacle', at Bishop's Storford, which probably took place near the new tabernacle it was helping to pay for.

Some priests held such elaborate ales that, as one of Henry VIII's Protestant advisers complained in 1544, 'with leaping, dancing and kissing thay maintain the profit of their church.' A few preferred not to hold ales at all, and only drank with their parishioners informally, at home and in taverns.

Often they collected money from 'gatherings', which were similar to ales but without any organised provision of ale. Like ales, gatherings took place on feast and holy days; they often accompanied church ceremonies and folk plays, and were held in churches and churchyards. The year of the tabernacle ale at Bishop's Storford, there was also a play of some sort, which featured a dragon, and was paid for by parish subscription and 'divers gatherings in the church which brought in 4/2d.'

There were umpteen secular ales and gatherings: gyst (manorial) ales, bridal, lamb, scot (tax), clerk and leet (court) ales. Some took place on village greens, or in the grounds of manor houses, but most took place in churchyards, which were the gathering grounds of every community. Processions, ales, gatherings, funerals, weddings, plays, dances, sports, markets and fairs followed each other in festive succession through medieval churchyards.

Churchmen enjoyed and encouraged churchyard celebrations

that emanated directly from church ceremonies, and tried to forbid any others. Churchwardens were always telling people to remove their poultry and washing from churchyards, but priests kept their muckheaps, and often their poultry too, in them. There were all sorts of odds and ends in hospitable churchyards. In 1468 a woman called Katherine Pocock died in York, and left in her will a black gown with fur on it to a blind widow living in the cemetery of St Mary's church, Castlegate. Hermits, anchorites, the helpless and the homeless were all churchyard occasionals.

Sermons were preached from churchyard scaffolds, listened to by congregations seated on the grass, leaning on the walls, and refreshed by cherries and nuts bought from salesmen walking up and down amongst them. It was in a sermon of this sort that the Dominican preacher, Étien de Bourbon, denounced the thirteenth-century faithful for singing lewd songs at holy places and dancing lascivious dances 'treading down the bodies of holy Christian folk in the churchyards.'

The use of churchyards as market and fair grounds was officially condemned, but often winked at because of its connection with feastday celebrations. Big processions went all round the parish before coming back to refresh themselve with festive ale, and sometimes a meal as well, in the churchyard. Piemen and fruiterers set up churchyard stalls on feast days and Sundays.

The best place to catch the hungry and thirsty faithful was just outside the church door, and the church porch was the parish gossip and refreshment centre. In 1387 the Master of St Thomas's hospital in Southwark 'appropriated a plot outside his church . . . he has built thereon two shops on the north side of the church porch.' But commerce as remote from religious ceremony as this was frowned upon by church and lay authorities alike.

In 1285 Edward I decreed that 'neither fairs nor markets be held in churchyards, for the honour of the Church.' But profit had a more apparent appeal than honour, and Sunday markets continued to be held right through the period.

Churchyard fairs originated in the same way as markets, but the refreshment they provided was more gleeful. The basic origin of both was wakes. Pope Gregory the Great instructed his missionaries to let the English 'on the anniversary of the dedication or on the martyrdom days of the holy martyrs whose relics are placed there, make tabernacles out of tree branches around those churches which were formerly heathen temples, and celebrate the solemnity with religious festivity.' The form of religious festivity the English chose was the wake. Food and drink sustained the Medievals better at prolonged prayer than anything else did, except perhaps song and dance, which were incorporated along with food and drinks into the enthusiastic celebration of wakes. Official disapproval was more formal than committed. As long as paganism was subsumed into Christianity, the exuberance of celebration could be to some extent winked at.

But games with clear pagan associations were forbidden, among them racing, lewd dancing and erotic games which had honoured local pagan deities. Gerald of Wales described some games which he saw played in the cemetery of St Elined's church, near Brecknock, on the feast of Elired, the local virgin saint, August 1st, in the mid twelfth century. They were pagan fertility mimes such as the Church's synods were always denouncing, but Gerald's disapproval seems mild, almost admiring. 'Men and girls . . . run into the cemetery enclosure chanting . . . they do representations, before everyone, with their hands and feet. One might see a hand form a plough, and another one drive an oxen with a whip . . . One might see . . . a woman untangling spun threads as if to make cloth . . . they take offerings up to the altar, then go back to their places, amazed.'

Wake mimes were usually more exuberant than that, and included all kinds of folk dances and masques, as well as hobbyhorse riding, a vaguely pagan game that was popular throughout the period. [Illustration 64]

By the end of the Middle Ages, wakes were shows, presented with the help of professional entertainers. In 1388 the wake at St Peter's, Cambridge, was enlivened by performing historiones. Local troupes often performed at wakes, which developed distinctive local characteristics reflecting the performing skills of the local population and the legends surrounding the local saint.

By the fifteenth century the wake at Cowley, near Oxford, had become famous as the country's cudgel play centre. The wake at Congleton, Cheshire, developed more directly in connection with its patron saint, who was St Peter ad Vincula. At midnight on August 1st three acolytes began the celebration of his feast day by putting belts hung with chains over their shoulders, and running through the streets. The jingling of the bells represented the clanging of St Peter's prison chains, and exhorted the faithful to watch and pray.

Refreshment and entertainment quickly made wakes into fairs. The St Mary's fair at Salisbury was still being held in the cathedral precincts, where it had originated as a wake, in the fifteenth century. But most fairs moved out to open spaces nearby, and some never had church associations in the first place; they were the outcome of markets and royal grants. But even they had associations with the local saint; they were often held on his or her feast day. In Hedon, near York, the relics belonging to St Augustine's church were carried through the town several times a year, and on St Mary Magdalene's day, July 22nd, up through the middle of the fair being held on Magdalene Hill.

Religious processions apart, travelling shows were usually unwelcome at fairs. There were enough local minstrels, buffoons, jugglers and tricksters without outsiders arriving to threaten the perilously high-spirited peace. Constables and bailiffs patrolled fairs, to try and keep the peace, and wandering performers and vagabonds were one of their biggest headaches.

In 1325 the bailiffs of St Ives fair in Cambridgeshire fined one of its stallholders, Richard Brewhouse, sixpence because he 'received merry-andrews into the midst of the fair, to the disturbance and peril of the merchants.' Thirteen years earlier the fair had been disrupted by a band of frenzied carollers, and nine years before that by a group of unruly local knights who tried to stage a tournament as a closing ceremony. Lepers from the nearby Stourbridge leper hospital used to include the St Ives fair in their illegal begging circuit of Cambridgeshire fairs. Little bands of sick, beggars, gleemen and pickpockets did annual circuits of fairs, sometimes over considerable distances.

So did prostitutes. On a single day in 1287 the fair bailiffs fined sixteen prostitutes sixpence each. Most of them claimed to be bath attendants, which was the usual medieval cover for prostitutes, but one of them was proud of her profession, and called herself by the evocative name of Dulcia (the sweet one) of Oxford. She had travelled a wide circuit to grace St Ives with her fair favours. [Illustration 65]

During big fairs, shops nearby were forbidden to open for business, there were sports on surrounding commons, and church processions and ridings to watch. The monks of St Werburg's in Cheshire used to perform mystery plays for the people going to the fair there.

Feast days often coincided with fair days, and were the high-points of the local year. Religion being the lifeblood of medieval Christendom, the Church was captive to criticism, familiarity bred festive contempt, and the typical parish festival, whether religious, civic or both, was a mixture of good humour and irreverence.

There were innumerable processions, ridings and pageants in medieval towns, as well as re-enactments of martyrdoms and local incidents of history, all of them individually characteristic but at the same time with features in common. Pilgrimages took their individual characteristics from the saints they honoured, but they all had a festive purpose, whether their associations were penitential, longsuffering, healing or light-hearted. They were a group quest for grace, and when the pilgrims had visited and prayed for grace at the shrine of their choice, they wore badges to prove it: palms, gloves, ears of wheat, cockle shells and simple initialled buttons.

Pilgrims with badges were members of a folk élite. Pilgrims setting out were members of a band united by singing and story telling, eating and drinking, praying and listening to sermons, and staying in pilgrim inns on their journey. Some identified their membership of this band by wearing pilgrim uniform: a slavein (long, coarse tunic), a long staff with a metal toe, and a scrip (shoulder-bag). For many Medievals, pilgrimage was their only chance to travel any distance, and they banded together to make the festive best of it.

Weddings were similar folk celebrations. Bishop Richard Poore of Chichester decreed that weddings should be celebrated 'reverently and not with laughter and sport or in taverns or at public potations or feasts.' To rule out drinking altogether would have been unthinkable. The Hereford Missal advocated the drinking of hot ale at weddings, from a cup blessed by a priest, with pieces of wafer cake immersed in it. The better off sometimes chose wine instead. The festive cup, like the bridal kiss, was intrinsic to every wedding.

As soon as the married couple came out of the church, into the churchyard, the celebration became public, and little offerings were thrown over them at the church door: money if the family was wealthy; ears of wheat, symbolising plenty and fertility, if the family was poor. Oliver de Bordeaux and Lady Maud Trussel were showered with money 'during the celebration of their nuptials, at the door of the chapel within the park at Woodstock.' Beggars gathered at church doors in case they could catch some of the money, or beg some off the guests. As the party became public, bridal ales were drunk and all the church bells rung.

They were all rung at funerals too, and one of them at the moment of death, when a soul passed from this life to the next, which is why they were known as passing bells. The parish was supposed to pray for the passing soul, and the whole parish would go to the funeral, and to the wake in the home of the deceased the night before it. A thirteenth-century Church council forbade 'singing, games and choruses while a dead person lies in the house.'

Parishioners were usually buried on the south side of the church, the cold north side left empty as the devil's quarter. There were no gravestones until the later Middle Ages. Only a cross in the south corner distinguished the cemetery from the rest of the churchyard. Though tradition has it that King Arthur was buried in a tree trunk, and though Abbot Warin of St Albans directed in the twelfth century that his monks should be buried in stone coffins, most medieval corpses were simply wrapped in strong cloths, made of linen if the family was quite well off, made of a religious habit if the deceased was a monk or nun, and made of rough canvas if the family was poor. Monastic graveyards were often north of the abbey church, planted with flowers and shaded with trees, watched over by a crucifix, and often with a cross marking each grave. They were as quiet and secluded as parish graveyards were populated and busy.

On funeral days, graveyards were full of people holding bunches of flowers, sprigs of evergreen, especially bay laurel and, in the later Middle Ages, rosemary for remembrance. As the corpse was lowered into the ground, the sprigs were thrown in with it, or perhaps roses, or if the corpse was that of a child or a virgin, white flowers symbolic of purity. The funeral procession often went round the whole parish.

The hearse was made of human hands, a bier, a horse's back, or some sort of cart. The word hearse comes from the French herse, meaning a harrow, and early hearses were harrow-like spiked frames fitted with candles. The bier fitted over the corpse while it lay in church, and was sometimes carried to the grave with it: 'a hearse shall be put about the body with thirteen square wax lights burning at the *Placebo* [Vespers in the Office of the Dead] and the dirge and mass. And there shall be four angels and four banners of the Passion, with a white border, and scutcheons of the same powdered with gold, and offerings shall be made; and as many masses shall be said for the soul of dead as there are brethren and sisters in the gild' [Funeral instructions of the fifteenth century Gild of the Resurrection in Lincoln].

Christenings, solemn blessings and church proclamations or Civic proclamations were celebrated with gregarious enthusiasm as parish events. The privilege of sanctuary at Durham was the biggest and most famous in the north of England, and anyone claiming it was given a black gown with the yellow St Cuthbert's cross on the left shoulder, a grate to sleep on, and food and bedclothes for thirty-seven days, in the south-west corner of the cathedral nave. Admittance to the privilege was proclaimed by the tolling of the great Galilee bell over the north porch; it was a privilege that belonged equally to church and town.

Church festivals often coincided with folk and town festivals. Many of them were careful to do so; the Church took over the old fertility festival of first spring, and Christianised it as Plough Monday, celebrated on the Monday after the Epiphany. Ploughmen decked out a 'fool plough' and dressed up in festive colours to drag it round the village lanes, preceded by a Betsy, a fool, and in the later Middle Ages, Morris dancers. On their way round, they collected money with plough ales and gatherings, to pay for the 'plough lights' they burnt before the statues of their favourite saints in church. The procession ended with a blessing in church, and a play or mumming about wooing and marriage, or about the death of the old and the birth of the New Year, in the churchyard. The sowing and growing season had begun.

But not yet the season of warmth and light; there was still a long way to go until spring. Candlemas, celebrated on February 2nd, was a festival of light, banishing the winter darkness from the fields and from souls alike, looking forward to spring. There was a candle-lit procession before mass, and the candles were held alight during mass until the Offertory.

The approach of spring meant Lent, for which the final preparation was Shrove Tuesday. Shrove was the Old English word for shrive, to confess; Shrove Tuesday was the last chance to confess before Lent began. For those in religious orders and for the devout laity, it was also the last chance to eat meat. Church bells rang before dawn to wake people in time to be shriven. The last scraps of meat from the winter stores were chopped up and made into pancakes, the traditional carnival dish.

Apprentices celebrated less austerely. They had a holiday, and spent it horse- and foot-racing, playing football or cock-fighting. Some of the more boisterous Shrove Tuesday sports developed into riots, even political rebellions. In 1443 there was a start-of-Lent celebration in Norwich in which, according to the chronicler, 'John Gladman . . . made a disport with his neighbours having his horse trapped with tinsel and otherwise disguising things . . . afore him each month disguised after the season thereof, and Lenten clad in white with red herrings and his horse trapped with oyster shells after him, in token that sadness and absence of mirth should follow and an holy time; and so rode in diverse streets of the city . . . making mirth and disport and plays.' These soon turned into an uprising known as 'Gladman's Insurrection.'

People played hard at Shrovetide because Lent was a grim season, religiously, socially and, often, climatically. Religiously, it began the day after Shrove Tuesday with a mid-afternoon procession to be ashed, followed by a penitential mass. Socially, it was austere, with relentless sermons and no marriages. Climatically, it often brought the worst February and March weather.

Any relief was welcome, but it was not until the late fourteenth century that St Valentine's day was celebrated with seasonal wooing songs on February 14th. Chaucer first mentioned St Valentine's day as the one 'When every bird cometh there to chose his mate'. [*Parliament of Fowls*] By the fifteenth century it was established at court as a feast of love poetry competitions and games.

When March 1st was a Sunday it was much more widely celebrated, because it was often mid-Lent or Simnel Sunday. The word simnel is probably derived from the Latin *simila*, meaning fine flour, or possibly from the Anglo-Saxon ʃymbel, meaning a feast or banquet: it was the day for breaking the Lenten fast with cakes made of fine flour, and any sweet bits and pieces that had survived storage. 'Farthing simnels' were standard mid-Lenten fare by the thirteenth century.

March 25th was the feast of the Annunciation, Lady Day, a great medieval favourite, and the official new year's day, in the eyes of the Church and of the Law, until the late seventeenth century. It was a rent day and a high spring festival, celebrated with votive masses to Our Lady in flower filled churches.

Palm Sunday marked the beginning of the end of Lent, and began Holy Week, which neared its Easter climax on Maundy Thursday, as spring softened into warmth. Maundy is a corruption of mandate, and the feast commemorates the Lord's command to his apostles to wash the feet of others as he had washed theirs. The Medievals carried out his maundy with alms giving and processions, and it became a popular folk festival. Ever since Anglo-Saxon times it had been the custom of monastic brethren not only to wash each other's feet but also the feet of as many poor folk as there were monks in the monastery. The King and Queen soon imitated this custom on behalf of the secular world, washing the feet of thirteen subjects, representing Christ and the twelve apostles. In 1212 King John gave '14/1d. in alms to thirteen poor persons, each of whom received 13d. at Rochester, on the Thursday of the Lord's supper.' It was the thirteenth year of his reign.

Church altars were stripped and washed, the Blessed Sacrament being removed to an 'altar of repose'. But at least one Medieval was determined to turn the focus from sacrifice to feasting, and commemorated the Lord's last supper by stipulating in his will in 1491 that the churchwardens of his parish, St Andrew Eastcheap, should spend 'five shillings each Holy Week entertaining people in St Clement's parish who were at variance with each other, to beget brotherly love among them.' If there were no such people, they were to 'entertain the parishioners in a tavern on the day of Our Lord's supper'.

Next best after a tavern supper or drinking session was a procession, and the Durham monks had one every day of Holy Week until Good Friday, when processions consisted simply of 'creeping to the cross', to kiss the feet of the crucified Saviour. Churches were bare. In the afternoon, Easter sepulchres were buried, to be watched until Easter Sunday morning. In 1483 the watchers at St Augustine's, Hedon, were supplied with 'faggotts' by the churchwardens, probably to make torches, but possibly to make a fire to keep them warm.

As darkness fell on Easter Saturday, the mood became excited. The Paschal candle, wound round with evergreens, was lit, to provide a point of light in a dark church. At Durham it was so massive that it had to be lit through a hole in the roof, and stood on a stand decorated with metal flowers and smaller candles. There had been a festival in honour of the spring goddess Eostre in pagan times, and in honour of the Passover among the Jews. Both these, together with the feast's pagan name, were taken over by the Christians. Easter was always an elemental spring festival, its date fixed according to the moon and the spring equinox, its ceremonies centering on the ritual blessing of fire and water. It was a great folk festival.

As well as sepulchre plays, there were Easter miracle plays, especially in the north of England. At their simplest they were no more than 'liftings' in imitation of the resurrection: on Easter Monday the men of the parish lifted the women into the air three times; on Easter Tuesday the women lifted the men. At their more sophisticated, they were Peace Egg plays or mummings.

People of every class gave Easter eggs as presents, sometimes dyed green, the colour of longevity and hope. Eggs were ancient symbols of new life, and were eaten as a final farewell to meatless Lent. Easter Monday was the first day of the after-Easter festive season and was a sports day all over the country. Lower clergy played hand-ball against their superiors, and girls played it against boys. Chester has long been famous for its Easter Monday football matches. Its sheriffs also organised an early morning archery match, after which they ate a communal breakfast of calves' heads in the town hall.

From Easter until the Saturday after Whitsun was a festive season. Paschal candles burned during every mass; priests wore white vestments; churches were hung with spring flowers and branches of evergreen.

Two weeks into these festivities came Hocktide. It was a two-day folk festival, and one of the most vigorous of the year. Tradition holds variously that hocking commemorated Ethelred's victory over the Danes, and an ensuing massacre, the death of Hardicanute and the accession of Edward the Confessor, and simply an old Easter custom. The last may well be the true tradition, Hock Monday and Tuesday being fixed as the second Monday and Tuesday after Easter; the money collected on them was given to the Church.

On Hock Monday women tied up any man they could catch, and only released them if they paid a fine. On Hock Tuesday it was the mens' turn. The women always collected more than the men. Perhaps they had less money to forfeit; perhaps they tied up their victims more efficiently, or perhaps they were allowed to buy their liberty with kisses. Hocking was popular with everyone from the thirteenth century, if not before. Edward I was 'taken in bed' by ladies of the court 'on the morrow of Easter' and made to pay a forfeit. In April 1464 Sir John Howard was caught and bound while riding home, and paid '16d. in hocking at Sudbury.' When he got safely home to Stoke Neyland, he gave '12d. to the hock-pot.'

In 1498 the churchwardens at St Mary-at-Hill rewarded the women there for their superior efforts at hocking with a hock supper of two ribs of beef, bread and ale. Several churches gave hock suppers, usually for hockwives. Hockdays were always ebullient and alcoholic; often they were rough too. In 1406 the London city council banned hocking 'within house and without', and when they repeated the ban three years later they classed hocking with football and cock-threshing as criminally extortionate.

As spring reached its height, the Church celebrated a series of rogation days. Priests led their congregations round the parish boundaries on the Monday, Tuesday and Wednesday before Ascension Day, asking God's blessing on the earth and the harvest to come. They carried shrines and relics, and sometimes symbols that were both pagan and Christian, like the dragon carried in the 1439 Ripon Ascension procession, and they sang litanies to God and the saints. Rogations were a mixture of primitive pagan and Christian prayers, magic rites and the traditional beating of the parish bounds.

Ascension Day was sometimes known as Bounds Thursday. It often fell close to the date of St Mark's Day, April 25th, which was celebrated with Lesser Litanies, following the Greater Litanies of the rogations. In some parts of England, notably Lincolnshire, it was customary to celebrate St. Mark's Day with a midnight vigil in the church porch, which was supposed to be rewarded with a vision of the ghosts of all those who would die during the coming year, walking silently past. The first touch of summer magic was in the air.

On Mayday it took hold of everyone, and there were victory celebrations for the fertile season of summer. The Medievals danced the old fertility and phallic dances of the Druids and Romans around Maypoles which they dragged in from the woods by means of oxen hung with flowers and with flowers tied to their horns, as had been the custom on the Roman feast of Floralia. The parishioners of St Andrew the Apostle, Cornhill, erected such a tall maypole before the church on May morning that the church became known as St Andrew under Shaft. Our Lady of the May was a new queen but an old goddess, honoured with old rites, of which the Church was, not surprisingly, apprehensive.

Grosseteste, the Oxford theologian, rebuked the clergy for joining in 'maying' in rural areas. They collected branches and flowers from the countryside to decorate altars, churches, maypoles and doorways. Everyone from courtier to cottager went maying, and most of them joined in the dancing, drinking and debauching that accompanied it. [Illustration 66]

'Mayers' danced in couples, processions and whole villages round the maypoles and through the streets, for prizes of rush rings, garlands and promises of marriage. Processional dances were often led by a hobby-horse rider like the 'May's child' at St Andrew Hubbard's, Eastcheap, whom the churchwardens paid twopence in 1459 'for dancing with the hobby-horse.' Summer was welcomed in dance and mime, probably to the tunes of shepherds' airs and songs, sometimes with the help of minstrels. There may have been plays about Robin Hood, established by the later Middle Ages as the King of the May.

The festivities took place at traditional nature shrines: trees and wells. For centuries there was a great old oak about three miles from Great Ilford, in Essex, near the town's Maypole Inn; the May games took place under the oak, and the attendant drinkings in the inn.

Whitsun usually followed close on Mayday, and was a great summer feast at court.

Trinity Sunday, shortly after Whitsun, is said to have been established as a feast by St Thomas Becket soon after his consecration. Wherever Becket was popular, it was celebrated with childrens' processions. The following Thursday was Corpus Christi, the great summer procession day. Midsummer Eve is on June 23rd, the summer solstice, an ancient feast-day and the one chosen by the Church to be the feast of one of its most important saints, John the Baptist. Greenery was hung round doorways, the favourite countryside plant being St John's wort. Some townsmen defied the law and cracked the street paving to plant little trees in front of their houses, in tribute to the season's growth. Lanterns were lit, and in many towns bonfires too, outside entrance doors. In 1409 the corporation of London decreed that every householder was to keep a barrel of water in front of his house, and an iron crook suitable for pulling down burning thatch. Every ward was to have a fire alarm horn. Wealthy Londoners set out tables before their front doors, next to their bonfires, to feast their neighbours. The old gods of fire and fertility held brilliant sway.

One of the friars in Winchelsea Priory in the fifteenth century described the St John's Eve celebrations he saw nearby one year. They included all the usual feasting, drinking and dancing, and the distinctively sun-worshipping games of torchlit processions, flaming wheels being rolled down hills, and bonfire leaping, and the distinctively fertility-seeking ones of adorning with flowers, divining the future, bathing in hot water, and what the friar discreetly described as sex rites. Some of these could be given a Christian interpretation: priests dedicated midsummer fertility fires to St John the Baptist because he was a bright, shining light preparing the way for Christ in a dark world. But the coating was thin. Bonfires are much older than Christianity, and are so called because in the days when they were used to scare away evil spirits, they were often made of bones, to add to their power. Jumping through flames might be symbolic of expiating one's sins, but it was traditionally a rite of Moloch and Baal.

On St John's Eve, homes and churches were hung with St John's wort, trefoil, rue, roses and vervain, symbolic of the patron saint, the trinity, grace, Our Lady and herbal cure-alls. Girls pulled the petals off these old love flowers to see how many loves they would have; they wore bunches of them in their hair and threw them into fires, to help them win love; they bathed in petal baths, to ensure fertility.

But the most spectacular midsummer game was the midsummer 'marching' or 'watch', with its midnight procession. The city watch, or band of waits, was sworn in for the year after a festive wake. An Oxford inquest in 1306 heard how 'on Thursday the eve of St John last past, the tailors of Oxford and other townsfolk with them held a wake in their shops the whole night through, singing and making their solace with citherns, fiddles and divers other instruments, as the use and custom is to do there on account of the solemnity of the feast.' Solemnity but not sobriety; after midnight the tailors 'held their dances in the High Street', and in the course of them fought with a clerk called Gilbert of Foxlee, who struck at them with his sword. The tailors responded in good midsummer style: one of them wounded him in the right arm with a sword, one in the back with a misericord, one on the head, and one in the left leg, inflicting a wound four by two-and-a-half inches, of which Gilbert died later, with a spar-axe.

Some midsummer watches and wakes were quieter. 'Paid to four men to watch with the Mayor and to go with him at nights 16d.' is a typical midsummer accounts entry, in this case from the London accounts of 1460. The inaugural 'going' or 'going about' of the waits was followed by the Mayor and Corporation, lit by cresset and torch bearers, and accompanied by music, dancing and pageantry. In Coventry the Mayor, Corporation and craft gilds processed round the town in scarlet and velvet robes, carrying huge straw figures of giants which they burnt in bonfires. The streets were hung with flowers and birch boughs, and there was an orgy of eating and drinking which went on into the next day.

After a start like this, high summer was relatively quiet, with only local feast days. Everybody was busy cutting hay and preparing for the harvest. June 29th was the feast of Saints Peter and Paul, and many people left their midsummer decorations up for this feast too. July 2nd was St Thomas Becket's day, and in Cornwall there were 'Bodmin ridings' in his honour on the Sunday and Monday after it. Becket was the most popular martyr saint in medieval England, and there were processions, plays, pilgrimages and pageants in his honour all over the country.

July 15th was St Swithun's Day. He was a popular Anglo-Saxon saint, and some churchwardens' accounts record 'gatherings and the collection of St Swithun's farthings.' In 1534 the townsmen of Worcester did a 'show of St Swithun's,' which Prior More rewarded with a tip of 20d.

St Kenelm's Day, July 17th, was also a big day in Worcester, since Kenelm came from Clent, in the parish of Hales Owen, Worcestershire. A wake was held there in his honour every year. July 25th was St James's Day, celebrated in many places with wakes and parties. August 1st was what is nowadays called a national or bank holiday. Everyone went to the loaf-mass, which gave the day its nick-name: Lammas Day, to offer up the first loaf made of the new corn. Sometimes servants were given a pair of new gloves, or the money to buy a pair, on Lammas Day. One of the cellarers at Bury Abbey used to give his clerk 2d.

glove-silver, his cowherd 1d., his granger (barn-keeper) 11d., and his squire 11d.

August was a feverishly busy month. Women and children helped with the harvesting, and the biggest festival was the movable one of Harvest Home, when the last wagon of corn was brought into the barn amidst singing, dancing and drinking. The pressure of harvesting over, people played boisterous games. They did the same after hay cutting, when landlords released a sheep into a field of stubble for the labourers to catch if they could, fortified by bread and beer.

The Assumption was the big August feast. It was celebrated on August 15th, which was often just about the date of Harvest Home, and people took bundles of herbs, fruits and vegetables to church, to offer them up in thanks and to ask for blessings on them, as they had done with the first corn on Lammas Day.

August 24th was the feast of St Bartholomew, and the climax of the huge international fair named after him for which Rahere, Henry I's jester, had been granted licence by his king in 1133, after his retirement from royal service and his foundation of St Bartholomew's Priory, Smithfield. Naturally, St Bartholomew was popular in London; less so elsewhere. The monks of Crowland Abbey, Lincolnshire, used to hand out little knives on his feast day, in memory of the knife with which he was flayed.

St Giles, whose feast day was September 1st, was more popular. In the later Middle Ages he was one of the most popular saints in Europe; over 150 churches were dedicated to him in Britain alone. He was the patron saint of cripples and down-and-outs, and one of his biggest churches in England was St Giles Cripplegate, in London. He probably won this attribution because he protected a pet hind which he kept near his hermitage in the woods outside Arles, in Provence. One day, when the king was hunting there, he came upon St Giles sheltering the hind in his arms; it had been pierced by one of the king's arrows. From that time on, people prayed to St Giles, and made pilgrimages to his shrine, on behalf of the wounded and crippled.

More important and more popular still was St Cuthbert, the patron saint of Durham and pretty well the whole of the Celtic north-east, which he had helped to convert to Christianity. Over much of the north of England Cuthbert was supreme. He had two feast days: one on March 20th and one on September 4th, commemorating the transference of his remains from Lindisfarne to Durham. Both were festive occasions in the north. The Nevills tried to inaugurate a new custom at Durham for the feast on September 4th. They took a freshly caught stag to the cathedral church and presented it to the Prior, requesting a feast from him in return. The Prior and his monks refused the request, the Nevills tried to force their way in, the monks defended themselves with heavy candles, and the custom was abandoned. St Cuthbert was honoured enough without being used as the patron of an ambitious family.

September 8th was the birthday of the Blessed Virgin, a religious and gently romantic feast marked by votive masses offered in churches full of late summer flowers. Summer began to give way to Autumn on September 14th, Holyrood (Holy Cross) Day, when it was customary to go out nutting. It gave way completely on September 29th, when the new accounting year and rent-term began. In agricultural administration, Michaelmas was New Year's day. Festively, it was the day to eat a Michaelmas goose. Sometimes the two were combined, tenants like John de la Hay of Lastres, Herefordshire, presenting their landlords with rents like '20d. and one goose fit for his lord's dinner on the feast of St Michael the Archangel' (1470).

Shoemakers had a holiday on their patron Saint Crispin's Day, October 15th. Crispin and Crispinian were third-century converts to Christianity, who were reputed to have made shoes and sold them to the poor at low prices, to support themselves while they preached the gospel. The leather was supplied by an angel. They were martyred under Maximian, and honoured by shoemakers everywhere in the Middle Ages; in Britain especially at Faversham in Kent, where local tradition has it that they fled from persecution.

Almost every craft had a patron saint, as did almost every town, village, community and individual. A patron saint's day was like a birthday, and was celebrated like one.

Less personal feast days were less personally celebrated. When the shoemakers had finished celebrating St Crispin's Day, they joined in the general celebration of All Hallows' Eve, in preparation for the feast of All Hallows, or All Saints, the next day. There were bonfires to fend off evil spirits, and it was the day when the fires in monastic warming-rooms were lit for the winter. The next day, November 2nd, was All Souls' Day, and began winter with a remembrance of the dead. Churches rang their passing bells to call people to masses for the dead. Women baked soul-mass cakes and gave them to the poor. It was the feast of the forgotten.

Martinmas, nine days later, was the last feast before fresh provisions ran out, and the last chance to stock in winter ones. The wealthy tasted the new wine just harvested and drawn from the lees. They killed their stock and hung, salted and pickled their meat. They ate fresh fat geese. Everyone dried peas, beans and herbs for winter use. Just as Candlemas was an end-of-winter rent-day, so Martinmas was a start-of-winter one, and the checking of the Michaelmas accounts for the year was completed. The York Corporation made Martinmas a really festive corporation day, with a procession second only to the one they held at Corpus Christi.

St Brice was celebrated in Lincolnshire as the patron saint of bull running, on November 13th, St Clement was celebrated by mariners, on November 23rd; he was said to have been martyred by being lashed to an anchor and thrown into the sea. St Catherine, whose feast day was November 25th, was immeasurably more popular than either of these two. Her feast day was the high point of November. She was the patron saint of spinsters, the many medieval women who spun wool at home, and they took the day off in her honour. The first recorded saint's play in England was in honour of St Catherine, staged by an Anglo-Norman schoolmaster called Geoffrey, who borrowed the costumes from the nearby monastery of St Albans. St Catherine's appeal never dimmed. In 1490 the Coventry gilds did a 'play of St Catherine given in the Little Park' as well as their Corpus Christi cycle. On her feast day women and girls processed to her shrines and altars, carrying wheels, doves and images of Christ, in memory of the Catherine wheel on which she was tortured and the doves who are said to have fed her in prison.

The last day of November is St Andrew's Day, and it shared with St Catherine's Day something of a reputation for being a time to foresee the future, a piece of old pagan magic that gave it the same sort of support as the cult of the returning dead gave to All Souls. The Church welcomed all the support it could get at this time, when the month of preparation for Christmas was dauntingly close.

Advent was first mentioned at the Council of Tours in 567, when it was declared a fasting season for monks. By the seventh century it was a fasting season for the whole Church, so that by the time Christmas came, 'for lack of meat we were nigh dead . . . from stinking fish not worth a louse' [fifteenth-century carol].

Christmas was first celebrated in the Eastern Church, as an aspect of the Epiphany, one of their most important festivals. It was celebrated in Rome before 336, and quickly spread through Western Europe. It is hard to tell whether the Celtic Christians in Britain made much of Christmas, but Augustine of Canterbury certainly did; on Christmas Day 598 he baptised the chroniclers relate, over 10,000 Christian converts. In 1043 the Anglo-Saxon chroniclers referred for the first time to Christmas, rather than the Nativity, Midwinter Mass or Midwinter. Christmas meant the twelve days between the Nativity and the Epiphany, not just Christmas Day. This was a slack time, with little work in the fields, and had been a festive respite for the Romans and Anglo-Saxons; the latter called it Yuletide. The Christian Christmas was probably fixed on December 25th because that was the middle of the Roman winter solstice, the birthday of the unconquered sun, and of the northern Yuletide. Like Easter, Christmas had good pagan foundations.

On to these the Church built the preparatory season of Advent and the fun-loving feast of St Nicholas, the patron saint of children and Christmas burlesques. From the eleventh century onwards, St Nicholas was one of the most popular saints of Western Christendom; later he became Father Christmas. The legend of his saving three girls from prostitution by throwing three bags of gold, to pay their dowries, through their father's window at night, merged with later legends of his saving three murdered children by restoring them to life. Merchants, sailors and pawnbrokers claimed his patronage, and his feast day was celebrated with the giving of gifts, the mumming and acting of plays and the games of Masters of Revels and Boy Bishops.

Even when gift giving was moved from St Nicholas's Day to Christmas Day, in the later Middle Ages, it was still St Nicholas who brought the gifts. His feast day was a first taste of Christmas.

As far as food and drink were concerned, the Christmas taste was indulgently meaty and alcoholic. After a dry and salty Advent, everyone's idea of a feast was fresh meat and beer. Even the few who had to work on Christmas Day had a bit of a feast. One thirteenth-century Somerset manor entitled its shepherd to a white loaf and a dish of meat on Christmas Day, and his dog a loaf too. Bishop Swinfield celebrated the Christmas of 1289 at Prestbury more splendidly, with what his accounts describe as 'great brewing'. His household was issued with clean linen, to mop up the grease from their three meat meals, an 'unscored' amount of beer and red wine, and just a little white wine.

Opulent eaters like Swinfield often gave pride of place on their Christmas table to the traditional boar's head, the boar being the old sacred animal of the Norsemen and the centrepiece of their Yule feast. One of the most popular late medieval carols was the boar's head carol. Henry III was a gargantuan feaster, just the man for boars' heads. In 1247 he kept Christmas at Winchester Castle with '48 boars, with heads entire', 1,900 fowls, 500 partridges 'put in paste (pastry)', 41 swans, 48 peacocks, 260 hares, 24,000 eggs, 300 gallons of oysters, 300 rabbits, 'as many birds, whitings and conger eels as could be had, . . . 100 mullets fat and heavy' and £27/10/- worth of bread, at a time when bread cost a farthing a loaf. The 'fowls' eaten may have included turkey, but this was never singled out for mention until about 1524, when turkeys had been introduced into Europe from the New World.

Such feasts were accompanied by all the usual music and dancing, often by mummings too. The medieval Christmas priorities are summed up by these three short entries in a late medieval Christmas account roll, from a noble household:

Item, paid to the preacher 6/2d.,
Item, paid to the minstrel, 12/-.,
Item, paid to the cook, 15/-.

Good cooks had to earn their money with more than just roasting, though in a big household this was a vast enough task. They also had to make meat pies, like the 'most choice paste' the London Salters' cook made for the company at Christmas 1394. In was in the shape of a bird, and contained a pheasant, a capon, two partridges, two pigeons, two rabbits, offal and egg in huge quantities, 'a goodly portion' of seasoning spice, pickled fungi and bone gravy. Medieval mince pies were made of minced meat, like this one, though by the fifteenth century they were more like the sweet modern ones because prunes, raisins and currants were more easily available to be added in and to make the sweet and sour mixture, sharpened with wine or verjuice (grape vinegar), that all Medievals relished. Dried fruits and spices were the only sweet foods available at Christmastime, and they were mashed together to make frumenty, a rich, sweet, holiday porridge. Beer and ale, often sweetened with honey, sweet herbs and spices, were the favourite Christmas drinks. Henry III's powers of eating were matched only by his powers of drinking, and he had his own favourite Christmas drinks: gariofiliac, wine flavoured with gillyflower petals, and claret, a mixture of two parts white to one part red wine, sweetened and spiced.

Now every man at my request
Be glad and merry at all this feast.
Let no man come into this hall,
Groom, page nor yet marshal,
But that some sport he bring withall;
For now is the time of Chrismas.

[Fifteenth-century carol]

Being 'glad and merry', hospitable and sociable, were the Christmas virtues. Nothing combined them better than the wassail. This was a cup of spiced ale, carried from door to door during the Christmas season, New Year's eve in particular, by young women who sang verses and offered people a sip of the ale, hoping for some payment in return. The wassail became a Christmastide toast of well-being, at which every feaster sang and drank in turn, passing the cup round the table. It survived in some parts of England until the nineteenth century, and was always closely associated with the expulsion of the old year, the 'forthdrove', and the welcoming of the new one. In 1401 the community at Bury paid 'two shillings for forthdrove and wassail at Christmas.' The earliest known English Christmas carol, a thirteenth-century Anglo-Norman one, ends with the words:

> Here then I bid you all wassail,
> Cursed be he who will not say 'Drink hail!'

The main religious figure was the child Jesus, serenaded in carols that were religious versions of popular love songs: 'Come and look upon her child nestling in the hay!' sang Jacopone da Todi (1228–1306), an early Franciscan writer,

> Little angels all around
> Danced, and carols flung.

The German mystics were the first to write carols in this romantic and earthly spirit with which the Franciscans invested Christmas; the English did not to any extent until the fifteenth century, when they wrote a great many. They preferred to express the Franciscan Christmas in drama.

Shepherds' plays were performed in churches and churchyards, or in the still, silent form of the crib. Christmas cribs had existed since the seventh century, but it was St Francis who brought them to popular life and made them part of Christmas folklore, complete with an ox and an ass. The Mayor and Borough of King's Lynn presented some 'religious Tableaux' before Lord Scales in the yard of Middleton Castle in 1445, and these may well have been a series of crib scenes.

All Christmas dramas had music and costume, often with masks and disguises. They were performed in the highest of spirits, often boosted with masses of alcohol. Inside the houses visited by mummers and Christmas players, people played the usual indoor games, between bouts of feasting, staying up later than usual while they waited for Midnight Mass. On St Paul's manor in Somerset, one of the tenants had to watch all night over Christmas and keep up a good fire in the hall.

Christmas presents were given in an atmosphere of festive excitement and tension. They were extorted in the same way. In 1419 the City of London forbade its sergeants and other officers to beg for Christmas gifts because in previous times they had extorted them from brewers, bakers, cooks and other city gildsmen with threats and violence. Private present-giving is only occasionally recorded, in the records of big households, where the presents were usually money, food or exotic birds that could soon be turned into food. They were given any time between St Nicholas's Day and Candlemas, to which date the Christmas season had been unofficially extended by the end of the Middle Ages.

The evergreen decorations could be left up for the whole season. The favourite was mistletoe, which had been cut and handed round at Christmas ever since Druid times. It was symbolic of fertility. Medieval Christmases were a blaze of fertility, festivity and plenty, under the blessing of religious rebirth.

The religious climax was Midnight Mass on Christmas Eve, to which most people went, and at which many people received communion for the only time in the year. On Christmas morning there was a dawn mass and a midday mass, the three masses together symbolising the three-fold birth of Christ, eternally in the bosom of the Father, physically from the womb of the Virgin, and mystically in the souls of the faithful.

The day after Christmas was a rest day, played away with skating and horse racing. St Stephen, whose feast day it was, was the patron saint of horses, and it was a day for racing and for bleeding horses, the latter to purge them of germs and to get them in condition for spring sports and work.

December 28th was the feast of the Holy Innocents, the children slain by Herod, and mourned with special affection by the English. Childermas, the other name for this feast, was the height of misrule, and Edward IV is said to have postponed his coronation from its original date of Sunday until Monday, because the Sunday was Childermas, when hierarchy was turned upside-down and the only king was a foolish king.

New Year's eve brought presents and wassails. New Year's day even more so, following the Anglo-Saxon custom of beginning a new year with plenty and generosity. The very last chance to wassail was Epiphany eve. The Epiphany was a major feast, much bigger than it is today. It was the last and most exotic day of Christmas. Decorations were burnt, Kings of Misrule and Boy Bishops dethroned, the last of the Christmas food eaten, and the hard business of cultivation faced for a new year. In some parts of England the end-of-holiday feeling caused the day after the Epiphany to be nicknamed St Distaff's day, because it was then that women went back to their spinning and distaffs after their holiday.

The Medievals loved their holidays, and their number increased steadily through the period, until the calendar was packed with minor and local feastdays. In the fifteenth century in particular, new devotions and patron saints sprang up apace.

The only modern routes back to the medieval life that celebrated its saints in this way are the medieval routes of gleeful prayer and song. The best medieval songs are drinking songs, and in honour of whichever saint has his or her feastday today, or had it on this day in the Middle Ages, these are the opening lines of a medieval drinking song. Like many medieval drinking songs, it was written by a cleric, in this case the Cistercian monk Walter Map. Its refrain is a transport straight back to the festive thirteenth century: "Tis my intention, gentle sir, to perish in a tavern.'

qnt len se part de la cite de cali
anf qne dit nous ay desus si che
nanche len sui. iournees par
poient tontes sois tronuant
chastianx et cites asses. ou il a
grans nmrchandises de draps. et mnns bianx
iardinis et mnanr bianx champs tons plains de
moners dont len fait la soie. la gent tnit sont

63 A pole-wife looking for custom. From Marco Polo's *Travels. Bodleian Library, Oxford* MS. Bodl. 264, fol. 245v.

solennitate beatorum martyrum
dyonisii rustici & eleutherii passio
ne decorasti concede nobis famuli
tuis digna veneratione eorum me
moriam celebrare vt quorum do
ctrina exēplo tibi gallorum sub
didisti colla fauertica ipsorum i
teruentione assidua mereamur
adipisti gaudia sempiterna. Per.
De Sancto Martino. Antiphō.
Bea
tu
virum cu
ius anima
paradisu
possidet
vnde ex
ultant angeli letantur archangeli
chorus sanctorum proclamat turba
virginum inuitat mane nobiscum
ineternum. ℣l9 Amauit eum dns

64 Boys riding hobby-horses. *Bodleian Library, Oxford* MS. Douce. 276, fol. 124v.

65 A prostitute inviting a client into her hut. From the Alexander Romance. *Bodleian Library, Oxford* MS. Bodl. 264, fol. 83, fol. 204.

66 A couple Maying, he is carrying a blossomy bough, she has hers carried by a servant. *The British Museum* 2467 Add. Ms. fol. 46.

Index